RENAISSANCE DRAMA

*New Series* XXIX        1998

# Renaissance Drama

NEW SERIES XXIX

## Dramas of Hybridity: Performance and the Body

Edited by Jeffrey Masten and Wendy Wall

Northwestern University Press

EVANSTON 2000

# Contents

# Editorial Note

R*ENAISSANCE* D*RAMA,* an annual interdisciplinary publication, invites submissions that investigate traditional canons of drama as well as the significance of performance, broadly construed, to early modern culture. We particularly welcome essays that examine the impact of new forms of interpretation on the study of Renaissance plays, theater, and performance. There are no fixed chronological or geographical limits.

Volume XXIX, "Dramas of Hybridity: Performance and the Body," includes essays that focus on historically specific early modern bodies, analyzing staged representations of bodies as they spectacularly unfold, determine, negotiate, and erode various social categories. In particular, these essays introduce us to moments of hybridity in drama and performance: the squeaking and stammering voice of the boy actor at the threshold of normative masculinity; the diseased body and its encoding of national pathologies; the threatening amalgam of foreignness and femininity in the figure of the actress; the shifting conceptions of miscegenation and race marked on bodies; the myriad crossings between genre and sexuality. "Dramas of Hybridity" thus both reflects recent critical attention to historicizing the body (its disorderly humoral interior, its vulnerable substantiations onstage) and works to show the complicated movements across social, political, and dramatic categories in early modern culture.

*Reniassance Drama* conforms to the stylistic conventions outlined in the most recent MLA Style Manual. Scholars preparing manuscripts for submission should refer to this book. Manuscripts should be submitted in triplicate; those accompanied by a stamped, self-addressed envelope will be returned. Submissions and inquiries regarding future volumes should be addressed to *Renaissance Drama,* c/o Professors Jeffrey Masten and Wendy Wall, Department of English, 215 University Hall, Northwestern University, Evanston, IL 60208, USA.

Jeffrey Masten and Wendy Wall
Editors

RENAISSANCE DRAMA

*New Series* XXIX     1998

# "The Enterprise Is Sick": Pathologies of Value and Transnationality in Troilus and Cressida

## JONATHAN GIL HARRIS

T HE RECENT PANIC in global markets about the so-called Asian flu or Asian contagion and its potentially epidemic effects offers a timely reminder that the discourses of economics and pathology have long been mutually entwined—a linkage revealed also by such crucial economic terms as "inflation" and "consumption," each of which has a pathological provenance.[1] This essay plots the coordinates of one such discursive overlap in early modern England. Shakespeare wrote *Troilus and Cressida* very shortly after the publication of a pioneering treatise of mercantilist philosophy, Gerard de Malynes's *Treatise of the Canker of England's Commonwealth* (1601); both texts display strikingly similar preoccupations with, and uncertainties about, disease and value. What follows is an attempt to connect the dots of pathology and economics both in and between the two texts. By way of introduction, I first consider generic critical approaches to the disease imagery of plays that, together with *Troilus and Cressida*, are conventionally assigned to that most pathological of Shakespearean dramatic categories, the "problem play"; then I propose an alternative mercantile and transnational framework in which to decode *Troilus and Cressida*'s references to disease.

### I

Shakespeare's problem plays are, if nothing else, utterly sick.[2] As numerous critics have noted, syphilis, its symptoms, and its colloquial discourses

3

seem to have thoroughly infected the plays' vocabularies, whether expressly (the "pocky corses" of *Hamlet*'s graveyard scene, Lucio's banter about "French crowns," Thersites' caustic remarks about "Neapolitan bone-ache" as well as Pandarus's disclosure of his ailments at the end of *Troilus and Cressida*)[3] or more obliquely (the "tetter" that coats the poisoned body of King Hamlet and that crops up again in Thersites' railings, the "sciatica" and "serpego" referred to in both *Measure for Measure* and *Troilus and Cressida*).[4] But a battalion of other diseases are name-checked in the plays. *Measure for Measure* offers us "gout" and "rheum" (3.1.31), "palsied eld" (3.1.36), and a "strange fever" (5.1.152); in *Hamlet* we encounter "contagious blastments" (1.3.42), a "vicious mole of nature" (1.4.24), a "leprous distillment" (1.5.64), "pestilent . . . vapors" (2.2.322–23), a "sense . . . apoplexed" (3.4.72–73), "the ulcerous place" (3.4.147), "the hectic in my blood" (4.3.66), "th' imposthume of much wealth and peace" (4.4.27), "plague" (4.7.13), "the quick of th' ulcer" (4.7.123), and a "canker of our nature" (5.2.69); and *Troilus and Cressida*, the most disease-ridden of them all, bequeaths to its audiences and readers a virtual compendium of early modern ailments: "ulcer of my heart" (1.1.54), "plague" (1.1.94, 1.3.96, 3.3.264, etc.), "jaundies" (1.3.2), "biles" (2.1.2), "botchy core" (2.1.6), "red murrion" (2.1.19), "scab" (2.1.29), "colic" (4.5.9), "tisick" (5.3.101), and in one nonpareil of Thersitean virulence alone, "rotten diseases of the south, the guts-griping, ruptures, catarrhs, loads a'gravel in the back, lethargies, cold palsies, raw eyes, dirt-rotten livers, whissing lungs, bladders full of imposthume, sciaticas, lime-kills i' th' palm, incurable bone-ache, and the rivell'd fee-simple of the tetter" (5.1.18–23).

What are we to make of these images? When confronted with the problem plays' extensive pathological vocabularies, twentieth-century critics have tended to adopt either of two distinct approaches. The first has consisted of occasionally lurid speculation about the state of Shakespeare's mind and health in or around 1601. In her enduringly influential study *Shakespeare's Imagery and What It Tells Us*, Caroline Spurgeon notes that Shakespeare's interest in plague and hidden diseases such as cancer "became stronger in middle age," reaching its height in *Hamlet* and *Troilus and Cressida* (129, 131). Developing the implications of Spurgeon's observations more than half a century later, Johannes Fabricius suggests that the pathological imagery of these plays might be "explained as a predictable reaction to the poet's midlife crisis," but adds that the plays' pervasive disgust at sex and atmosphere of "rottenness, disease, death and corruption" point strongly to Shakespeare's having contracted syphilis (231, 234).[5] By contrast, a quite different tradition of criticism has tended to view the plays' images of disease as metaphors for social and symbolic breakdown, whether universally or in turn-of-the-century Tudor England. This approach's most influential avatar is René Girard, who in a series of essays on mimetic desire and *Troilus and Cressida* offers variations on his more general claim that, throughout literature, "plague is universally presented as a process of undifferentiation, a destruction of specificities" ("Plague" 136).[6] Girard's ideas have been developed and lent greater historical context by Eric S. Mallin, whose brilliant topical readings of *Troilus and Cressida*'s and *Hamlet*'s pathological imagery are grounded in a specifically sixteenth-century assumption that "disease offers a structural template that produces unstructuring" (65).[7]

As illuminating as these two very divergent strains of interpretation might be, they nonetheless share a substantial limitation: each tends to condense the plays' many diseases into Disease, either by interpreting illness as a generic metaphor with one symbolic valence (be it autobiographical or sociopolitical) or by implicitly regarding one disease—usually syphilis or plague—as the model of all others. But as careful scrutiny of *Hamlet*'s, *Troilus and Cressida*'s, and *Measure for Measure*'s pathological imagery makes clear, the problem plays contain a multiplicity not only of illnesses but also of implied forms and etiologies of disease in general. The differences between these two pathological models, I shall argue, are highly significant and can be grouped into two broad paradigmatic camps.

In all three plays, there are references to illnesses that demonstrate Shakespeare's familiarity with humoral discourse.[8] The latter, codified largely in the work of Galen, modeled disease not as a determinate, invasive organism but as a state emerging primarily from *dyskrasia,* or internal bodily imbalance. So in the midst of his long lecture in *Measure for Measure* about the diseases to which the body is prone, Duke Vincentio tells Claudio that "thy complexion shifts to strange effects" (3.1.24); Hamlet observes that a "vicious mole of nature" emerges from "the o'ergrowth of some complexion" (1.4.27, 30); and *Troilus and Cressida*'s Greek characters similarly suffer from complexional dysfunctions, to the point where it can seem as if the play were at least initially conceived of as a comedy of humors. Alexander describes Ajax as "a man into whom nature hath so crowded humors . . . He is melancholy without cause, and merry against the hair" (1.2.21–22, 26–27), a diagnosis that Ajax himself applies to

Achilles (2.3.87); and when Agamemnon asks his men, "What grief hath set these jaundies on your cheeks?" (1.3.2), he alludes to a humoral condition commonly believed to be caused by obstruction of the bile.

While these afflictions are all construed as endogenous states arising from internal imbalance, the problem plays refer also to certain illnesses that seem to offer a more modern, ontological conception of disease as a determinate thing contracted from an external source.[9] This is particularly the case with the plays' multiple references to syphilis, which more than any other disease tested the humoral assumption that illness was an internally derived state. The customary names for syphilis in early modern England—Spanish pox, *morbus gallicus* or the French sickness, the Neapolitan disease—make clear how it was understood to derive from *elsewhere,* to reside in and be transmitted by foreign bodies that had infiltrated English bodies politic and natural.[10] This protomicrobiological conception of the disease was formally articulated on the continent during the mid-sixteenth century by both Girolamo Fracastoro and Paracelsus, who separately attributed the origins of syphilis as well as plague to invasive "seeds" of infection rather than to humoral imbalance.[11] Although Shakespeare displays no knowledge of Fracastoro's theories and only a passing familiarity with those of Paracelsus,[12] the emergent ontological perception of syphilis is powerfully present in *Troilus and Cressida:* Thersites anachronistically refers to it as the Neapolitan bone-ache (2.3.18–19), and Pandarus's concluding reference to the Winchester Goose (5.10.54), a colloquial name for the pustules of syphilitic infection, notably figures the disease not only as an organism but also as migratory—an illness one might "bequeath," to use his term (5.10.56).[13]

There are other diseases mentioned in the plays, however, whose etiology is less easy to pigeonhole. The affliction of serpego, a skin condition referred to by both Duke Vincentio and Thersites, provides a notable case in point. The Scottish physician Andrew Boorde believed serpego to have a humoral origin, arguing that it stems from "hote and corrupt blode myxt with coler"; Joannes De Vigo associated it with an excess of phlegm (Boorde sig. Hh4v; De Vigo fol. cxxxix^v). Yet like other cutaneous afflictions, the disease increasingly had come to be associated with syphilis, and serpego's etymological root—the Latin *serpere,* "to creep"—helped model the disease less as an endogenous state of imbalance than as an affliction that migrates, both within the body and from body to body.[14] Diseases and their causes are thus contradictorily (dare one say problematically?) figured in the problem plays. The confusions surrounding the form and origin of an ailment like serpego resonate with the more general confusion of Shakespeare's peers about the origins of epidemic disease. In his *Treatise of the Plague* (1603), Thomas Lodge asserts that plague is caused by a "great repletion, or a general deprauation of the humours"; yet he also insists that the cause is "the ayre which we sucke, which hath in it self a corrupt and venemous seede, which we draw with our in-breathing."[15] Galenic humoralism, Hippocratic miasmic theory, and a Paracelsan proto-microbiologism here blur indeterminately into one another.

I have argued elsewhere that the significant if incomplete displacement of humoral pathology in the sixteenth and seventeenth centuries by mod-els of disease entailing the agency of foreign bodies cannot be disentan-gled from larger social developments and reorganizations of knowledge.[16] Seemingly unrelated domains of discourse, especially those of politics and religion, provided conceptual reservoirs for the often contradictory rethinking of disease. I would like to extend this argument here by suggest-ing that *Troilus and Cressida*'s pathological images evince an uncertainty specific to the mercantilist moment of early-seventeenth-century England. The play's contest between residual humoral and emergent ontological models of illness, I shall argue, bespeaks a larger tension between differing paradigms of not just disease but also value—a tension strained to the break-ing point by the growth of global trade and foreign currency exchange. The questions with which *Troilus and Cressida* and Shakespeare's culture alike grapple are these: are the origins of disease and value intrinsic and endogenous, or are they external and exogenous? And if "the enterprise is sick," to borrow Ulysses' suggestive coinage (1.3.103), what exactly is the nature of economic sickness, and where does it originate? These questions surface also in *The Canker of England's Commonwealth*, written by the merchant and later Assay Master of the Mint Gerard de Malynes. In plotting the links between the two texts, I seek to show that early modern discourses of pathology and mercantile economics are to a certain extent mutually constitutive, each providing the other with one of its horizons of conceptual possibility.

## II

Gerard de Malynes's *Treatise of the Canker of England's Commonwealth* was published in the same year that many believe Shakespeare to háve begun writing *Troilus and Cressida* (1601). Regardless of whether Shake-speare had read it, Malynes's treatise conjoins analysis of commercial exchange with images of disease in ways that are highly pertinent to a reading of Shakespeare's play.

Malynes endeavors to explain the cause of England's depletion of wealth, which he attributes to the unchecked outflow of specie from the country. English merchants, he argues, prefer to ship coin to their overseas clients instead of purchasing bills of foreign exchange; they do so because English currency is terribly undervalued, which means the pound sterling's inter-national exchange rates are far poorer than the value of its component metals. Because merchants save more by sending their money directly to overseas factors instead of buying foreign currency at present exchange rates, England's supply of treasure cannot help but hemorrhage—and this, he argues, is the "unknowne disease of the politicke body" (*Canker* sig. B2).[17] Malynes employs an altogether more ambiguous model of disease than those favored by earlier sixteenth-century economic writers. Whereas the latter often invoked the conventional humoral illness of consumption, implying that economic ailments derive entirely from internal imbalances in the body politic such as unequal distribution of resources or insufficient levels of production,[18] Malynes resorts to a disease whose form and etiol-ogy in much sixteenth-century writing entails both humoral disarray *and* the agency of pathogenic foreign bodies.

Such confusion is not immediately obvious from his choice of the term "canker." Since antiquity, cancer had been believed to have an exclusively humoral and hence internal origin: Hippocrates and Galen both attributed it to an excess of *atra bilis,* or melancholy, a diagnosis that survived well into the sixteenth century.[19] Nevertheless, certain subtle semantic shifts in the meanings of "canker" had helped lend it new metaphorical possibilities. Early modern medical authorities frequently reminded their readers that the term derived from the tumor's resemblance to a crab, both in its physical appearance and in its migratory and gustatory habits; as one English physician remarked, "it is called Canker because it goeth forth like a Crab" (Paynell sig. T2v). Such images of a creeping, devouring crustacean invader doubtless contributed to the emergence in the fifteenth century of the term "canker worm," or simply "canker," to designate a parasitic caterpillar that destroys plants by eating their buds and leaves. Through a process of reverse influence, canker the parasite arguably began to affect popular perceptions of canker the disease. Instead of designating an exclusively endogenous, humoral disorder, the now multivalent term more readily suggested a hostile, even foreign, organism that invades and consumes the body.

An equally if not more decisive factor in the transformation of the popular etiology of cancer was its association during the sixteenth century with the symptoms of syphilis. The pustules of syphilitic infection were known by a variety of names, including "bosses," "tetters," and the "Winchester goose"; they were also commonly called "chancres," French for canker. The French and English terms were, in fact, readily interchangeable. In his *Dictionarie of French and English* of 1611, Randle Cotgrave defines the "Bosse chancreuse" as *"A cankered byle; pockie sore, Winchester goose"* (sig. P5v);[20] as early as 1543, in *The Most Excellent Workes of Chirurgerye*, Bartholomew Traheron listed "lothsome cankers" as one of the prime symptoms of "that moste fylthy, pestiferous, & abominable dysease the Frenche or spanyshe pockes" (De Vigo, dedication, sig. +ii). If the names for syphilis helped challenge the assumptions of humoral pathology by explicitly locating its origins in foreign agents, "canker" also acquired something of the disease's exogenous associations. This perception was to gain medical legitimacy in the early seventeenth century, when the German pathologist Daniel Sennert theorized that cancer was a communicable condition, and the Flemish Paracelsan J. B. Van Helmont suggested that the disease derived from an "external contagion"—an attitude that was in no small way responsible for European hospitals refusing admission to cancer patients well into the nineteenth century.[21]

I would argue that it was "canker" 's twin connotations of complexional imbalance and external agency in the production of illness that attracted Malynes to the term. In his treatise, the cause of the canker of England's commonwealth might seem at first glance compatible with humoral etiology. He insists that England's illness derives from unhealthy imbalances within the body politic's internal mix of elements: "The right course of exchange being abused . . . causeth an *ouerballancing* of forrain commodities with our home commodities" (sig. C1; emphasis mine). But it soon becomes apparent that Malynes believes such imbalances to stem from the plottings of malevolent aliens, European bankers whom he accuses of manipulating the rates of exchange to England's detriment: "these Bankers which commonly are in league with the financiers of the low countries . . . do vse, or rather abuse the exchange, & make of it a trade for monies" (sigs. D8v, E4). This attribution lends Malynes's treatise something of a tabloidesque, scaremongering tone. Everywhere on the continent that he casts his worried gaze, he spies evil foreign bankers conniving to destroy England's economic health:

But when the exchaunge goeth high, our merchants are inclined to buy forraine commodities, or to barter their commodities for the same, which oportunities is not onely obserued by the Bankers, but also procured. To which end they follow by the meanes of their factors, our merchants at all places, euen as the Eagle followeth her pray. (Sigs. D5v–D6)

This conspiratorial narrative of rapacious "Eagle" bankers and their hapless English prey sheds further light on Malynes's choice of pathological terminology: canker's semantic freight, not to mention its suggestive but perhaps unintentional rhyme with "banker," facilitates Malynes's attribution of economic illness to predatory foreign bodies.[22]

Malynes's invectives against the foreign Banker Canker betray an anxiety prompted by a good deal more than the alleged depletion of England's treasure. The sense of emergency that pervades *The Canker of England's Commonwealth* is demonstrably fueled less by the physical migrations of specie out of the nation than by the more ineffable migrations of money's *value*—a phenomenon endemic to the growing, turbulent cash economy of the sixteenth century, which witnessed the repeated debasement and devaluation of England's currency along with unprecedented volatility in international exchange rates.[23] As a prophylactic measure against such turbulence, Malynes reiterates Aristotle's conviction that money should be a *"Publica mensura"* (sig. B6), or common measure of value, and hence exempt from fluctuation:

[M]oney was deuised to bee coyned of the finest and purest mettals, to be the rule or square, whereby all other things should receiue estimation and price, and as a measure whereby the price of all things might be set. And to maintaine a certaine euenhood or equality in buying & selling, and the same to haue his standing valuation onely by publicke authority: to the end that all things might equally passe by trade from one man to another. (Sig. B4)

For Malynes, money's capacity to measure value derives from the supposedly fixed, intrinsic value of its component metals, a conviction that he expresses also in his later, more extensive theorization of mercantilist philosophy, the *Lex Mercatoria:* "the last propertie of Money is, to haue an internall value in substance, whereupon the Exchanges of Money are grounded" (*Consuetudo* 1:254).

As the above passage from *The Canker of England's Commonwealth* concedes, however, the putatively endogenous value of money needs to be fixed by a "publicke authority"—specifically the prince—who therefore functions somewhat paradoxically as both the protector of money's "internall value in substance" and the external *fons et origo* of such value. With this schema, Malynes brokers a deft compromise between the residual medieval model of intrinsic value, whose most influential formulation can be traced back to Thomas Aquinas, and the powerfully emergent mercantile intuition of the arbitrary, extrinsic nature of value.[24] In a subtle yet significant deviation from the traditional medieval scholastic distinction between the preexisting *bonitas intrinseca,* or metallic value of the coin, and the *bonitas extrinseca,* or face value given it by the prince, Malynes models the will of the prince rather than money itself as the gold standard that stabilizes exchange: in effect, it is now the *bonitas extrinseca* imposed by the prince that produces and protects money's fixed intrinsic worth.[25] Malynes is thus able to acknowledge implicitly the inadequacy of endogenous value, while repudiating the epistemological dislocations to which an unreservedly exogenous model of value might commit him.

But this compromise stumbles upon one major obstacle. As Malynes recognizes, money's value is anything but fixed, even with the allegedly stabilizing influence of the prince. He regards certain cases of money's revaluation as inevitable and even desirable: the practices of clipping coins and transforming their ratios of gold to silver necessitate adjustments of money's value that reflect its component metals' intrinsic values as determined by "publicke authority." Malynes reserves his outrage for another widespread practice of currency revaluation, one notably based not on changes in the physical constitution of coins but on what he calls "merchandizing exchange"—that is, the alteration, authorized by foreign bankers, of national currencies' exchange values. For Malynes, this practice not only represents an egregrious usurpation of royal prerogative ("the valuation or alteration of money, concerneth only the soueraignty and dignity of the Prince or gouernor of euery countrey, as a thing peculiar vnto them" [sig. B7v]); even more problematically, it transforms value into something *transparently* external and arbitrary bestowed by private foreign agents—a canker—rather than a *seemingly* essential or intrinsic quality legitimized by "publicke authority." The currency revaluations entailed by "merchandizing exchange," he maintains, can lead only to crises of multiple or indeterminate value:

[T]he merchandizing exchange which thus ouer-ruleth the course of commodities & mony, is intollerable: for we shall find in effect, that one summe of mony, of one sort and kinde of coine, hath two prices, & two valuations, at one time, exchanged for one distance of time; differing only by the diuersities of place & countrie: whereby priuate men alter as it were the valuation of coines. (Sig. E4v)

Failing to respect ideals of intrinsic value, the stabilizing authority of princes, or the sovereignty of nations, bankers therefore, in effect, make laws out of their own arbitrary wills or appetites.[26] This derogatory yoking of commerce and unbridled private will aligns Malynes's economic "canker" at least in part with syphilis, a disease whose ready association with prostitution entailed a similar freighting of appetite and trade.

In Malynes's explanations of the origin of money's value, we can glimpse the outlines of a telling pair of related confusions, both of which testify to the increasingly transnational nature of early modern trade and disease. He insists on money's "internall value in substance" yet complains that he is helpless to stop its revaluation by foreign agents; similarly, his campaign to secure the health of England's economy by balancing the mix of domestic and imported commodities as well as regulating exchange rates, both of which have pronounced affinities with humoralism, is at odds with the protomicrobiological paradigm of infection implied by the continental Banker Canker. A comparable pair of confusions, I shall argue, afflicts *Troilus and Cressida.*

### III

When Viola gives Feste a coin in *Twelfth Night,* he begs another: "I would play Lord Pandarus of Phrygia, sir, to bring a Cressida to this Troilus" (3.1.51–52). The comparison of Cressida and Troilus to money provides a suggestive point of connection with which to begin unraveling the more substantive links between Malynes's and Shakespeare's texts. Feste's remark makes explicit what is in *Troilus and Cressida* a perhaps surprising subtext: Shakespeare's play about the long-gone heroic age is obsessed with decidedly contemporary mercantile issues of currency, trade, and valuation.[27] More specifically, both its principal female characters are coded as public yardsticks of value who, like Malynes's *publica mensura,* money, are nevertheless themselves subject to revaluation in the course of foreign exchange. The play's concern with value has attracted considerable attention from scholars, who have often viewed Shakespeare as offering a proleptic Hobbesian vision of market economy.[28] *Troilus and Cressida*'s ruminations on value, however, couched in the contradictory terms of a pathological discourse torn between exogenous and endogenous etiologies of disease, resonate much more closely with the language, concerns, and confusions of Malynes's *Canker of England's Commonwealth.*

Malynes's anxiety about the unregulated private origins of value is echoed throughout the play. This may be the war of heroes—but too many heroes means too many sources of value, as becomes apparent in the epidemic of emulousness that has "crept" like serpego through the warriors of the Greek camp. The unlicensed production of value is the subject of the Trojans' forensic debate concerning Helen's worth. To Troilus's question, "What's aught but as 'tis valued?" (2.2.52), Hector replies:

> But value dwells not in particular will,
> It holds his estimate and dignity
> As well wherein 'tis precious of itself
> As in the prizer. 'Tis mad idolatry
> To make the service greater than the god,
> And the will dotes that is attributive
> To what infectiously itself affects,
> Without some image of th' affected merit.
>                                        (2.2.53–60)

In insisting that any object's value ought to be "precious of itself" rather than arbitrarily derived from "particular will," Hector echoes Malynes's complaint that the overvaluation of currencies in foreign exchange produces "but an imaginatiue wealth, consisting in the denomination and not in substance" (sig. F6v).

Hector's characterization of "attributive" value ("inclineable" in the Folio edition) notably resorts to a pathological vocabulary: the will's fanciful imposition of value upon an object, he insists, is performed "infectiously." Early modern English usages of the adverb and its cognates participated within a decidedly slippery array of meanings that bespeaks the broader cultural confusion about the nature and origins of disease. "Infect" had retained the connotations of its Latin etymological root, *inficere,* "to stain or pollute"; in Galenic discourse and Shakespeare's plays alike, the term is often used to refer to the pollution of the body by ill or superfluous humors. A complexional understanding of infection is apparent in *Timon of Athens,* for example, when Apemantus characterizes Timon as suffering from "a nature but infected; / A poor unmanly melancholy" (4.3.202-3). A related but slightly different sense of infection, which can be traced back to Hippocrates' miasmic theory of pathogenic pollution, crops up frequently in early modern English writing about the plague, a disease often believed to be contracted by inhaling foul vapors that disturb the body's humoral balance; Shakespeare uses "infection" in this miasmic sense when Leontes wishes in *The Winter's Tale* that "The blessed gods / Purge all infection from our air" (5.1.168-69).[29] By virtue of its exogenous model of pathogenesis, miasmic theory was conceptually closer to the more recognizably modern sense of infection that gained currency within the discourses of syphilis during the sixteenth century. As I have noted, most physicians regarded syphilitic infection less as a humoral affliction than as the infiltration of a determinate, invasive disease. Writing of syphilis in 1596, for example, the surgeon William Clowes offers what looks uncannily like a protomicrobiological account of infection: "the disease is taken by externall meanes. . . . Any outward part being once infected, the disease immediately entreth into the blood, and so creepeth on like a canker from part to part" (sig. U1).[30]

Hence, by 1601, "infectious" was by no means a clear or self-explanatory term: it variously designated bodies that were humorally imbalanced, miasmically polluted, or protomicrobiologically invaded by determinate, pathogenic entities. These multiple possibilities present the reader of *Troilus and Cressida* with an intriguing problem, one that has been insufficiently addressed: how to decode the "infectiousness" of valuation. Is the attributive will's infectiousness humoral and endogenous—a spontaneous disease confined to the subject and caused, like "jaundies," by *dyskrasia?* Or is it ontological and exogenous like the Winchester Goose, transmitted over a distance from the will to its object? In this confused and confusing play, it is arguably both.

It is certainly difficult to resist an exclusively protomicrobiological reading of Hector's infectious valuation. Fierce though Hector's commitment to the ideal of endogenous value may be, *Troilus and Cressida* struggles to present that ideal as a viable alternative to the rival, exogenous codes that he critiques. Just as Malynes is powerless to protect the value of money from the foreign Banker Canker of unregulated currency revaluation, so the supposedly intrinsic values of *Troilus and Cressida*'s objects are similarly vulnerable to external recoding; as goods circulate from owner to owner, they change, seemingly infected by the wills that evaluate them. Take, for example, the sleeve Troilus gives Cressida as a love token; in the space of less than a hundred lines it degenerates from a "pretty pledge" (5.2.77) to a "greasy relic" (5.2.159), its value altered less by its passage from Cressida to Diomedes than by the unstable nature of Troilus's intense investment in it, an investment which barely conceals a pathological capacity for disgust.[31] Something similar seems to take place with Hector's valuation of the armor of the Unknown Soldier: the sumptuous casement, which he claims to prize (5.6.28), reveals a "putrefied core" (5.8.1)—as if Hector's will has itself infected the armor's previously battle-ready occupant. Appetite, then, seems to have the power to debase its objects throughout *Troilus and Cressida.* In an equation perhaps typical of an age in which venereal disease had irrevocably transformed attitudes toward desire and its physical consequences, to "affect" is to "infect," as Hector's earlier remarks in the Trojan debate about Helen's worth imply.

If the protomicrobiological reading of Hector's "infectiously" derives considerable support from contemporaneous developments in early modern epidemiology, the radical transformations of pathology that characterize the period were arguably linked also to concurrent economic developments. As Malynes's *Canker of England's Commonwealth* hints, the steadily growing inclination of laypeople during this time to view diseases as originating less in internal states of imbalance than in determinate foreign bodies was, if not directly caused, then certainly facilitated by the growth of a global mercantile economy in which commodities, currencies, and individuals alike had become unprecedentedly migratory and the sources of their market value extrinsic. Syphilis's customary names— French disease, Neapolitan bone-ache, or Spanish pox—found counterparts in the names of a growing number of foreign goods available to early modern English consumers. "French cloth," "Italian books," and "Spanish fruit" all acquired a widespread pathological valence in political and didactic writing as the external causes of the body politic's economic and moral ills.[32] Moreover, the very practice of foreign exchange necessitated the external attribution of variable value to any commodity, including money itself, according to fluctuating demand or appetite. And such revaluation is precisely what befalls the play's two exchanged women, Helen (taken hostage by the Trojans as a countermeasure to the Greeks' kidnapping of Hesione) and Cressida (traded to the Greeks in exchange for Antenor), as they cross their national borders.

Helen is the male characters' yardstick of value, the *publica mensura* of their exploits in war and in love. Her value is nonetheless extrinsic: "Helen must needs be fair," complains Troilus, "When with your blood you daily paint her thus" (1.1.90–91). As Linda Charnes has noted, this remark foregrounds the play's retroactive remodeling of Helen's *bonitas extrinseca* as inherent worth (81). Like the unstable value of English coin in foreign markets lamented by Malynes, moreover, Helen's "painted" value is shown to vary across the national borders over which she has been transported. She is the "theme of honor and renown" (2.2.199) to the Trojan men, while the Greek Diomedes damns "every scruple / Of her contaminated carrion weight" (4.1.71–72). The latter's extraordinarily suggestive phrase freights the economic and the pathological: weighing her by the "scruple," or one twenty-fourth of an ounce (a standard unit of measurement for apothecaries and merchants), Diomedes proclaims her "contaminated," a synonym—particularly in the discourses of venereal disease—for infected.[33] In what is for Diomedes an intolerable and even syphilitic mingling of rival valuations, therefore, Helen is pathologically marked by two men, Menelaus and Paris, and by two nations.

Similarly, even as Diomedes insists that Cressida "to her own worth / . . . shall be priz'd" (4.4.133–34), her value emerges not from her "own" intrinsic qualities but from patriarchal markets of fluctuating value and demand, as she herself realizes: "Men prize the thing ungain'd more than it is" (1.2.289). Such "prizing" is neither singular nor stable, thanks to the rival foreign agents who determine her worth. By the fifth act, Cressida is simultaneously Troilus's Cressida and Diomedes' Cressida, possessed of two extrinsic values; hence the "bifold authority" at work in Troilus's famous "This is, and is not, Cressid" (5.2.144, 146), which provides a striking counterpart to Malynes's complaint that "one summe of mony, of one sort and kinde of coine, hath two prices, & two valuations, at one time, exchanged for one distance of time; differing only by the diuersities of place & countrie: whereby priuate men alter as it were the valuation of coines" (sig. E4v).[34] Hence also what has been for many readers Cressida's distressing lack of agency as her location, loyalty, and worth are altered by "priuate men." Although Douglas Bruster has argued that Cressida attempts to control her commodity function and maximize her value as she is trafficked from Troy to Greece, she still cannot avoid becoming whoever her male evaluators determine her to be (98–99). Ulysses' disgusted assessment of her while she is circulated among the men of the Greek camp—"There's language in her eye, her cheek, her lip / Nay, her foot speaks; her wanton spirits look out / At every joint and motive of her body" (4.5.55–57)—henceforth fixes her literal face value as "sluttish" (4.5.62) in her own eyes ("O false wench!" [5.2.71]) as much as those of the play's male characters, despite the discrepancy between Ulysses' evaluation and the Cressida of earlier scenes. What Ulysses attributes to Cressida's intrinsic character, or at least to her body, can be read critically as an act of ventriloquism; the "language" that her body allegedly speaks is, after all, his own. But this ventriloquism is the prerogative, perhaps even the constitutive principle, of a patriarchal economy in which the *bonitas intrinseca* of women is the product of their male evaluators' infectious wills.[35]

Thus far, *Troilus and Cressida* might appear to articulate an unreservedly modern conception of value as exogenous and mutable. Ulysses' extended speech to Achilles about time (3.3.145–90), for example, is not just a meditation on mutability but a proto-Marxian reflection on the market fluctuations of honor and virtuous deeds;[36] Cressida's exchange for Antenor, or Helen's for Hesione, corroborates Georg Simmel's insistence that economic value is an extrinsic, variable, but definite sum which results from the commensuration of two intensities of demand (67).[37] Inasmuch as *Troilus and Cressida* offers such striking parallels to modern conceptions of market value, it would appear to support the prolepticism that has characterized analysis of the play's economic preoccupations. W. R. Elton and Gayle Greene, for example, both see Shakespeare's play as anticipating Hobbes's assertion that "*value* . . . is not absolute; but a thing dependent on the need and judgment of another" (3:76)[38] Hugh Grady goes further, finding in *Troilus and Cressida* not only a "masculine prefiguration of Hobbes's state of nature" but also "a prescient exposition of the corrosive powers of instrumental reason and the related autonomous logic of Foucaultian power" (58–59).[39]

Yet even as the play disqualifies the possibility of fixed and intrinsic worth, it is important not to forget that it also literally pathologizes attributive value. And, in this respect, *Troilus and Cressida* offers a much more complicated, less prescient vision of modernity and the market than critics have on occasion intimated. The play's pathologization of externally derived value, I have suggested, is confusing and contradictory, resisting singular interpretation. At the same time as Hector's "infectiously" invites a protomicrobiological reading, its meanings can be seen to derive at least in part from the discursive field of humoral pathology. This much is made clear by one of *Troilus and Cressida*'s other references to infection. Speaking of the metaphorical illnesses that have afflicted the Greek camp and rendered them incapable of winning the war against Troy, Agamemnon observes that

> . . . checks and disasters
> Grow in the veins of actions highest rear'd,
> As knots, by the conflux of meeting sap,
> Infects the sound pine and diverts his grain
> Tortive and errant from his course of growth.
>                                         (1.3.5-9)

Here the infection to which Agamemnon alludes is manifestly derived from an internal disorder, a pathological "conflux" of elements located in the "veins."

The humoral counterdiscourse of infection glimpsed in Agamemnon's speech surfaces elsewhere in the play's treatment of valuation. Thersites' mocking assessments of his superiors, for example, are revealingly imaged in humoral as well as monetary terms: Nestor refers to him as a "slave whose gall coins slanders like a mint" (1.3.193). Such humoral coding of the "coining" of value might also help explain a significant departure Shakespeare makes from his sources. Despite the seeming communicability of the infectious will elsewhere in the play, and despite her precarious status as the object of rival male evaluations, Cressida does not contract any overt infection as does her leprous counterpart in Robert Henryson's *Testament of Cresseid,* with her "bylis black ouirspred in hir visage" (line 395).[40] Instead the play's burden of disease is shouldered by one of the men: Pandarus. From where, or whom, did he contract the aching bones and "whoreson tisick" (5.3.101) of which he complains at the play's end? According to Frank Kermode, from himself. Alone among critics in arguing that the play's pervasive pathological imagery is symptomatic of the attributive will, Kermode offers a decisive diagnosis of Pandarus's ailments: "[T]he war is being fought for Opinion, the delusive power which makes Helen seem what she is not—a valuable person, worth many men's lives. This disastrous error is produced by the dominance of blood over reason, imaged again and again as a disease of which Pandarus, at the end of the play, is a walking emblem" (182). Kermode thus sees the twin problems of externally imposed value and Pandarus's syphilitic ills through what amounts to a humoral prism; anyone suffering from unbalanced blood is captive to the infectious delusions of his or her own will. In this respect, Kermode echoes those few obstinate Galenists of the sixteenth century who persisted in attributing syphilis to humoral infection rather than to external agents; the German physician Ulrich von Hutten, for example, remained convinced that "this infirmite cometh of corrupt, burnt, & enfect blode" (fol. 4).[41]

To illustrate his point, Kermode cites Ulysses' diagnosis of Achilles' self-destruction, which is surprisingly redolent of von Hutten's language:

> . . . Imagin'd worth
> Holds in his blood such swoll'n and hot discourse
> That 'twixt his mental and his active parts
> Kingdom'd Achilles in commotion rages,
> And batters down himself. What should I say?
> He is so plaguy proud that the death tokens of it
> Cry "no recovery."
>
> (2.3.172–78)

Ulysses presents infectious valuation as a complexional disease of the blood, and hence more lethal to the evaluator than to the object of value (unless, as in this case, the evaluator and the object are one and the same). He thus concurs with Nestor's observation that those Greek princes who aspire to speak with an "imperial voice"—that is, who not only inflate their own worth but also set themselves up as authoritative evaluators—are "infect" (1.3.187). In this reading, to "affect" is less to infect than to *become* infected. If Pandarus is for Kermode "a walking emblem" of the play's pathologies, it is because Pandarus's will has succumbed to the disease of coining and inflating market value, an affliction on display in his flagrantly flawed assessment of the Trojan heroes' relative worths in act 1 scene 2. Thus when Pandarus "mark[s] Troilus above the rest" (1.2.183–84), it is arguable that he also infectiously "marks" himself—another term that potentially conjoins the economic ("mark" as a unit of measurement or currency) and the pathological ("mark" as a scab or pustule).

As this interpretation of Pandarus implies, the humoral reading of infectious valuation leaves open the possibility that an object does possess a *bonitas intrinseca* misapprehended or unacknowledged by the sick

evaluator. Ulysses' speech about Achilles would certainly seem to corrobo-
rate Kermode's conviction that the "plaguy" Myrmidon, his body in a state
of humoral disarray analogous to the internecine strife of civil war, has a
deluded sense of self-worth fatally at odds with his true intrinsic value.
But this is to make the essentialist assumption that Achilles—or any other
object of deluded desire—*has* an intrinsic value, a position that the play
repeatedly problematizes, not least in Ulysses' own insistence to Achilles
that no man can "make boast to have that which he hath, / Nor feels what he
owes, but by reflection" (3.3.98–99).[42] Whatever "true" value Achilles fails
correctly to intuit remains suspiciously extrinsic and mutable, therefore,
determined by "reflection" in another. Inasmuch as the consequences of
will or appetite are repeatedly shown to be pathologically destructive to the
desiring subject, Kermode is right to detect a residue of humoral discourse
in the play's presentation of valuation; but his singularly endogenous diagnosis as much as any singularly exogenous reading of the infectious will
speaks to only one side of *Troilus and Cressida*'s pathological transactions
of desire. The viability of *both* humoral *and* protomicrobiological readings
of the play's infectious valuations makes clear how *Troilus and Cressida*'s
pathological wills infect inwardly as much as outwardly.

## IV

Anxiously stranded between the failure of endogenous value and the
double-edged infectiousness of imposed or attributed value, between a
defunct (if ever extant) feudal order in which all things have a fixed *bonitas
intrinseca* and the inescapably protean world of market capitalism in
which price is calibrated with fluctuations of appetite and the dynamics of
"merchandizing exchange," *Troilus and Cressida* concocts a compromise
comparable to Gerard de Malynes's: a theory of value that integrates the
two opposed paradigms within a third, by means of which feudal stability
can seemingly be reconstituted within the constraints imposed by the
new mercantile dispensation. The play thus gestures toward an alternative
model of value that is neither quite intrinsic to the object nor quite derived
from the external imposition of the wills of multiple, potentially competing
subjects. Instead, value is assessed and fixed by a single, sovereign will that
can be equated with the "publicke authority" of the prince in Malynes's
schema. As is the case with its double coding of "infectious" valuation,

however, *Troilus and Cressida*'s presentation of the sovereign will is mediated by a conflicted pathological vocabulary.

The notion of the sovereign will may be glimpsed in Ulysses' critique of Ajax's and Achilles' idolatrous investment in the *machina* above the *deus* of war. "The ram that batters down the wall," complains Ulysses, "For the great swinge and rudeness of his poise, / They place before his hand that made the engine" (1.3.206–8). To Ulysses, the ram has no value in and of itself; rather, it derives its worth contagiously—not from the infectious wills of its evaluators, however, but from the "hand" of its creator. To the extent that Ulysses identifies the source of an object's worth in an external agent who "made" it, he seems to anticipate Locke's, Smith's, and Marx's labor theories of value. But his model is different in one crucial respect: value is for Ulysses, as for Malynes, a product not of bodily labor but of an ineffable, sovereign designer.[43] This alternative model is more fully elaborated within Ulysses' Tillyardian set piece about degree. The latter might seem to suggest that everything has a fixed, intrinsic value within a cosmic hierarchy. But upon closer inspection, Ulysses' cosmos displays a pathological (and recognizably humoral) predisposition to disorder, one that is corrected only by the intervention of the sun-king:

> And therefore is the glorious planet Sol
> In noble eminence enthron'd and spher'd
> Amidst the other; whose med'cinable eye
> Corrects the ill aspects of planets evil,
> And posts like the commandment of a king,
> Sans check, to good and bad.
>
> (1.3.89–94)

The sun-king plays a contradictory role within this world picture: correcting the "ill aspects"—or face values—of wandering planets, he is both the protector of intrinsic order and its external origin. Ulysses' choice of pathological language to describe the curative effect of sovereign power, "med'cinable," works to model the sun-king's will as the polar opposite of Hector's infectious will. But here we might also recall Paracelsus's conviction that "every poison is good for some use" (*Selected Writings* 107).[44] There is little in fact to separate the sun-king's "med'cinable" will from the private agent's infectious one, other than its being the sun-king's. Like the infectious will of the private evaluator, the sun-king's "med'cinable" power entails, contrary to Hector's and Aquinas's conceptions of the origins of *bonitas intrinseca,* a value that "dwells . . . in particular will." Rather than being the straightforwardly conservative articulation of the Elizabethan worldview that most readers have believed it to be—no matter whether they regard Ulysses as hierarchical degree's passionate advocate or as its Machiavellian manipulator[45]—the Ithacan prince's view of the cosmos is in fact very close to the mercantilist compromise of Malynes's *Canker of England's Commonwealth,* according to which the "publicke authority" of the sovereign is likewise the sole, not to mention paradoxical, external source of intrinsic value in a universe composed of migratory, mutable elements.[46] Like Malynes's compromise between exogenous and endogenous theories of value, moreover, Ulysses' conception of the sovereign will has an explicitly transnational mercantile agenda: without it, he insists, there would be no "peaceful commerce from dividable shores" (1.3.105).

Also like Malynes's compromise, however, Ulysses' vision of "med'cinable" valuation proves unrealizable. Nowhere in the play does any putative sovereign will succeed in either stabilizing the worth of the elements under its jurisdiction or warding off the outbreaks of unlicensed, infectious attribution that render value fugitive within and across its national boundaries. Neither of the two camps' nominal sun-kings, Agamemnon or Priam, is capable of stamping even any temporary order on the "ill aspects" of his polity; each is largely displaced by rival "imperial voices"—Agamemnon by Ulysses and Achilles, Priam by Hector and Troilus. The two leaders' surrogates fare no better, Troilus in particular providing a case study of the failed would-be sovereign will. In a revealing speech, he resorts to a Malynesian image of imperial creation, the production of coin's face value, to characterize his truthfulness: "Whilst some with cunning gild their copper crowns," he somewhat boastfully tells Cressida, "With truth and plainness I do wear mine bare" (4.4.105-6). Troilus vouches here for the enduring value of his currency, which at this point—at least metaphorically—is, and is not, Cressida. Troilus's very language betrays the delusion of his will, however. His unwavering "truth" ironically damages rather than stabilizes his coins: in wearing them "bare," or ungilded, he "wears" them bare, that is, depreciates their value. Just as much as Achilles, then, Troilus's "imperial voice" is "infect."

The depreciating effects of the would-be sovereign will are brought to light persistently in *Troilus and Cressida,* and in a fashion that ultimately implicates not only the play's "orgillous" princes (Prol. 2), but also poets and playwrights as aspiring creators of enduring national literary value.

The Trojan story and its characters provided writers across Europe with the materials for very different myths of nation and empire. Vergil mythologized the Trojan Aeneas as the father of Roman imperialism; Geoffrey of Monmouth propagated the apocryphal legend of the Trojan Brutus as the founding British patriarch; similarly, writers from France, Denmark, Ireland, and Saxony all traced their nation's origins back to characters in the *Iliad.* In a particularly insightful study, Heather James has characterized the Trojan myth as the coin of national identity formation, subject to competing "stampings" as it circulated through the literary marketplaces of classical, medieval, and early modern Europe.[47] What distinguishes Shakespeare's treatment of the myth in *Troilus and Cressida,* James argues, is how it makes explicit this history of rival valuation. Rather than simply perform another singular, nationalist stamping of the Trojan coin, Shakespeare deliberately highlights the multiple and mutually contradictory currencies he encountered in his source materials: "the play zealously exploits its various textual and generic resources with the goal of self-deformation" (James 91). As a consequence, *Troilus and Cressida*'s genre and characters alike are garish alloys minted from a treasury of ill-matched metals—among them, Homer's epic saga; Ovid's satiric debunking; Chaucer's romantic comedy; and Henryson's moral redaction.

The characterological disruptions wrought by Shakespeare's multinational literary sources have a pathological dimension. Consider Alexander's striking description of Ajax:

They say he is a very man *per se.* . . . This man, lady, hath robbed many beasts of their particular additions. He is as valiant as the lion, churlish as the bear, slow as the elephant: a man into whom nature hath so crowded humors that his valour is crushed into folly, his folly sauced with discretion. There is no man hath a virtue that he hath not a glimpse of, nor any man an attaint but he carries some stain of it. He is melancholy without cause and merry against the hair; he hath the joints of everything, but everything so out of joint that he is a gouty Briareus, many hands and no use, or purblind Argus, all eyes and no sight. (1.2.15, 19–30)

This description is and is not humorous, at least in the early modern sense of the term. Alexander appears to describe Ajax's internal mix of elements, those "crowded humors" within which are blended complexional opposites such as "melancholy" and "merry" sanguinity. But upon closer inspection, the illusion of humoral interiority reconfigures itself as a bricolage of mutually contradictory versions of Ajax derived from the pens of multiple authors: Alexander's Ajax is an amalgam of the "valiant" Telamonian Ajax of Homer, the "churlish" aggressor of Vergil, and the "slow" dunderhead of Ovid.[48] In a fashion that both parallels the undermining of the play's Trojan and Greek "imperial voices" and implicitly rereads European literary history from the perspective of his own mercantile moment, therefore, Shakespeare transmutes the sovereign wills of his predecessors into rival, infectious sources of value. Any assumption that the play's women alone are the protean, recodable coin of the realm thus becomes highly questionable. If *Troilus and Cressida*'s female characters are multiply marked by their Trojan and Greek evaluators within the play, so are its male characters multiply valued by their transnational authors within the Iliadic literary tradition. Here we might recall that for Feste, Troilus as much as Cressida is coin.[49]

Hence just as there is no one stabilizing sovereign will among *Troilus and Cressida*'s characters, neither does the play uphold any single authority among the rival purveyors of the Trojan legend. Whatever originary, fixing power Homer might command elsewhere within the Troy canon is dissolved in *Troilus and Cressida* by the play's many explicit transnational markings and contaminations of the *Iliad*. In this respect, Shakespeare's treatment differs greatly from that of George Chapman, who, insisting on the primacy of a sovereign, unpolluted Homer, sternly warned the readers of his translation of the *Iliad* against infecting its eminent author "with foul hands" or "other poet's slights" (which prompted his memorable and perhaps unique command that all readers should "Wash here" before reading) (1:xiii).[50] By contrast, Shakespeare's Homeric coin is already irrevocably infected by later "foul hands" and "poet's slights," as the medieval provenance of the Troilus and Cressida story makes clear. The transnational contaminations of Homer are pungently highlighted by the play's anachronistic references to those diseases whose names, postdating the *Iliad,* trace the historical and geographical trajectory of the legend from Greece through the Italian peninsula and finally to England: Thersites' "diseases of the south" (5.1.18) and "Neapolitan bone-ache" (2.3.18–19) yield at play's end to Pandarus's "goose of Winchester" (5.10.54).

*Troilus and Cressida* is not the only play in which Shakespeare subjected classical Greek and contemporary English settings to deliberately anachronistic and anatopistic mingling. But the final scene's Londonizing of Pandarus and his diseases is of a very different order from the celebratory Anglo-Athenian gallimaufry of *A Midsummer Night's Dream*. The latter's mythical Greek aristocrats and English "rude mechanicals" spring from the tidily hierarchized worlds of court masque and antimasque. By contrast, *Troilus and Cressida*'s transnational contaminations reproduce the altogether more unstable, centrifugal universe of Gerard de Malynes's Banker Canker, in which no object or *publica mensura* of value can be secured against infection by private foreign bodies. Tellingly, Shakespeare's Troy meets a different end from Homer's, and by means of a very different agent of invasion. In *Troilus and Cressida*'s global marketplace of "traders in the flesh" (5.10.45)—an epithet that can be applied just as much to Shakespeare and his rival Iliadic storytellers as to Pandarus and his ilk— the majestic Trojan Horse has been superseded by the hissing Winchester Goose.[51] For Shakespeare, therefore, Troy is irremediably contaminated by England.

Interestingly, Troy was by 1601 not only an infected *publica mensura* of national literary value; it had also become an equally problematic gold standard for the measurement of weight. In *The Canker of England's Commonwealth,* Malynes asserts that Scottish coin is "inferiour vnto ours, and likewise their weight lesser then ours by foure peny weight full vpon the pound troy" (sig. F7v). Here Malynes invokes the troy system of measuring weight and bullion as a kind of meta-*mensura,* a yardstick with which to measure money's ability to measure value. But he does so to register the financial and epistemological crises generated by the *lack* of any standardized system of measurement. Sixteenth-century English minters and merchants tended to vacillate between three systems: the offical Mint or Tower system, whose pound was equal to 5,400 troy grains; the avoirdupois system of general traders, more widely used on the continent, which divided pounds into sixteen ounces and was equal to 7,000 troy grains; and troy weight itself, which posited a pound divided into twelve ounces and equal to 5,760 troy grains. Complicating matters further, the Scottish ounce was one sixty-fourth less than the English troy ounce. With twenty pennyweights to the ounce and twelve ounces to the pound in both systems, the difference between the two national pounds amounted to four English pennyweights, as Malynes acknowledges.[52] Such discrepancies in measurement of the pound inevitably rendered any notion of money's fixed, intrinsic value—already substantially undermined by sixteenth-century currency devaluations and fluctuations of foreign exchange rates—all the more elusive.

The troy system probably derived its name from the French town of Troyes, not the city of classical legend. But that didn't stop Malynes's and Shakespeare's contemporaries from thinking otherwise, particularly when they sought to make sense of the confusions engendered by rival, nationally coded systems of measurement. In the collaborative play *The Old Law* (c. 1618), a character observes that "Cressid was Troy weight, and Nell was haberdepoise [avoirdupois], she held more by four ounces than Cressida" (Middleton and Rowley 4.1.77–79). Here may be heard an uncanny echo of Malynes's remark about the disparities between English and Scottish coin that, finding personification in Shakespeare's Trojan and Greek women, serendipitously aligns the shared concerns of the two writers. Confronted in 1601 with the mounting dislocations wrought by foreign exchange as well as variable mercantile and literary systems of valuation, both Malynes and Shakespeare invoked—and found wanting—a gold standard named "Troy." With its allegedly prophylactic power comprehensively called into question, even multiply pathologized, the two writers' enterprises could not help but be sick.

V

There is no evidence to indicate that Shakespeare ever read Malynes. The threads of connection that I have teased out between *The Canker of England's Commonwealth* and *Troilus and Cressida* are not the cause-and-effect relations of source study but filaments in a more elusive network of contact or, at least metaphorically, contagion. Malynes's treatise and Shakespeare's play are infected—in both humoral and microbiological senses—with their shared historical moment. Each text endogenously produces a distinctively pathologized vision of late Tudor "merchandizing exchange" nominally held in check by a "publicke authority" of questionable power; yet each is also exogenously marked by the effects of early modern globalization, which included the increasingly transnational circulation of not only commodities and epidemic diseases but also competing discourses of value.

The Shakespeare that I have sketched in the process might seem an all-too-familiar figure. By styling Troilus's oxymoronic "This is, and is not, Cressida" as symptomatic of the play's self-contradictory complexity—that is, by asserting that what Shakespeare offers audiences or readers is and is not humoral (or ontological) infection, is and is not intrinsic (or attributed) value, is and is not Homer's (or Henryson's) Troy—I have arguably reproduced the hoary old myth of the playwright who cannot help but present the multiple sides of any story. Whether as a new-critical exemplum of open-mindedness, a post-structuralist producer of texts divided from themselves by the vicissitudes of undecidability, or a new-historicist subject straddling the fault lines between shifting, colliding discursive formations, the "is, and is not," Shakespeare continues to have currency across a wide variety of potentially adversarial critical methodologies. Is there no alternative to this coin of the realm (no matter how many different stampings it may have undergone)? Should we—could we—reject it?

While I am apprehensive about retelling what might seem to be an overly familiar story about Shakespeare, I am equally reluctant to jettison it just because it has been told before. Rather than regard the "is, and is not," Shakespeare as a critical desideratum worth debunking or fighting for, however, I would suggest that we treat it as a strategic construction that continues to be useful when it enables the telling of other, previously unheard stories. What I have sought to do in this essay is shed new light upon the occulted historical conditions in which those notions of disease and value we now take for granted first appeared. The "is, and is not," Shakespeare I have produced here—or, for that matter, the "is, and is not," Malynes—affords us a glimpse of a moment when dominant understandings of disease and value were being put to an increasingly strong test by emergent and, to our twenty-first-century eyes, more familiar concepts and practices. To recognize as much not only allows us to recover the complexity and volatility of that moment's transnational (re)organizations of knowledge; it also helps us to acquire a clearer understanding of the long-established mutual implication of discourses of pathology and economics that persists into our own millennial moment of the "Asian flu." Telling an old story, then, can be the means toward a more comprehensive engagement with and questioning of the present—a possibility that would not have been lost on the author of *Troilus and Cressida.*

## Notes

An earlier version of this essay was prepared for the 1999 Shakespeare Association of America seminar directed by Thomas Cartelli entitled "New Problems, Old Plays: *Hamlet, Troilus,* and *Measure for Measure.*" For their helpful comments and criticisms, I am grateful to Shilpa Prasad, Henry Turner, an anonymous reader at *Renaissance Drama,* my fellow seminarians Linda Charnes, Rachana Sachdev, and Mike Torrey, and, most particularly, Heather James.

1. The term "inflation" derives from the early modern medical term for "swelling"; and the use of "consumption" as an almost invariably negative economic term in the sixteenth and seventeenth centuries depended on its pathological freight, i.e., as a practice that wasted the resources of the body politic. I discuss the multiple discursive determinations of consumption in Harris, " 'Canker.' "

2. The "problem play" category is, of course, itself problematic. In the century since F. S. Boas applied the label to *All's Well That Ends Well, Measure for Measure, Troilus and Cressida,* and *Hamlet* in *Shakespeare and His Predecessors* (344-408), there has been an ongoing debate—the contributions to which are too voluminous to itemize here—about which plays from this list are or are not "problems," and what indeed a "problem play" might be. A useful summary of the debate's highlights is offered by Jamieson. As readers will notice, I am somewhat cavalierly adapting the category in order to focus critical attention on a group of three plays from the period 1601-4 that share a distinctive pathological vocabulary. For that reason, I omit discussion of the "traditional" problem play *All's Well That Ends Well,* which despite its own fair share of references to illness—most notably, the king's fistula (1.1.34) and the "French crown" fit for a "taffety punk" referred to by the clown, i.e., syphilis (2.2.22)—does not evince the same sustained interest in pathology shown by the other three plays. All references to Shakespeare's works, unless specified otherwise, are to *The Riverside Shakespeare.*

3. *Hamlet* 5.1.166; *Measure for Measure* 1.2.52; *Troilus and Cressida* 2.3.18-19, 5.3.101-6, and 5.10.35-56.

4. *Hamlet* 1.5.71; *Troilus and Cressida* 5.1.23; "sciatica" and "serpego" ("suppeago" or "sapego" in some editions) are referred to in both *Measure for Measure* (1.2.59, 3.1.31) and *Troilus and Cressida* (5.1.21, 2.3.74). Although they were traditionally regarded as discrete illnesses, tetters (pustules), sciatica (pain in the groin, hips, and upper leg), and serpego (skin disorders ranging from rashes and boils to ringworm) had all come to be associated with the symptoms of syphilis; see also n. 10.

5. See Fabricius, chap. 11, "Shakespeare's Midlife Crisis."

6. See also Girard, "Politics" and Girard's chapters on *Troilus* in *Theatre.* Compare Bentley: "Shakespeare uses syphilis as one of the central images, in fact the *ne plus ultra* of individual, social, and political decay. It is the word picture [*sic*] that he consistently and coherently employs to satirize the physical, moral, and spiritual degeneration of English society" (4).

7. In her important essay, " 'So Unsecret to Ourselves': Notorious Identity and the Material Subject in *Troilus and Cressida*" (chap. 3 of *Notorious* [70-102]), Linda Charnes offers a celebratory psychoanalytic variant of this approach, arguing for the "subversive signifying power" of *Troilus and Cressida*'s pathological imagery (72), which she reads as symptoms of the erosion of a symbolic order that never existed in the first place.

8. On Shakespeare's adaptations of humoral discourse, see Hoeniger, esp. 175-89; Paster.

9. On the emergence of protomicrobiological or "ontological" notions of disease, see Pagel, esp. 134-40; Nutton; Harris, *Foreign Bodies,* chap. 2, esp. 22-30.

10. Hence a committedly Galenic physician such as Andrew Boorde, whose *Breuiary of Helthe* is a compendium of largely humoral etiologies and remedies, was forced to conclude about syphilis: "The Grecians can nat tell what the sicknes doth meane wherfore they do set no name for this disease for it did come but lately into Spayne & Fraunce and so to vs

about the yere of our lorde. 1470" (sig. Y3). On the foreign origins implied by the disease's customary names, see Quétel 16.

11. See Fracastoro, esp. 34–35; Paracelsus, "Von Blatern, Lähmi, Beulen, Löchern und Zitrachen der Franzosen und irs Gleichen," in *Sämtliche Werke* 6:301–479, esp. liber 2, cap. 10.

12. See Hoeniger 189–90. Shakespeare implicitly alludes to the battle between humoralism and the new pharmacies when he makes satiric reference to the followers of "Galen and Paracelsus" in *All's Well That Ends Well,* 2.2.12.

13. Although Shakespeare's editors tend to gloss "Winchester goose" as "prostitute," the term had a specific pathological application. In *The Nomenclator,* a "bubo" is defined as "a sore in the grine or yard, which if it come by lecherie, it is called a Winchester goose, or botch" (439); John Taylor refers in his "Praise of Cleane Linnen" to "A Groyne Bumpe, or a Goose from *Winchester*" (sig. Pp2v).

14. In Thomas Heywood's *The Royall King and Loyall Subject,* e.g., a virtuous captain scolds a prostitute whose customers include men who have "the French Fly, with the *Sarpego* dry'd" (*Dramatic Works* 6:50). In his *Breuiary of Helthe,* Boorde explains that "serpego" is the Latin term for the English "tetter"—another common term for the syphilitic pustule (sig. Hh4v). Perhaps Shakespeare unconsciously picks up on serpego's etymology when he has Hector speak about the fever of emulousness that afflicts the Greek army in *Troilus and Cressida:* "Their great general slept, / Whilst emulation in the army *crept*" (2.2.212–13; emphasis mine).

15. See also Harris, *Foreign Bodies* 24.

16. See Harris, *Foreign Bodies.*

17. For discussions of Malynes's economic theories, see Appleby 41–47; Harris, " 'Canker' "; Heckscher 2:238–48; Muchmore; Roover, "Gerard de Malynes"; Spiegel 100–6.

18. See Harris, " 'Canker' " 312–15.

19. On Hippocrates' and Galen's diagnoses of cancer, and the history of attitudes toward cancer and oncology in general, see Ackerknecht; Rather, esp. 9–21; Sontag. Thomas Paynell observed in 1528 that "[a] canker is a melancholy impostume, that eateth the parts of the body" (sig. T2v). Andrew Boorde replicated this view: "This infyrmyte doth come of a melancoly humour, or a coleryke humour adusted" (sig. G4v).

20. For discussions of the origins of the term "chancre," see Fabricius 185–86; Keil.

21. For Sennert's and Van Helmont's theories of the etiology of cancer, see Rather 28–29.

22. My discussion of Malynes's criticism of practices of foreign exchange owes a great deal to the work of Raymond de Roover, especially "What Is Dry Exchange?" and to B. E. Supple. For a fuller version of my argument here, see Harris, " 'Canker,' " esp. 318–20.

23. On early modern English coin, its minting, and its fluctuations of value, see Challis; Fischer.

24. My treatment of Malynes's compromise is indebted to Pierre Macherey and Etienne Balibar's theory of the linguistic compromise formation, which they outline in "Literature as an Ideological Form" 43–58, esp. 48. For an illuminating application of Macherey and Balibar's theory to Shakespeare's presentation of artisanal labor in *A Midsummer Night's Dream,* see Kavanagh.

25. In this respect, Malynes performs what Julie Robin Solomon has identified as one of the

characteristic gambits of mercantilist discourse: the coordination of royal and private interests through the representation of "the monarch as the disinterested representative of the public weal, while casting aspersions upon the unregulated pursuit of private interests" (75). For a useful discussion of the distinction between *bonitas intrinseca* and *bonitas extrinseca,* see Spiegel 71.

26. On the fixed versus fluid values of money in seventeenth-century mercantilist discourse, see Appleby 42-47. See also Foucault's discussion of the seventeenth-century epistemic shift in representations of value, "Exchanging," in *The Order of Things* 166-214.

27. *Troilus and Cressida*'s pervasive mercantile metaphors have been the subject of a large number of essays from an almost equally large variety of critical perspectives. See Southall; Stafford; Wilson; Barfoot; Bruster, " 'The Alteration of Men': *Troilus and Cressida,* Troynovant, and Trade," chap. 7 of *Drama and the Market in the Age of Shakespeare* (97-117); Engle, "Always Already in the Market: The Politics of Evaluation in *Troilus and Cressida,*" chap. 7 of *Shakespearean Pragmatism* (147-63); Grady, " 'Mad Idolatry': Commodification and Reification in *Troilus and Cressida,*" chap. 2 of *Shakespeare's Universal Wolf* (58-94).

28. Discussions of the play's presentation of the origin of value include Nowottny; Kermode's very useful riposte to Nowottny (including her invocation of Hobbes), "Opinion, Truth, and Value"; Elton's enduringly illuminating essay "Shakespeare's Ulysses and the Problem of Value"; Greene's pair of essays, "Shakespeare's Cressida," which approaches the question of value from the point of view of patriarchal economies of female subject formation, and "Language and Value in Shakespeare's *Troilus and Cressida,*" which reapplies her argument to issues of signification; Girard, "Politics," which analyzes value in terms of mimetic desire and violence; Engle, which relates Shakespeare's treatment of ancient codes of value to the emergence in the late sixteenth century of a ubiquitous market economy; Charnes, " 'So Unsecret to Ourselves,' " which provides a powerful development of and corrective to Greene's and Girard's arguments through an analysis of value as it is produced within the play's male homosocial structures of desire; and James's " 'Tricks We Play on the Dead': Making History in *Troilus and Cressida,*" chap. 3 of *Shakespeare's Troy* (85-118), which treats value through the prism of the play's heterogeneous, conflicting literary sources.

29. The most extensive treatment of early modern theories of plague transmission, including miasmic models of infection, is Barroll; see esp. chap. 3. On Shakespeare's largely miasmic understanding of infection, see Hoeniger 187-90.

30. Fabricius discusses Clowes's theories of the causes and cures of venereal disease (106-12).

31. Compare James's argument (110-11) that Troilus's desire for Cressida is complicated by his investment in a "truthful" ego-ideal predicated on her faithlessness; according to this reading, his Petrarchan love already teeters on the brink of sanctimonious disgust.

32. See, e.g., Starkey, who suggests that the body politic suffers from "palsy" as a result of merchants' importing foreign "trifles and conceits," especially "French cloth" (82, 92); Gosson, who complains about "wanton Italian bookes, which being translated into english, haue poysoned the olde manners of our Country with foreine delights" (sig. B6); and Tryon, who declaims against Spanish fruits, arguing that "the eating and drinking of *Forreign Ingredients*" is what most "destroys and hurts [the] health" of bodies natural and politic (90).

33. "Contamination" derives from the same etymological root as "contagion"; in medieval

Latin, "contamen" meant "infection." Hence "contaminate" and its various cognates appear repeatedly in early modern medical discourse, most notably in relation to syphilis: the English translation of Oswald Gaebelkover's *Boock of Physicke* (London, 1599) analyzes "Contamination in [the] bodye, be it either of the French disease, or of anye other such like infectious diseases" (sig. Bb3v). Interestingly, both "infect" and "contaminate" came to have a twinned medical and numismatic application: in his *Metallographia; or, An History of Metals* (London, 1671), the physician John Webster speaks of "imperfect metals" which have been "infected, or contaminated with terrestrial faeculency" (sig. S2v). My thoughts on Helen's "contamination" by her male evaluators owe a great debt to Heather James's astute reading of Diomedes' lines; see James 104–5.

34. By contrast, Robert Weimann has argued that *Troilus and Cressida*'s "bifold authority" springs from the divided *locus* and *platea* of the Elizabethan platform stage (see "Bifold Authority" and "Representation and Performance").

35. In her important essay "Unbodied Figures of Desire," Cook observes that Cressida's lines elsewhere in the play sound "like an effect of ventriloquism" (51). See also Alan Sinfield's reading of Cressida's "character" (54).

36. Compare Marx and Engels's famous epithet about the transformations of value by capitalist production: "all that is solid melts into air, all that is holy is profaned" ("The Communist Manifesto," in *The Marx-Engels Reader* 476). Elton writes of the "market fluctuations" that underwrite the play's theme of mutability in general and Ulysses' speech on time in particular (104). Engle likewise sees Ulysses' speech as espousing a "market ethic" (157).

37. For an illuminating explication and adaptation of Simmel's theory of the commensuration of demand in the production of value, see Appadurai.

38. See Elton, esp. 100–7; Greene, "Language and Value" 272.

39. See also Newlin, who documents the many early-twentieth-century stage treatments of *Troilus and Cressida* that viewed the play as addressing fundamentally "modern" concerns.

40. Cressida may have been depicted as leprous also in Henry Chettle and Thomas Dekker's lost *Troilus and Cressida* (1599). A fragmentary "plot" of Chettle and Dekker's play has survived, and it indicates a great debt to Henryson's poem; as in the latter, Cressida is shown to enter "w[th] Beggars," which suggests strongly that Chettle and Dekker followed Henryson in afflicting Cressida with leprosy. If so, Shakespeare's deviation from this tradition, given its freshness in his audience's minds, would have been all the more noteworthy. See Jenkins 222.

41. As Greg Bentley points out, other writers attributed the causes of syphilis to melancholy; but the humoral etiologies they proposed were often confusingly interarticulated with exogenous models of infection. Von Hutten's humoral explanation of the disease, for example, is blended with a miasmic one, inasmuch as he attributes the complexional disarray causing syphilis to bad vapors. See Bentley 10.

42. Kermode's assumption of an objective value that the deluded will misapprehends has been repeated by subsequent critics. Greene says of Troilus and the other male evaluators, "[A]ssuming that value is assigned by 'will,' these characters subvert reason with passion and invert the proper working of the mind" ("Language and Value" 277); Wilson similarly asserts that "Shakespeare's play directs a world of trivial combat and mannered passion where infected will strains to replace objective merit" (15). For a critique of the implicit essentialism of such presumptions, see Charnes 70.

43. Ulysses' theory of value is in many respects a precursor of a phenomenon that was to emerge with increasing forcefulness throughout the seventeenth century: that is, the valuation of a commodity not by any allegedly intrinsic use-value it might possess but by an appeal to an ineffable source outside it that determines its market or exchange value. Perhaps the best example of such an appeal is provided by not the play itself but by the epistle to the 1609 quarto edition, dedicated by the "Never Writer" to the "Ever Reader." *Troilus and Cressida,* the Never Writer claims, has avoided the taint of the stage, where it would have been "stal'd" or contaminated by its audiences' assessments, both contagiously ("clapper-clawd with the palmes of the vulger") and miasmically ("sullied, with the smoaky breath of the multitude"). The Never Writer insists that the play's "scape" from the stage to print has been necessary for it not only to avoid such infection but also to disclose a stable value that derives from an external "sovereign" source, the playwright's "power of wit." All quotes are from *Troilus and Cressida,* ed. Kenneth Palmer (London: Methuen, 1982), 95. For more on the tendency to attribute an artistic commodity's market value to the power of an external creator, see Ann Rosalind Jones and Peter Stallybrass's recent work on fetishism and the origin of value in early modern Europe, particularly "Borrowed Robes: Clothes and the Making of the Renaissance Theater," chap. 7 of their forthcoming *Worn Worlds.*

44. For a discussion of the broader application of this notion in late Elizabethan and early Stuart political discourse, see Harris, *Foreign Bodies,* chap. 3. The reversability of the sun's curative and noxious properties is hinted at in *Timon of Athens* when Timon exhorts the "blessed breeding sun" to "infect the air" (4.3.1, 3).

45. On the ambivalent politics of the speech, see Cartelli 147-51.

46. It is worth noting that Hobbes proposes a similar compromise. Although he endorses an exogenous notion of value, he is disturbed by its civil consequences, which he notably figures in pathological terms: "[T]he *diseases* of a commonwealth . . . proceed from the poison of seditious doctrines, whereof one is, *that euery private man is judge of good and evil actions.* This is true in the condition of mere nature, where there are no civil laws. . . . But otherwise, it is manifest, that the measure of good and evil actions, is the civil law" (3:310). For Hobbes as for Malynes, in other words, subjection to civil law imposed by a monarch arrests the potential anarchy of multiple valuation. See also Elton 106-7.

47. "Drawing attention to the narrative techniques—rhetoric, genre, and disposition—that stamp interpretive values on the legendary events and heroes at Troy, [Shakespeare] exposes lack of authenticity in a legend which exists only to bequeath authoritative origins. . . . In the play's very dramatic construction, Shakespeare reiterates Troilus' notorious query, 'What's aught but as 'tis valued?' " (James 89-90). For a related reading of the intertextual ensembles that constitute character in *Troilus and Cressida,* see Cook 52. Compare Engle's richly suggestive argument that "aesthetic evaluations of the two major sources, Homer's *Iliad* and Chaucer's *Troilus and Criseyde,* and personal evaluations within the play are subject to a forceful thought experiment in perspective reversal" (23).

48. Compare Homer, *Iliad* 17.123; Vergil, *Aeneid* 2.438; and Ovid, *Metamorphoses* 13.291.

49. Compare James's remarks about Achilles' valuation of Hector (105).

50. See also Loewenstein for similar conclusions about Shakespeare's contamination of his Iliadic materials. In Hamlet's rendering of the "rugged Pyrrhus" set piece before the players, Loewenstein argues, "one can easily find a furiously empowered effacement of all distinction

between Trojan Homer, Trojan Virgil, and Trojan Shakespeare . . . the speech conflates the manner of ranting tragedy and of Virgilian epic. This is *contaminatio,* practiced in such a way that it elides the distinction between *imitatio* and the adoption of stylistic fashion" (75-76).

51. Pandarus may indeed have bequeathed the Winchester Goose to the play's audiences or readers. His syphilis is perhaps responsible for what is widely regarded as a compositor's error in the first published version of John Marston's *The Insatiate Countess:* a line from Signior Claridia's extended admonition to husbands in 5.1, which editors agree should read, "The box unto Pandora is given," was rendered in the 1613 quarto edition, "The poxe is unto Panders given." See Marston 3:81.

52. These figures are taken from Craig, esp. xv, 133. On the vicissitudes of coordinating competing systems of measurement in the sixteenth and seventeenth centuries, see Heckscher 1:110-27. Challis provides a useful comparative breakdown of troy, avoirdupois, and tower weight systems (appendix 1, 303). For a suggestive discussion of troy weight in relation to *Troilus and Cressida,* see Bruster 100-1.

# Works Cited

Ackerknecht, Erwin H. "Historical Notes on Cancer." *Medical History* 2 (1958): 114-19.

Appadurai, Arjun. "Introduction: Commodities and the Politics of Value." *The Social Life of Things: Commodities in Cultural Perspective.* Ed. Arjun Appadurai. Cambridge: Cambridge UP, 1986. 3-63.

Appleby, Joyce Oldham. *Economic Thought and Ideology in Seventeenth-Century England.* Princeton: Princeton UP, 1978.

Barfoot, C. C. "*Troilus and Cressida:* 'Praise Us as We Are Tasted.' " *Shakespeare Quarterly* 39 (1988): 45-57.

Barroll, Leeds. *Politics, Plague, and Shakespeare's Theater: The Stuart Years.* Ithaca, NY: Cornell UP, 1991.

Bentley, Greg W. *Shakespeare and the New Disease: The Dramatic Function of Syphilis in "Troilus and Cressida," "Measure for Measure," and "Timon of Athens."* New York: Peter Lang, 1983.

Boas, F. S. *Shakespeare and His Predecessors.* New York: Scribner's, 1896.

Boorde, Andrew. *Breuiary of Helthe, for All Maner of Syckenesses and Diseases the Whiche May Be in Man, or Woman.* London, 1547.

Bruster, Douglas. *Drama and the Market in the Age of Shakespeare.* Cambridge: Cambridge UP, 1992.

Cartelli, Thomas. *Marlowe, Shakespeare, and the Economy of Theatrical Experience.* Philadelphia: U of Pennsylvania P, 1991.

Challis, C. E. *The Tudor Coinage.* Manchester: Manchester UP, 1978.

Chapman, George. *The Iliads of Homer Translated According to the Greek.* 2 vols. London: J. M. Dent, 1898.

Charnes, Linda. *Notorious Identity: Materializing the Subject in Shakespeare.* Cambridge, MA: Harvard UP, 1993.

Clowes, William. *A Briefe and Necessary Treatise, Touching the Cure of the Disease Now*

*Usually Called Lues Venera, by Unctions and Other Approued Waies of Curing, in a Profitable and Necessarie Booke of Obseruations.* London, 1596.

Cook, Carol. "Unbodied Figures of Desire." *Theater Journal* 38 (1986): 34–52.

Cotgrave, Randle. *A Dictionarie of the French and English Tongues.* London, 1611.

Craig, John. *The Mint: A History of the London Mint from* A.D. *287 to 1948.* Cambridge: Cambridge UP, 1953.

De Vigo, Joannes. *The Most Excellent Workes of Chirurgerye, Made and Set Forth by Maister John Vignon.* Trans. Bartholomew Traheron. London, 1543.

Elton, W. R. "Shakespeare's Ulysses and the Problem of Value." *Shakespeare Studies* 2 (1966): 95–111.

Engle, Lars. *Shakespearean Pragmatism: Market of His Time.* Chicago: U of Chicago P, 1993.

Fabricius, Johannes. *Syphilis in Shakespeare's England.* London: Jessica Kingsley, 1994.

Fischer, Sandra K. *Econolingua: A Glossary of Coins and Economic Language in Renaissance Drama.* Newark: U of Delaware P, 1985.

Foucault, Michel. *The Order of Things: An Archaeology of Human Knowledge.* London: Tavistock, 1970.

Fracastoro, Girolamo. *De Contagione at Contagiosis Morbis et Eorum Curatione.* Trans. Wilmer Care Wright. New York: G. P. Putnam's Sons, 1930.

Gaebelkover, Oswald. *Boock of Physicke.* London, 1599.

Girard, René. "The Plague in Literature." *"To Double Business Bound": Essays on Literature, Mimesis, and Anthropology.* Baltimore: Johns Hopkins UP, 1978. 136–54.

———. "The Politics of Desire in *Troilus and Cressida.*" *Shakespeare and the Question of Theory.* Ed. Patricia Parker and Geoffrey Hartman. New York and London: Methuen, 1985. 188–209.

———. *A Theatre of Envy: William Shakespeare.* Oxford: Oxford UP, 1991.

Gosson, Stephen. *Playes Confuted in Fiue Actions, Prouing That They Are Not to Be Suffred in a Christian Common Weale.* London, 1582 [?].

Grady, Hugh. *Shakespeare's Universal Wolf: Postmodernist Studies in Early Modern Reification.* Oxford: Clarendon Press, 1996.

Greene, Gayle. "Language and Value in Shakespeare's *Troilus and Cressida.*" *Studies in English Literature* 21 (1981): 271–85.

———. "Shakespeare's Cressida: 'A Kind of Self.'" *The Woman's Part: Feminist Criticism of Shakespeare.* Ed. Carolyn Ruth Swift Lenz, Gayle Greene, and Carol Thomas Neely. Urbana: U of Illinois P, 1980. 133–49.

Harris, Jonathan Gil. "'The Canker of England's Commonwealth': Gerard de Malynes and the Origins of Economic Pathology." *Textual Practice* 13 (1999): 311–28.

———. *Foreign Bodies and the Body Politic: Discourses of Social Pathology in Early Modern England.* Cambridge: Cambridge UP, 1998.

Heckscher, Eli F. *Mercantilism.* Trans. Mendel Shapiro. 2d ed. 2 vols. London: George Allen and Unwin, 1955.

Henryson, Robert. *Testament of Cresseid.* Ed. Denton Fox. London: Thomas Nelson, 1968.

Heywood, Thomas. *The Dramatic Works of Thomas Heywood.* 6 vols. London: John Pearson, 1874.

Hobbes, Thomas. *The Collected Works of Thomas Hobbes.* Ed. Sir William Molesworth. 2d impression. London: Routledge/Thoemmes Press, 1994.

Hoeniger, F. David. *Medicine and Shakespeare in the English Renaissance.* Newark: U of Delaware P/Associated Press, 1992.

Homer. *The Iliad.* Trans. Richmond Lattimore. Chicago: U of Chicago P, 1951.

James, Heather. *Shakespeare's Troy: Drama, Politics, and the Translation of Empire.* Cambridge: Cambridge UP, 1997.

Jamieson, Michael. "The Problem Plays, 1920–1970." *Shakespeare Survey* 25 (1972): 1–10.

Jenkins, Harold. *The Life and Work of Henry Chettle.* London: Sidgwick and Jackson, 1934.

Jones, Ann Rosalind, and Peter Stallybrass. *Worn Worlds: Clothes and the Fashioning of the Renaissance Subject.* Cambridge: Cambridge UP, forthcoming.

Kavanagh, James H. "Shakespeare in Ideology." *Alternative Shakespeares.* Ed. John Drakakis London: Methuen, 1985. 144–65.

Keil, Harry. "The Evolution of the Term Chancre and Its Relation to the History of Syphilis." *Journal of the History of Medicine* 4 (1949): 407–16.

Kermode, Frank. "Opinion, Truth and Value." *Essays in Criticism* 5 (1955): 181–87.

Lodge, Thomas. *A Treatise of the Plague: Containing the Nature, Signes, and Accidents of the Same, with the Certaintie and Absolute Cure of the Fevers, Botches and Carbuncles that Raigne in These Times.* London, 1603.

Loewenstein, Joseph. "Plays Agonistic and Competitive: The Textual Approach to Elsinore." *Renaissance Drama* 19 (1988): 63–90.

Macherey, Pierre, and Etienne Balibar. "Literature as an Ideological Form: Some Marxist Hypotheses." *Praxis* 5 (1980): 43–58.

Mallin, Eric S. *Inscribing the Time: Shakespeare and the End of Elizabethan England.* Berkeley: U of California P, 1995.

Malynes, Gerard de. *Consuetudo, Vel, Lex Mercatoria; or, The Ancient Law-Merchant.* 3 vols. London, 1622.

———. *A Treatise of the Canker of England's Commonwealth.* London, 1601.

Marston, John. *The Plays of John Marston.* Ed. H. Harvey Wood. 3 vols. London: Oliver and Boyd, 1934–39.

*The Marx-Engels Reader.* Ed. Robert C. Tucker. 2d ed. New York and London: W. W. Norton, 1978.

Middleton, Thomas, and William Rowley. *The Old Law.* Ed. Catherine M. Shaw. New York and London: Garland, 1982.

Muchmore, Lynn. "Gerrard de Malynes and Mercantile Economics." *History of Political Economy* 1 (1969): 336–58.

Newlin, Jeanne. "The Modernity of *Troilus and Cressida.*" *Harvard Library Bulletin* 17 (1969): 353–73.

*The Nomenclator, or Remembrancer of Adrianus Junius.* London, 1585.

Nowottny, Winifred M. T. " 'Opinion' and 'Value' in *Troilus and Cressida.*" *Essays in Criticism* 4 (1954): 282–96.

Nutton, Vivian. "The Seeds of Disease: An Explanation of Contagion and Infection from the Greeks to the Romans." *Medical History* 27 (1983): 1–34.

Ovid. *Metamorphoses.* Trans. Rolfe Humphries. Bloomington: Indiana UP, 1955.

Pagel, Walter. *Paracelsus: An Introduction to Philosophical Medicine in the Era of the Renaissance.* Basel: S. Karger, 1958.

Paracelsus. *Sämtliche Werke.* Ed. Karl Sudhoff. 14 vols. Munich: R. Oldenbourg, 1922.

———. *Selected Writings.* Ed. Jolande Jacobi. Trans. Norbert Guterman. New York: Pantheon, 1958.

Paster, Gail Kern. *The Body Embarrassed: Drama and the Disciplines of Shame in Early Modern England.* Ithaca, NY: Cornell UP, 1993.

Paynell, Thomas. *Regimen Sanitatis Salerni; or, The Schoole of Salernes Regiment of Health.* London, (1528) 1649.

Quétel, Claude. *History of Syphilis.* Trans. Judith Braddock and Brian Pike. Baltimore: Johns Hopkins UP, 1992.

Rather, L. J. *The Genesis of Cancer: A Study in the History of Ideas.* Baltimore: Johns Hopkins UP, 1978.

Roover, Raymond de. "Gerard de Malynes as an Economic Writer: From Scholasticism to Mercantilism." *Business, Banking, and Economic Thought in Late Medieval and Early Modern Europe.* Ed. Julius Kirshner. Chicago: U of Chicago P, 1974. 346–66.

———. "What Is Dry Exchange? A Contribution to the Study of English Mercantilism." *Business, Banking, and Economic Thought in Late Medieval and Early Modern Europe.* Ed. Julius Kirshner. Chicago: U of Chicago P, 1974. 183–99.

Shakespeare, William. *The Riverside Shakespeare.* Ed. G. Blakemore Evans et al. 2d ed. Boston: Houghton Mifflin, 1997.

———. *Troilus and Cressida.* Ed. Kenneth Palmer. London: Methuen, 1982.

Simmel, Georg. *The Philosophy of Money.* Trans. Tom Bottomore and David Frisby. London: Routledge, 1978.

Sinfield, Alan. *Faultlines: Cultural Materialism and the Politics of Dissident Reading.* Berkeley: U of California P, 1992.

Solomon, Julie Robin. *Objectivity in the Making: Francis Bacon and the Politics of Inquiry.* Baltimore: Johns Hopkins UP, 1998.

Sontag, Susan. *Illness as Metaphor.* New York: Farrar, Straus, and Giroux, 1978.

Southall, Raymond. "*Troilus and Cressida* and the Spirit of Capitalism." *Shakespeare in a Changing World.* Ed. Arnold Kettle. London: Lawrence and Wishart, 1964. 217–32.

Spiegel, Henry William. *The Growth of Economic Thought.* 3d ed. Durham, NC: Duke UP, 1991.

Spurgeon, Caroline F. E. *Shakespeare's Imagery and What It Tells Us.* Cambridge: Cambridge UP, 1952.

Stafford, T. J. "Mercantile Imagery in *Troilus and Cressida.*" *Shakespeare in the Southwest: Some New Directions.* Ed. T. J. Stafford. El Paso: Texas Western Press, 1969. 36–42.

Starkey, Thomas. *Dialogue between Reginald Pole and Thomas Lupset.* Ed. Kathleen Burton. London: Chatto and Windus, 1948.

Supple, B. E.. "Currency and Commerce in the Early Seventeenth Century." *Economic History Review,* 2d ser., 10 (1957): 239–55.

Taylor, John. *All the Workes of Iohn Taylor the Water Poet.* London, 1630.

Tryon, Thomas. *The Good Housewife Made Doctor.* London, 1685.

Vergil. *The Aeneid.* Trans. L. R. Lind. Bloomington: Indiana UP, 1963.

Von Hutten, Ulrich. *De Guaiaci Medicina et Morbo Gallico.* London, 1533.

Webster, John. *Metallographia; or, An History of Metals.* London, 1671.

Weimann, Robert. "Bifold Authority in Shakespeare's Theatre." *Shakespeare Quarterly* 39 (1988): 401-17.

———. "Representation and Performance: The Uses of Authority in Shakespeare's Theatre." *PMLA* 107 (1992): 497-510.

Wilson, Douglas B. "The Commerce of Desire: Freudian Narcissism in Chaucer's *Troilus and Criseyde* and Shakespeare's *Troilus and Cressida.*" *English Language Notes* 21 (1983): 11-22.

# "Thy Voice Squeaks": Listening for Masculinity on the Early Modern Stage

GINA BLOOM

ERHAPS BECAUSE OF the burgeoning industry of Shakespeare films and the late-twentieth-century fascination with everything Elizabethan, new students of early modern English drama often are surprisingly familiar with the conditions under which Shakespeare's plays were originally performed, even the very unmodern convention of using boys to play female parts. And though some consumers of Shakespeare still echo Stephen Orgel's query about why the English stage took boys for women, a more intriguing question seems to be one of process: not why but *how* was gender negotiated on an all-male stage? Whereas work by Orgel and other scholars has been most attentive to the visual aspects of early modern gender performance, this essay examines how the aural dimensions of the Elizabethan theater shaped its representations of gender.[1]

The impact of sound on the performance of gender is at the heart of two recent popular interpretations of Shakespearean theater, John Madden's *Shakespeare in Love* and Michael Hoffman's *A Midsummer Night's Dream.* In each of these Hollywood films, the major turning point of the plot involves a male actor realizing that his physiological state prevents him from mimicking a woman's voice effectively, a failure that threatens to undermine the success of the play. Although Madden's and Hoffman's films approach the Bard in distinct ways and are located in different historical moments, they resolve this play-within-the-film vocal crisis in strikingly

39

similar ways. In *Shakespeare in Love*, the cast of *Romeo and Juliet* is surprised to hear a few minutes before the curtain rises that the voice of the boy who will play Juliet has begun to change. The film maintains that this is cause enough to pull the actor from the part, even though the only possible substitute for him is a woman, whose presence on the stage thwarts royal decree.[2] *A Midsummer Night's Dream* imagines what would happen if a postpubescent male actor, with a fully cracked voice, were allowed to play the female role. When the deep-voiced Flute uses a falsetto vocal style to personate Thisbe in the play within the film, his audience breaks into laughter at his aesthetically unpleasant, squeaking sound. The solution here is not to bring in a real woman's voice, as in *Shakespeare in Love,* but to allow the grave voice to be used. Flute completes the play in his natural voice and the performance, like that of *Romeo and Juliet,* is portrayed as a smashing success. In Madden's and Hoffman's assessments of the boy-actor stage convention, the success of a play is contingent on the physiological state of the male body and its capacity to produce a satisfying aural experience for the audience. Both films suggest that it is better to risk legal censure or the audience's distraction than to allow an unstable, squeaking male voice on stage.

In their displacement of squeaking voices, these modern performances diverge from early modern theatrical practice. For in contrast to today's audiences, early modern theatergoers had ample opportunity to hear unstable male voices. Whether the frequent enactments of squeaking voices in early modern plays point to a dramatic convention or offer evidence of a theatrical custom (that boy actors continued to perform while their voices were changing), there is much at stake in noting the role of these voices on the stage and in the culture at large.[3] On stage or off, a squeaking voice announced a boy's transition into manhood at the same time that it indicated that the transition had yet to be completed. As it attested to a boy's liminal position in a gradual process of pubescent development, the squeaking voice exposed the fragile condition of young male bodies and, as a corollary, the aleatory nature of gender differentiation. This essay examines precarious vocality as a cultural concern in early modern England and considers how the presence of unstable male voices shaped the representation of gender on the stage.

Whereas most critics interested in boy players and the enactment of gender have focused on the ramifications of boys playing the parts of women, I am interested in the implications of boys playing the parts of adult men.

This would necessarily have been the case in all-male children's companies. As some of the boys in these companies were likely to have been on the verge of puberty, their voices were liable to crack at any time. I argue that these unstable voices would have been a source of uneasiness for male actors and audiences, for in early modern England, vocal control was a signifier of masculinity. Thus, the successful performance of masculinity on the stage would have been undermined by the particular vocal proper-ties of the actors responsible for representing manliness. Unlike modern theatrical interpretations—wherein concerns about vocal instability are manifested in the decision to keep unstable voices off the stage—early modern theatrical practices allowed a space for unstable voices on the stage. The theater played on early modern men's already present fears of losing control over not only the production of voice but the production of gender identity as well.

## Listening for Masculinity

To understand the role of the voice in cultural and dramatic performances of masculinity—that is, to listen for masculinity—we must recognize a historical difference between early modern and contemporary represen-tations of the relation between gender identity and voice. Contemporary popular culture stereotypes masculinity aurally through a bass voice. In Hoffman's *Midsummer Night's Dream,* to take one convenient example, the hypermasculine Oberon (played by Rupert Everett) sports not only buff pectorals but a deep, sultry voice as well. Early modern texts also equate masculinity with a deep voice, but at stake in their understanding of this voice feature is more than aural aesthetics. According to early modern humoral theories, the quality of a man's voice, as it testifies to the physio-logical state of his body, also denotes the condition of the social, political, and cosmic world he inhabits. Order in these macrocosmic spheres—order that is vital to a smoothly functioning patriarchal system—is intertwined with the body's maintenance of a humoral equilibrium (balanced amounts of heat versus coldness; of wetness versus dryness).

Varying levels of body heat and moisture, explains Francis Bacon in *Sylva Sylvarum* (1626), determine the deepness of the body's voice:

*Children, Women, Eunuchs* have more small and shrill *Voices,* than *Men.* The reason is . . . from the Dilation of the Organ; which (it is true) is . . . caused by Heat. But the Cause of *Changing* the *Voice,* at the yeares of Puberty, is more obscure. It seemeth to be, for that when much of the Moisture of the Body, which did before irrigate the Parts, is drawne downe to the Spermaticall vessells; it leaveth the Body more hot than it was; whence commeth the dilatation of the Pipes. (52)

An increase in the body's heat—which may be brought on by a decrease in moisture—causes the vocal pipes to dilate and a deeper voice to be produced. This, Bacon explains, is why boys going through puberty begin to speak with graver voices. Levinus Lemnius in *Touchstone of Complexions* (1576) considers how the body's changing levels of heat have implications for vocal aesthetics and for character:

They therefore that have hoate bodyes, are also of nature variable, and chau[n]geable, ready, pro[m]pt, lively, lusty and applyable: of tongue, trowling, perfect, & perswasive: delyvering their words distinctly, plainlye and pleasauntlye, with a voyce thereto not squekinge and slender, but streynable, comely and audible. The thing that maketh the voyce bigge, is partlye the wydenes of the breast and vocall Artery, and partly the inwarde or internall heate, from whence proceedeth the earnest affections, vehemente motions, and fervent desyers of the mynde. (qtd. in Smith 100)

The ideal voice being described in this passage, Bruce Smith points out, is a man's voice, for according to humoral theory, only men have enough heat to produce what the passage suggests are aesthetically desirable vocal features (100-1).[4] Women and children, having bodies that tend to be colder than men's, are endowed with smaller vocal instruments; rather than producing a voice "perfect, & perswasive . . . comely and audible," delivered "distinctly, plainlye and pleasauntlye," women and children produce unpleasant, "squekinge and slender," inaudible voices.

If the body, as early modern men and women believed, is a microcosm with concordances to macrocosmic spheres of family, nation, and God, then a man unable to keep his voice from squeaking manifests a breakdown in patriarchal order. Male identity and, concurrently, male superiority are contingent on men maintaining control over their vocal sounds. A scene from John Marston's play *Antonio's Revenge* suggests as much. When Antonio, Pandulfo, and Alberto—the drama's three disempowered men— join together to wail against the injustices that have brought disorder to their social and political lives, Antonio asks a page if he will "sing a dirge." But Pandulfo discourages the singing: "No, no song; 'twill be vile out of tune" (4.2.88-89).[5] Alberto thinks that Pandulfo is referring to the physiological state of the boy's voice: "Indeed, he's hoarse; the poor boy's voice is cracked" (90), but Pandulfo, lamenting his failure to obtain retribution for the murder of his son and his banishment from the dukedom, has a more profound thought in mind:

> Why, coz, why should it not be hoarse and cracked,
> When all the strings of nature's symphony
> Are cracked and jar? Why should his voice keep tune,
> When there's no music in the breast of man?
> (4.2.91–4)

The boy's hoarse voice is symptomatic not only of a physiological disturbance but of a social, political, and spiritual one as well. The pubescent boy's inability to control the microcosm of his body is figured as homologous with Pandulfo, Antonio, and Alberto's failure to maintain macrocosmic order.

When Marston's play was originally performed, we must not forget, a hoarse voice was not only a fictional concern for the pubescent boy represented in this scene; it may have been a real source of uneasiness for the pubescent actors playing the parts of Pandulfo, Antonio, and Alberto. Their fragile physiological conditions threatened to disrupt their enactments of masculine character. Since voice changes were considered in this period an inevitable experience of puberty, representations of and dramatic allusions to the inevitability of a cracked male voice served as reminders that the "homeostatic masculine body" was an impossible ideal (Breitenberg 53). If early modern patriarchal systems were, as scholars have argued, predicated on clear and fixed differentiation between the sexes, then the pubescent voice—unpredictably modulating between (female) squeakiness and (male) gravity—not only upset binary gender systems but the logic and operation of early modern patriarchy itself. Attending to the material practice of voice on the stage enables us to unpack the relation between vocal control and masculinity, to consider how early moderns coped theatrically with the instability of the male performing body and concomitant anxieties about gender order.[6]

The social significance of the material voice and the theatrical production of gender difference have been examined as separate issues in feminist scholarship, but the relations between the two have rarely been discussed. Moreover, work on each of these topics has been focused, in the first case, primarily on women's bodies (Boose; Parker; Stallybrass) and, in the second

case, on spectatorship and visual practice.[7] One exception is Dympna
Callaghan's essay on the transvestite stage, in which she examines how representations of men's failure to control the voice can be read as attempts to
grapple with the fraught process of sexual differentiation.[8] For Callaghan,
the quality of the stage performer's voice is ultimately symptomatic of the
"presence or lack of male genital sexual equipment" (323). To be sure, male
genitalia and other body parts feature in early modern assessments of the
voice (see Mazzio on the tongue); however, the production of speech and
its relation to masculine identity were also thought to be influenced by less
localized bodily processes (including humoral equilibrium, the condition
of a speaker's soul, and the material composition of breath). Subject more
acutely to temporal and spatial contingencies, such processes cannot be
theorized in terms of a binary system of presence versus absence. Often
putting genitalia aside, early modern texts insist the cracking, squeaking
voice be understood as indexical of a body in flux, always in transition.
If the voice is a signifier of gender identity, then the squeaking voice that
betrays the liminal state of the male body also disturbs gender categories.[9]
Representations of men who lose control of their voices are not merely
signs pointing to an underlying, visually inflected crisis in identity but in
and of themselves figure ruptured masculinity.

   To contextualize my reading of the place of voice in theatrical representations of masculinity, I begin by surveying late-sixteenth- and early-
seventeenth-century representations of the voice as communicated by
writers interested in what I broadly term vocal training and performance.
I closely examine one text partly devoted to voice instruction for boys,
Richard Mulcaster's *Positions Concerning the Training Up of Children*
(1581). Written by a pedagogue whose theories of voice find their basis
in Galenic humoral theory, Mulcaster's treatise can be read in dialogue
with contemporaneous medical texts that address the precariousness of
young, male voices in similar terms. Furthermore, as it is authored by a
theater professional, Mulcaster's text helps define the nature of vocal crises
that arise on the early modern stage. With such vocal training in mind,
I then examine John Marston's early play *Antonio and Mellida* (1599–
1600). Written to be performed by an all-boy company, the drama enacts
the fraught vocal dynamics of the stage, self-consciously alluding to the
challenges of taming unruly boys' voices. In *Antonio and Mellida* the
physiologically unstable male voice of the actor is a persistent subtext in a
drama that defines masculinity as, in part, the ability to control one's voice.
Listening for the tension between the narrative action and the realities of

its dramatization in the theater, I examine the ideological implications of vocal instability for representations of masculinity in the play.

## Training the Unruly Voice

To get some sense of the terms by which early modern men and women conceived of the voice, one might note how often early modern writers figure the human vocal system as a musical instrument that can produce fine sounds when played properly. The analogy is especially pervasive in the period's drama. In Ben Jonson's play *Poetaster,* the ineloquent tongue is described not as naturally and permanently dissonant but as "untuned" (5.2.22). In Marston's *Antonio's Revenge,* a cough provides a "most pathetical rosin" for the voice, much as rosin on a bow helps produce a clear sound on the strings of a viol (3.3.41–42). And in *Antonio and Mellida,* the companion play to *Antonio's Revenge,* a melancholic lover requests a song of a page whom the lover compares to a musical instrument:

> Let each note breathe the heart of passion,
> The sad extracture of extremest grief.
> Make me a strain; speak groaning like a bell
> That tolls departing souls.
> Breathe me a point that may enforce me weep.
>                                                (4.1.132–36)

Though the commissioned singer may be like a bell, his human body and the sound it produces differ from this inanimate instrument and its sounds in significant ways. First, the material form of the young singer's music is breath; it is the breathing of notes that will enable this body-instrument to provoke weeping in the listener. Although instrumental music is capable of influencing listeners' emotions, the sounds produced by the human body are particularly potent insofar as human breath is a transporter of the soul. In Aristotle's *De Anima,* breath is conceived as the material substance responsible for transforming thoughts into spoken words that are then capable of affecting the minds and souls of listeners. The power of the vocalizer's breath to inspire emotion was much discussed in the early modern period, when classical theories of spiritual transmission had both learned and popular currency.[10]

But breath can only have these effects if it exits successfully from the body, carrying the harmonious voice with it. And such success, for many early modern writers, could not be taken for granted. A second difference writers note between vocal and instrumental sound is the material properties of the bodies that produce them. If one repeatedly strikes a bell made, say, of bronze or tin with the same force, in exactly the same place, and using the same baton, the bell will produce the same sound each time. The human body, however, was not considered so predictable. If the vocal cords or larynx had developed even minor irritations, the voice could emerge hoarse or raspy. Indeed, in making his musical request, the melancholic lover quoted above adds, "Thou has had a good voice, if this cold marsh / Wherein we lurk have not corrupted it" (4.1.128-30). The lover has heard the page's fine voice but knows that a "good voice" cannot be expected on every occasion. Because early modern humoral theory understood the body to be in a state of continual flux between cold and hot, moist and dry, an excess of coldness, such as that of the marsh, might allow a surplus of phlegm to accumulate on the larynx, corrupting the movement of the breath that carries vocal sound and preventing a "good voice" from emerging. This is not to say that an inanimate bell could not develop an "irritation"—it might fall from its tower and fracture. But alterations to the human vocal organs were considered more difficult to diagnose and more unpredictable in their development, given the complicated physiology thought to underlie them.

Despite the fact that the voice was often figured in physiological terms as unruly and resistant to training, or perhaps because of it, early modern writers interested in vocal instruction overwhelmingly insisted on its need to be disciplined.[11] Texts regarding oratory, for instance, emphasize the speaker's need to control vocalization. Charles Butler's *The English Grammar* (1633) describes volume as "the natural and ordinari force of each voic: which is to bee strained, or slacked" (55). Robert Robinson's *The Art of Pronunciation* (1617) explains in detail how the physiological processes of vocal articulation are an exercise in discipline:

A sound is an accident effected by the opposition of these two contraries, namely motion and restraint: motion of the ayre out of the inward parts of the body, and restraint of it in its motion. . . . Of the instrumentall causes of this motion. They are the lungs and hollow parts of the body, wherein the ayre is contained, which being drawne together by the motion, or rather the will of the mind, doe thereby expell the ayre, and cause it to be mooved through divers passages, as the throat, mouth, and nostrils. Of the instrumental causes of the restraint of this motion. They are the breast, throat, pallat, gums, tongue, lips and nostrils, stopping or hindering the free passages of the ayre in it's [*sic*] motion. (10–12)

For voice to happen, there must be a flow of air, of breath, from the lungs, through and out of the body cavity. But the art of speech, Robinson's tract explains, of producing sounds that will be comprehensible within a linguistic system, involves applying measured "restraint" on this flow of air. Robinson's manual is devoted to teaching the reader how to shape the oral cavity—how to purse the lips, hold the teeth, and organize the tongue so as to achieve the desired vocal sound. Speech, in effect, is disciplined voice.

Discipline is also central to the way early modern music theorists describe vocal practice. The preface to John Playford's *A Brief Introduction to the Skill of Musick* explains that grammar and music are taught

for the ordering their Voyce in Speech and Song; merely to Speak and Sing are of Nature, and this double use of the Articulate voyce the Rudest Swains of all Nations do make. But to Speak well, and Sing well, are of Art, neither of which can be attained but by the Rules and Precepts of Art. (A2r-v)

Anyone can produce sounds using the voice, but ordered sound—the art of singing and speaking—can only be created by the restrained vocalizer. Though published in 1658, Playford's passage concerning the difficulty of "ordering" the voice has much in common with the writings of voice pedagogues publishing earlier in the seventeenth century, during the heyday of the English professional theater. The preface to Charles Butler's *The Principles of Musik* (1636) discusses the need to build vocal skills because of the vagaries of singing—"the many Accidents of the Notes, the sudden changing, or rising and falling, of the voice." Musician John Dowland, translating Guido d'Arezzo's introduction to singing in 1609, explains that the natural tendency of most vocal performers is to articulate with too much fervor, loosening constraints in order to produce a forceful voice. But Dowland cautions, "Let the Singer take heed, least he begin too loud braying like an Asse, or when he hath begun with an uneven height, disgrace the Song. . . . It is not . . . the noyse of the lips, but the ardent desire of the Art, which like the lowdest voice doth pierce Gods eares" (Arezzo 80). Measured control over the voice, not unbridled expression, will be effective aesthetically and spiritually. Similar claims about the restraint essential for effective vocal performance appear in Richard Mulcaster's *Positions Concerning the Training Up of Children* (1581).

In this treatise concerning children's education, Mulcaster lays out an extensive program for the conditioning of children's voices, a program he claims will greatly benefit children's mental acuity in addition to their physiological well-being. Mulcaster's text is especially useful in the context of an account of vocal performance on the stage, for Mulcaster had an intimate connection with the theater industry. A preeminent educator in England at the end of the sixteenth and beginning of the seventeenth centuries, Mulcaster served as the master of the Merchant Taylors' school for twenty-five years (1561–85) and as the high master of St. Paul's School for a decade (1596–1608). In those capacities, he supervised the education of men who would later contribute in important ways to the English theater: writer Thomas Lodge, dramatist Thomas Kyd, and actor and playwright Nathan Field. As the director of a boys' company, Mulcaster was also directly responsible for theatrical productions. In the latter half of the sixteenth century, when children's companies were receiving tremendous favor at court, Mulcaster's students from the Merchant Taylors' school performed for Queen Elizabeth on at least six occasions (Barker).[12] And some historians suggest that when Mulcaster changed jobs later in his career and took on leadership of St. Paul's School around the turn of the century (1596), he might have helped revive the Children of Paul's, a company that, after a hiatus from the records, returned to popular status during the first decade of the seventeenth century.[13] To his contemporaries, then, Mulcaster was known for his skill at coaching young boys in the classroom and for the stage.[14] His dual interests are evident in his first major publication, *Positions*. Although scholars have tended to use the treatise to discuss Mulcaster's ideas about school curricula, as the text deals with performance-related matters, it is a useful piece of evidence not only for scholars of Renaissance pedagogy but for literary and theater historians as well.[15] Mulcaster's text helps map out some of the central issues at stake in a history of the voice: specifically, *Positions* reminds us that the male voices so important to early modern performance were understood in the period to be highly precarious and vulnerable to unpredictable alterations in character.

Mulcaster's theater experience seems to seep into the educational program he presents in *Positions*. Dancing, wrestling, walking, and running—all activities that would have had some place on the stage[16]—are among the nineteen exercises Mulcaster includes in his physical fitness program. Mulcaster is especially concerned with the fitness of children's voices, and he offers theories on and practical pointers for disciplining children's unruly vocal systems. Citing the practices promoted by ancient medical writers like Galen and early rhetoricians such as Quintillian,[17] Mulcaster's treatise urges supervised vocal exercise for all boys, and even for girls—though he much more carefully spells out the dangers of exercise where the "more weake" female body is concerned (176).[18] One of the exercises he prescribes is modeled after an ancient oratory practice called vociferation. The exercise consists of slowly and carefully increasing the volume and pitch of the voice, playing with its range, and then softening and deepening it:

[F]irst begin lowe, and moderatly, then went on to further strayning, of their speeche: sometimes drawing it out, with as stayed, and grave soundes, as was possible, sometimes bringing it backe, to the sharpest and shrillest, that they could, afterward not tarying long in that shrill sound, they retired backe again, slacking the straine of their voice, till they fell into that low, and moderate tenour, wherwith they first began. (58)

Like pedagogues Robinson and Butler, Mulcaster explains voluntary shifts in the character of the voice as resulting from the vocalizer's restraint: "strayning, of their speeche," "slacking the straine of their voice."

This language of discipline has cognates in early modern physiology. Sixteenth- and seventeenth-century medical writers conceive of vocal characteristics—such as pitch and volume—as a function of the size of the vocal organs, which can be manipulated to some extent by "strayning" and "slacking." Nicholas Culpeper's translation of Johann Vesling's *Anatomy of the Body of Man* (1653) explains how organ size and vocal quality are related: "[T]he larger the Larynx is, the larger is the Glottis, and as that is larger, so the Voyce is stronger and graver: The lesser . . . and narrower the Larynx is, the weaker, and shriller is the Voyce" (45). Anatomist Helkiah Crooke points out in *Microcosmographia* (1615) that the very structure of the vocal organs allows for their manipulation; the intersecting layers of gristle that make up the larynx, for instance, accommodate our "voluntary command" over constriction and expansion of the organ (634). The movable vocal organs produce an array of sounds when they are pushed, pulled, slackened, and strained, much like the strings of a viol. Of course, manipulation has limits; to a large degree, the body's age and sex determine the minimum and maximum size of its organs. According to early modern anatomy, the vocal organs of Mulcaster's prepubescent boys would have looked like those of women, and they would have been disposed toward producing a similar high-pitched, softer sound. Mulcaster's loud speaking exercise requires the young pupil to alter voluntarily the size of the vocal instruments as much as possible in order to experiment with range.

In addition to instructing the pupil in pitch and projection, exercises improve the overall quality or timbre of the voice by ridding the vocal organs of superfluous debris. Following Galenic physiology, Mulcaster writes that a clear voice results when "the sundry superfluities" that "darkened, weakened, and thickned the naturall heat" are "dismissed [from the body]" (56). Culpeper elucidates the relation between "superfluities" and vocal sound in further physiological detail: if the membrane covering the windpipe is "rough with flegm, the voice is hoarce" (44). This physiological process is especially important to Mulcaster, for his young male pupils, according to humoral theory, are naturally moist, and thus especially prone to accumulating too many "sundry superfluities."[19] Vocal exercises, by stimulating the larynx, vocal chords, windpipe, and lungs, increase the natural heat in these areas, allowing the body to dislodge superfluous phlegm. That speakers tend to expectorate when they talk is evidence, Mulcaster claims, that these humors are being expelled (56).

Because vocal exercises help regulate the body's humoral system, they not only improve the sound of the voice but simultaneously help the body maintain general levels of fitness. Excess moisture that remains on the vocal organs breeds disease, in addition to degrading the clarity of the voice. Because loud speaking exercises "encreaseth, cleanseth, strengtheneth, and fineth the naturall heat" (55), they can treat multiple somatic problems: "pewkishnesse of stomacke . . . vomiting . . . hardnesse of digestion . . . faintnesse . . . naughty constitution . . . painfull fetching their breath" (56), to name only a few. Mulcaster cites other "indoor" exercises that, operating under the same humoral ideology, have similar benefits. Loud singing, for instance, "sturreth the voice, spreadeth the instruments thereof, and craveth a clear passage" (59). An excellent cure for digestive ailments and headaches is the exercise of loud reading (60–61), discussed separately from loud speaking. Soft reading, though it works much less efficiently than does loud reading on the same parts, has the benefit of being sanctioned for practice directly after the pupil eats—loud reading after meals can interfere with digestion, and thus should be avoided (61). Talking, or, in Latin, *sermo,* remedies drowsiness (62). Cold heads and chests can be warmed up by the exercise of laughing, and further salutary benefits result from holding one's breath and weeping (63–71).[20] (Incidentally, stage directions in contemporaneous dramas indicate that all of these "indoor" activities were practiced on the stage.)

Mulcaster's modern editor, William Barker, remarks that these exercises likely strike today's readers as "unusual, even ridiculous" (xxiii). But these methods for loosening the humors in the throat and windpipe are less peculiar when we consider their historical company. For instance, Ann Brumwick's manuscript collection of home remedies offers a much more unusual cure "for dispersing anny humour gathered to the Thorat [*sic*] or for any soarnes in the same" (160). This involves blending dog dung with various organic powders, stuffing the mixture into a tobacco pipe, and then blowing the pipe into the patient's throat two or three times a day. As the patient is asked not to eat or drink for an hour after the treatment, it seems clear that the purpose is to provoke coughing, a stimulation of the lungs, throat, larynx, and windpipe, so as to achieve effects similar to the ones Mulcaster describes.

That recipe books are filled with treatments to dislodge excess humors from the vocal instruments suggests that vocal productions generated concerns for many early modern men and women and merited creative forms of attention. The kinds of patients who might use these cures are rarely mentioned, but it seems obvious that those who depended on healthy voices for their livelihoods would have been especially attentive to the functioning of their vocal organs. Though Mulcaster does not explicitly mention the benefits of vocal exercises for the voices of his performing children's troupe, such exercises could certainly be useful for warming up boys' voices before a play or concert. In fact, the original function of these exercises, as they were developed by ancient rhetoricians, was to prepare the voice for oratory competition and performance. Given Mulcaster's interest in training his pupils to perform at court and before a paying public, he most certainly knew the importance of voice to the success of a dramatic production. As a director of children, he would have been especially sensitive to the exertions of playing on a young voice: less physically mature boys would likely have had to strain their voices in order to be heard in noisy theaters, an action that could have detrimental long-term effects on boys' vocal instruments.

It is, however, impossible to know how or even if Mulcaster put into practice his vocal exercise program. Perhaps these exercises were only part of a utopian physical fitness program created by a pedagogue who never practiced on the stage what he preached on the page. How useful is Mulcaster's text, then, to the study of the early modern theatrical experience? I would suggest that it is highly useful, not necessarily to establish proof of particular stage practices—such as whether Mulcaster's boys actually trained with vociferation exercises—but in order to consider cultural attitudes toward vocal training and performance and to theorize the ideological implications of these attitudes. Before drawing out these implications, I would like to pause and consider what is at stake for theater history and performance studies in my proposed analysis of Mulcaster's text.

Theater history scholarship, notes William Ingram, often has been characterized by positivist approaches to evidence: the use of archival documents to write conclusive, event-centered narratives about the past.[21] One long-standing debate about vocal practices in the theater, for instance, has concerned what kinds of speaking styles were used by children's companies. Scholars who argue that the style was declamatory have claimed as evidence records of a strong relationship between stage acting and oratorical training, citing rhetorical manuals that taught boy actors how to modulate their voices during stylized oratorical address. Those who maintain that boys' delivery style was more "natural" advance as proof passages in city comedies or other plays written in colloquial language.[22] Of course, no matter what we include as evidence or how we integrate it, we cannot know what early modern listeners heard in the theaters or how they reacted to what they heard.[23] Though Mulcaster's text is not an accurate reflection of "how it was" and cannot with any certainty increase our knowledge of specific theatrical customs, it does help us consider what is at stake in early modern representations of vocalization as a material practice. What Mulcaster's pedagogical treatise shares with Ann Brumwick's recipe book and Culpeper's and Crooke's anatomical tracts is a view of human vocal organs as fragile and vulnerable to malfunction, a crucial observation for a materialist history of the stage.

The frailty of vocal instruments is most evident in Mulcaster's repeated warnings about the dangers of overstimulating the vocal organs; too much agitation "hurtes the voice" in addition to helping it. In fact, the more effective an exercise is in removing bodily humors that breed disease, the greater the risks that the exercise will create further problems, not only for the vocal instrument but for other areas of the body. For instance, the exercise of vociferation "filleth the head and make[th] it heavie"; it "causeth the temples [to] pante, the braines to beate, the eyes to swell, the eares to tingle" (57). The very processes that underlie the success of vocal exercises account for their dangers: the "chafing of the breath, and the breath instrumentes [in loud speaking] disperseth, and scattereth corrupt humours, thorough out the whole bodie" (57).

These dangers become even more pronounced when vocal exercises are practiced by young boys, who at the age of puberty experience a major shift in body temperament. As indicated above, an increase in heat is responsible for the comparatively graver and louder voice that mature men possess, for the influx of heat causes the vocal organs to expand, indeed to crack. Arviragus in Shakespeare's *Cymbeline* observes that a voice that has "got the mannish crack" (4.2.236) can still be manipulated to produce a range of sounds. But, as Arviragus's brother points out, the repertory of suitable songs cannot remain the same after puberty: the "notes . . . [will be] out of tune" (4.2.241).[24] The new size of the vocal organs, while enabling a louder, deeper sound, also limits the boy's ability to produce many of the shriller pitches that were once easily within reach.

This significant change in a boy's vocal sound, however, does not happen overnight. Because puberty involves a gradual metamorphosis of the body, the pubescent boy's voice has an unpredictable pattern of change. A high pitch impossible to sing one morning may again be in reach that very afternoon. This precarious state of boys' bodies is the basis for countless stage jokes about the cracked and squeaking male voice. After the character Firk in Thomas Dekker's *Shoemaker's Holiday* sings a round of "Hey down a-down derry," he apologizes for the "squeak" of his "organ-pipe" (13.9), claiming it needs liquoring. And, of course, most of us are familiar with Hamlet's address to the itinerant playing company that visits his palace. Turning to the young boy brought to play the women's parts, Hamlet gently mocks: "What, my young lady and mistress! by' lady, your ladyship is nearer to heaven than when I saw you last. . . . Pray God your voice, like a piece of uncurrent gold, be not crack'd within the ring" (2.2.424–28). The boy's growth in "altitude," or height and age, Hamlet hopes, has not been accompanied by a growth in his vocal organs, which might compromise his ability to play the part of the lady.

In its gloss of Hamlet's simile, the *Riverside Shakespeare* compares the actor's voice to a cracked ring: "a coin with a crack extending far enough in from the edge to cross the circle surrounding the stamp of the sovereign's head was unacceptable in exchange (uncurrent)" (1205n); that is, Hamlet hopes that the boy's voice is not cracked and, thus, unusable. Bruce Smith appreciates the material emphasis of this line, arguing that "ring" also puns on the shape of the actor's windpipe (229), a round organ that cracks as it expands during puberty, changing the boy's vocal range. Keeping in mind Smith's explication, I would suggest that the *Riverside* gloss be nuanced. Like a coin, the voice becomes "uncurrent" only when its crack reaches a certain point—when it is "crack'd within the ring." If the boy's voice is still in the early stages of changing, the boy may still be able to play the part of the lady; the partially matured voice, while it may portend an end to a boy's performance career, does not insist on its immediate demise. As the partially cracked coin has market value in spite of its degraded appearance, the boy's aesthetically unpleasant voice—which, according to Aristotle, is harsh or hoarse because of uneven expansion of the windpipe (Smith 227)—may have purchase power in the theater. Hamlet's comments suggest that only when the voice is fully cracked will the theater consider it "uncurrent."

Nevertheless, when Hamlet compares this cracked voice to "a piece of uncurrent gold," he reminds us of the value the early modern theater placed on boys' voices. Whether boys were so precious because they could approximate women's vocal sound on the all-male stage or because they had often been trained as choristers and could sing beautifully, the voice was part of a boy's "currency" in the theater, and a fully cracked voice altered a boy's worth in ways that we can never entirely know. Given the organizational and financial variables at issue, it must have been disconcerting that, in physiological terms, the rate of a boy's vocal growth was not easily predictable. Hamlet's speech suggests that a boy's height and age are not inherently linked to a particular stage in vocal development, and Mulcaster concurs when he writes that "ripenes in children, is not tyed to one time" (19). The precariousness of boys' voices likely made the jobs of directors like Mulcaster difficult indeed. Perhaps in rehearsals the boy playing Cleopatra had been able to use his uncracked or partially cracked voice to deliver the line "I shall see / Some squeaking Cleopatra boy my greatness" (*Antony and Cleopatra* 5.2.219–20) in a shrill pitch. But within a day, that range could exceed the actor's bodily capabilities, perhaps damaging his fragile vocal organs, or at least provoking laughter from the audience at the tragic climax of the play. The director of an all-boy theater company was, in a very real sense, playing with creatures of time.

Regardless of what the theater did with boys whose voices had cracked completely, we must account for the possibility that boys in vocal limbo were a presence on stage. How did the stage cope with the squeaking boys' voices that were a persistent feature of its industry? Let us explore the dramatic reaction of John Marston.

## Staging the Unruly Voice

Although it can be tricky to read for thematic elements across different literary genres, examining Mulcaster's treatise alongside Marston's play *Antonio and Mellida* proves useful.[25] For the young male voices that are the subject of Mulcaster's education program were also a key feature of the children's theater for which Marston wrote.[26] Many of Marston's plays ponder and showcase young male voices, but I take as exemplary *Antonio and Mellida,* a play that offers insight into the functioning of patriarchal systems and the manner in which gender identity and sexual difference were rendered intelligible in the theater and in English culture at large.[27]

Concerned with defining male identity—what it means to be a prince, courtier, father, son, indeed any man—*Antonio and Mellida* links failing patriarchal power structures of court and family with unstable male voices. This analogy weaves through the play not only thematically but performatively, for *Antonio and Mellida* frequently calls attention to the vulnerable vocality of boy actors. That self-conscious attention to boys' voices should be so evident in Marston likely comes as little surprise to his critics. Scholarship on Marston since the 1930s has noted the playwright's immersion in and self-conscious exploitation of the theatrical medium.[28] Anticipating the dramatic antics of modern playwrights like Tom Stoppard, Marston exposes his audience to the backstage realities of playing.[29] One critic writes of Marston that "no writer of the period . . . reminds us so persistently that we are in theatre watching a play" (Leggatt 119), and, I would add, hearing one too. A playwright who insists that his "scenes [were] invented merely to be spoken" and that the "life of comedy rests much in the actor's voice," Marston reflects on the bodily processes that enable, and sometimes disable, actors' vocality.[30] *Antonio and Mellida* figures the vulnerability of male voices and indexes male effeminacy not only by the early modern tropes that other scholars have noted—cowardice in battle, excessive love of women, and vanity—but also by an incapacity to control the voice.

The character who most exemplifies stock traits of early modern masculinity in *Antonio and Mellida* is Piero, the duke of Venice. We are introduced to Piero early in act 1, as he emerges victorious from battle. The stage directions describe a lavish procession, files of admiring courtiers, and Piero decked out in armor. He proceeds to give a bombastic speech detailing his great feats in overcoming his enemy, Andrugio, the duke of Genoa. Most of all, he boasts that in defeating Andrugio, he has prevented the marriage of his daughter, Mellida, to Andrugio's son, Antonio. He has, in one single sweep, secured his patriarchal interests in both the public and private realms: he has ensured, through battle, that the young lovers have no way to legitimize their desires for one another, and, at the same time, he has won the adoration of his subjects. No sooner has he testified to his victory and announced his decree to pay twenty thousand double pistolets to "whosoever brings Andrugio's head, / Or young Antonio's" (1.1.69–70), than the audience is invited to consider the dangers of the masculine excess that Piero exhibits. Cautioning Piero about displaying too much pride, court satirist Felice also warns against the use of "public power" to bolster "private fights" (1.1.85), drawing attention to potentially conflicting roles for the prince-father. Felice advises well, for, as the play unfolds, Piero's decision to continue using his power as duke to "prosecute [his] family's revenge" (1.1.88)—to keep Antonio away from Mellida—becomes problematic not only in terms of its ethical rectitude but of its practical feasibility. Because he conflates his two patriarchal roles, prince and father, Piero heightens performance pressure in both realms: should he slip up in his duties as a father, he will compromise his leadership of the state.

Indeed, this scenario almost comes to pass. In act 3, Piero discovers that Antonio, disguised as an Amazon woman, has infiltrated the court and that Mellida has run away with him. Piero's fury at the moment he learns of this threat to family and state manifests itself as a breakdown in vocal articulation. The swaggering soldier who earlier declared confidently, "My fate is firmer than mischance can shake" (1.1.41), now gives orders like a madman:

Run, keep the palace, post to the ports, go to my daughter's chamber. Whither now? Scud to the Jew's. Stay, run to the gates; stop the gondolets; let none pass the marsh. Do all at once. Antonio! His head, his head! [To Felice] Keep you the court.—The rest stand still, or run, or go, or shout, or search, or scud, or call, or hang, or d- d- do s- s- s- something. I know not wh- wh- wh- what I d- d- do, nor wh- wh- wh- where I am.

*O trista tradirice, rea, ribalda fortuna,*
*Negandomi vendetta mi causa fera morte.* (3.2.171–79)

Shouting out brief (mostly four- or five-syllable) orders to his men, Piero follows with a series of single-word imperatives, then falls into stuttering, and finally lapses into an Italian couplet that sums up his excitable state: "Accursed fortune, that with hard luck . . . What shall I do, what shall I say to escape so great an evil?"[31] (The very performance of this passage is likely to quicken the breathing of the speaker, simulating or even provoking frenetic emotions.) Piero's vocal confusion and distress reflect a concern that his inadequacies as a father and, by association, as a ruler have been exposed to his court. But the duke quickly regains his composure and his vocal control, at least for the moment, pledging to drink a toast to Genoa "in Antonio's skull" (3.2.229). The comment is delivered with such venom that one witness declares, "Lord bless us! His breath is more fearful than a sergeant's voice when he cries, 'I arrest' " (3.2.230). When Piero finds his renegade daughter, he publicly enacts his patriarchal authority, sending her back to the court and vowing to marry her off to a Milanese prince that very evening.

Piero's masculinity, displayed visually with armor and aurally through his (usually) controlled voice, is contrasted in the play with the effeminacy and frequent vocal failure of two Venetian courtiers, Castilio and Balurdo. Castilio and Balurdo manifest all the signs of early modern male effeminacy: they are cowards in battle, are enslaved by their passion for women, and exhibit excessive vanity. Whereas Piero is reputed to have bravely led his ships to victory over Genoa, Castilio and Balurdo cowardly hid their military rank to avoid being shot (2.1.29–30). Where Piero bravely dons his armor, Balurdo is reported to have wished for "an armour, cannon-proof" (2.1.32–33). Castilio and Balurdo's cowardice on the battlefield is accompanied by incurable and effeminizing lovesickness at home.[32] As desperate but unsuccessful wooers of Piero's niece Rosaline, Balurdo and Castilio willingly give up their masculine self-respect in exchange for Rosaline's affection.[33] In their efforts to attract Rosaline, the courtiers also exhibit vanity, a characteristic that, like cowardice and excessive passion, can turn men into women, according to early modern discourses of gender and sexuality.[34]

In addition to demonstrating what other critics have described as trademarks of male effeminacy, Castilio and Balurdo are characterized by a failure to control their voices.[35] Balurdo's difficulty in articulating himself before the woman he desires is figured literally as an emasculating experience. When asked by Rosaline whether he would like to be her servant, he stumbles to respond, "O God! Forsooth, in very good earnest la, you would make me as a man should say . . . as a man should say . . ." (2.1.67–68), and he is unable to complete the thought. Balurdo's statement, beginning and ending with "as a man should say," is revelatory. A man that cannot say what "a man should say" is not, by the logic of this sentence, a man. Balurdo reveals his unmanly rhetorical skills constantly, often stumbling to find the right words for his thoughts and frequently using other people's words incorrectly.

What compromises the courtiers' success in wooing women is not just a weak command over language but an inability to master the physiological production of voice. This is most evidently manifested in Castilio's failure to keep his voice from squeaking. In act 3, Castilio describes his plan to serenade Rosaline—"I will warble to the delicious concave of my mistress' ear, and strike her thoughts with the pleasing touch of my voice" (3.2.33–34). Castilio assumes he can impress Rosaline by pressing his "pleasing" voice into her ear, an ear that, by nature of its concave shape, seems ready and willing.[36] The only person affected by Castilio's voice, however, is Felice, who is awakened by Castilio's "treble minikin squeaks" (3.2.31). Castilio's failure at wooing and his related effeminacy are imagined to be a consequence not just of the high-pitched nature of his voice, its "treble" register, but of its squeakiness, which indicates his failure to manage his body's vocal systems.[37]

Male mastery over the physiological production of voice is put to the test in act 5 scene 2, when Rosaline, upon her own request, judges a singing contest that stalls her cousin Mellida's forced nuptials. Having granted Rosaline the authority to preside as "umpiress" over the competition for "music's prize," a gilded harp, Piero turns to several pages and commands, "Boys, clear your voice and sing" (5.2.6–8). According to Galenic theory, the "ahem" one uses to clear the voice before singing improves vocal sound by sweeping away humors that may have accumulated on the vocal organs. Piero's imperative, "clear your voice," thus gestures toward the humoral bodies of the singers, demanding what for some singers could be a difficult state of physiological readiness. If the young singer's humoral system is not balanced, then he will need much more than a cough to bring order to his vocal instruments, particularly if he wishes to prevent his voice from squeaking when he sings any high notes demanded by his song.

The conversation that follows the first page's song reflects further on the unstable voice. Rosaline, taking hold of the authoritative golden harp, presents her judgment:

ROSALINE: By this gold, I had rather have a servant with a short nose and a thin hair than have such a high-stretched, minikin voice.
PIERO: Fair niece, your reason?
ROSALINE: By the sweets of love, I should fear extremely that he were an eunuch.
CASTILIO: Spark spirit, how like you his voice?
ROSALINE: "Spark spirit, how like you his voice?"—So help me, youth, thy voice squeaks like a dry cork shoe.

(5.2.9-16)

Although Rosaline is charged with judging the voices based only on their singing merit, her first comment raises the stakes. A high-pitched sound renders the youth's voice unsatisfactory not only for Rosaline the music judge, but also for Rosaline the desirable woman—after all, Rosaline has been auditioning men to be her "servants" for much of the play. She begins by explaining that what disturbs her about the high-pitched voice is not the sound of the voice per se but what the voice might indicate about the state of the man's genital instruments: if a man has such a high voice, he might be a eunuch and thus will lack significant male anatomy. At first, the exchange seems to turn on what Callaghan describes as a correspondence of vocal sound, the phallus, and castration anxiety. But Castilio's interjection shifts away from this theme, reminding Rosaline that the subject at hand is the page's voice, not his genitalia. The function of Castilio's sudden comment is unclear, particularly since this is the only line he speaks in the entire act. Perhaps Rosaline's assessment of the singing youth's voice is portrayed as having personal ramifications for Castilio's character. Castilio has been trying to woo Rosaline since the play began, and he is on the verge of discovering what his beloved likes and dislikes in a man. If so, Rosaline's response to Castilio's question—"So help me, youth, thy voice squeaks like a dry cork shoe"—mocks the overpassionate courtier for his unattractive voice. Whether the line is delivered to the singing page or directly to Castilio, Rosaline's comment has consequences for Castilio's sense of masculine honor. When asked to describe what she doesn't like in a man's voice, Rosaline offers Castilio's marked vocal characteristics— "high stretched" and "squeak[y]"—as examples. Given that the restoration of Castilio's honor depends on his being able to win Rosaline's affections (thereby legitimizing his otherwise foolish wooing escapades), Rosaline's comments seal his failure. Castilio, who remains on stage for the rest of the play, does not say another word.[38]

Rosaline's comments about voice are borne out further in her own lengthy speeches, which serve to usurp her uncle's command over the aural register of the play.[39] Piero's inability to master Rosaline's voice (and her matrimonial course) is a prelude to his final emasculation. Not only is he outwitted by his archenemy, Andrugio, but he loses possession of his daughter to Antonio. Having refused to listen to Felice's earlier warning against the use of "public power" to bolster "private fights" (1.1.85), Piero suffers defeat in both spheres. The humiliation of these losses is figured as grounds enough for a sequel to the play, *Antonio's Revenge,* a drama motivated by Piero's desperate attempts to restore honor to his family and state. Compellingly, Piero's downfall in *Antonio's Revenge* is marked by a loss of vocal control: his tongue, his organ of speech, is ripped out by his enemies. Like *Antonio and Mellida* (albeit in a more gruesomely literal fashion), *Antonio's Revenge* reminds its audience that male voices, even those belonging to powerful dukes, have the propensity to fail, leading to (or at least being consequent with) a breakdown in masculine control in other respects.

This message would have been underscored when the plays were performed by St. Paul's boys, for whom vocal instability was an inescapable condition. "Anxious masculinity," to recall Mark Breitenberg's terminology, is an inevitable result when the world of these plays (in which controlling the voice is a masculine imperative) and the material space of the theater (in which the physiological vagaries of the voice elude the actors' command) intersect. This is most evident in the oft-discussed induction to *Antonio and Mellida.* The induction simulates a backstage conversation among the play's actors. With their "parts" in hand, the actors discuss their anxieties about not being ready for the production. Vocal performance is central to their concerns. "Piero" complains, "Faith, we can say our parts. But we are ignorant in what mould we must cast our actors" (3–4). From there, the characters advise one another about how to gesture, walk, pronounce— how to style their lines and movements. The actor most apprehensive about his capacity to play his part, however, is "Antonio," whose character must disguise himself as an Amazon for the first part of the play. Playing this "hermaphrodite" (65) role causes not only frustration but confusion, the actor explains, twice referring to this role as "I know not what" (65, 68–69). The actor's primary concern is that he does not have the voice to play the woman's part: "I a voice a play a lady! I shall ne're do it. . . . When use hath taught me action to hit the right point of a lady's part, I shall grow ignorant, when I must turn young prince again, how but to truss my hose" (69–76). Not having a naturally high-pitched voice, the actor fears he will have to fake "female" vocal sound. If he cannot successfully mimic a woman's voice, he will be, like Flute in Hoffman's *Midsummer Night's Dream,* the laughingstock of the stage. If he does mimic female sound effectively, he risks forgetting how to be a man, how to "truss his hose"—a common bawdy reference to boys' genital placement, a signature of manliness. But Antonio need not worry about "hit[ting] the right point of a lady's part," about reaching high notes with his voice, for, as his colleagues counsel him, the woman's part that he must impersonate is very similar to the part of the man that he plays: gendering an Amazon is not so difficult, they explain, for some women "wear the breeches still" (77) and, moreover, an Amazon's voice is not the typically shrill voice of a lady but has a man's gravity; it is "virago-like" (70). The gender identity of an Amazon, they point out, is like that of a "hermaphrodite" (65), neither man nor woman, but both.

It would be difficult to argue with W. Reavley Gair's reading of the induction as a metatheatrical reference to Paul's acting company, who, he submits, may have used *Antonio and Mellida* to announce their revival:

Marston is pointing out one of the special properties of the chorister company, that their physical condition, on the verge of puberty, allows them to be both sexes at once. The audience is made intensely aware that this performance is a debut for the Children of Paul's. In the ensuing action Antonio's inarticulate emotional crises will be a manifestation of the inexperience the cast admits to in the Induction. (45)

But the "propert[y]" that makes Paul's company "special"—that its actors are "on the verge of puberty"—also makes the company vulnerable. Like most critics, Gair assumes that the voice of the actor playing Antonio has matured (45), that it has now become "virago-like." But it is arguable that the actor's staged anxieties about his voice are less about coping with its altered state than with its unstable condition: if the actor playing Antonio is, indeed, "on the verge of puberty," he has no assurance that his voice will remain virago-like for the entirety of the performance, let alone that he will be able to switch voluntarily between the "right point of a lady's part" and the right point of a man's.

If a deep voice, like the categories of hermaphrodite and Amazon, blurs sexual difference, then how will "Antonio" enact the sexual identity of his masculine role? How will he portray manliness if he fails to keep his voice in order? The induction links the vocal instability of Paul's male actors with a breakdown in masculine identity explored further by the rest of the play. When Antonio reunites with Mellida for the first time, he feels unmanned by his Amazon disguise and by his passion for his beloved; "double all thy man" (1.1.161), he mutters, to shore himself against the vulnerabilities of his female character. Impersonating an Amazon, he feels incompetent, out of control; without a clear sense of his manly identity, he wishes to increase the portion of himself that is "man." Significantly, Antonio's masculinity is not communicated by the pitch of his voice—where a low voice denotes a man and a high voice denotes a woman. These categorical descriptions, the play insists, are not stable indicators of gender identity: an Amazon and a man can share vocal characteristics. Rather, it is the ability to control the voice that signals manhood. And Antonio lacks that from the onset. Even in the induction, the actor who plays him is plagued by stuttering. Describing the difficult part that Gallazeo must enact, he stammers: "Now as solemn as a traveller and as grave as a puritan's ruff; with the same breath, as slight and scattered in fashion as . . . as . . . as . . . a . . . a . . . anything. . . . Now lamenting, then chafing, straight laughing . . . then . . . Faith, I know not what" (117–24).

The link between Antonio's vocal breakdown and a disruption in gender differentiation is perhaps best articulated by a page who, witnessing Antonio and Mellida erupt into Italian, turns to the audience and remarks, "I think confusion of Babel is fallen upon these lovers that they change their language; but I fear me my master, having but feigned the person of a woman, hath got their unfeigned imperfection and is grown double-tongued" (4.1.209–12). Although the page explicitly refers to a regendering of Antonio's language, in the context of a play concerned with the physiology of speech, the lines also allude to the physiological instability of Antonio's voice. The observation that Antonio has adopted the traits of a woman after having "feigned the person of a woman" alludes to the play's induction even more acutely than most critics, who have discussed the strong relation between the induction and the play proper, have realized. The term "person" is derived from the Latin *persona*, meaning literally "through sound" (*per sona*).[40] The challenge of personating a woman is the risk involved in characterizing her sound, her voice: as the page points out, when a man performs womanliness through sound, he risks effeminization in other respects. No wonder "Antonios" 's primary concern about acting success is portraying the voice of an Amazon woman. For it is at the site of vocal production that the masculinity of Antonio, as a character and as an actor, is most vulnerable. Though we cannot know precisely how various participants in the theatrical experience reacted when a boy actor's voice squeaked mid-performance, it is clear that Marston's narrative builds up pressure around this moment of potential vocal instability, preparing audiences for its inevitability by scripting characters' vocal failure.

If the unstable voice was a source of uneasiness for early modern men, then we might wonder why Marston—a male playwright whose career may depend on winning the approval of male audience members—goes to such great lengths to dramatize it. Would his treatment not have offended theater patrons, or at least reduced their interest in his productions? Breitenberg's analysis of early modern masculinity and its attendant anxieties offers insight into these questions. He suggests that "staging or articulating anxiety" was "a way [for early modern men] to construct identity by naming a common experience and a shared adversary." As a result, the public articulation of anxiety "contribute[d] in a positive way to the formation and positioning of masculinity if only by upholding the discursive authority of the writer in relation to the supposed source of his anxiety and, in so doing, by linking him to fellow sufferers" (13). In a period in which interiority took on a somewhat different form than it does today, anxiety was experienced, Breitenberg explains, less as an individual psychic state than as a social condition. In effect, the venue of the stage operated as a public forum for the exploration of unstable gender systems and, concomitantly, for homosocial bonding over the fragile state of male identity.

Marston's theater might be understood as one such venue. *Antonio and Mellida* reminds playgoers and actors that their identities are subject to the whims of humoral physiology. The play recalls the uncomfortable fact that in a culture where vocal control instantiates male identity and superiority, the humoral body can be a liability. As the play dramatizes the vagaries of male identity, it forges a bond among male playgoers, actors, and playwright. By depicting men's shared pitiable state of vocal fragility, *Antonio and Mellida* offers a space in which the privileged subjects of early modern England can lament their fear of losing that privileged position. At the same time as the play unites its participants, it also sets the locus of discomfort—the boy actors—at a distance from theater patrons. The liminal nature of boys' bodies thus enables the adult male audience to identify and disidentify with these figures of gender anxiety. Through the use of boy actors, Marston's theater may open up a somewhat safer space for the negotiation of social concerns.[41]

The potential for modern performances of Elizabethan drama to put pressure on issues of normative masculinity is compromised by many modern directors' handling of actors' vocality. When *Antonio and Mellida* was revived in 1979 at the Nottingham playhouse, for instance, Peter Barnes chose not to enact Marston's induction (Weiss 91), the moment in the play where the audience is most self-consciously invited to step out of the play's fictional world and to consider theater as a live, volatile art created by unpredictable human bodies. Like other late-twentieth-century directors (including Hoffman and Madden), Barnes thus shields modern actors and audiences from considering their own potential for vocal breakdown. Contemporary directors' resistance to representing unstable voices, even when these voices are featured in the early modern playtexts that directors interpret, may suggest that despite the higher age range of actors, the voice remains a site of considerable anxiety in modern performance. Today's directors merely cope with unstable male voices in a different way than did their early modern counterparts: they suppress them. In comparison to Marston and Mulcaster's time, there are thus fewer opportunities to hear unstable voices on the professional stage, and, as a consequence, perhaps fewer opportunities for audiences to reflect on how the precarious voice problematizes gender categories.

# Notes

I am grateful to Linda Gregerson, Anne Herrmann, Bill Ingram, and especially Valerie Traub for their insights and commentary on this essay. I would also like to thank Carla Mazzio for responding to an earlier version that was presented in April 1999 to the University of Michigan's Early Modern Colloquium.

1. Although Orgel's *Impersonations* devotes some attention to the voices of boy actors, the study privileges visual signifiers of gender performance, such as costuming. The centrality of the visual is suggested by half of the chapter titles: "The Eye of the Beholder"; "Masculine Apparel"; and the concluding essay, "Visible Figures." There is, however, great debate in the period itself about whether playgoers should privilege their eyes over their ears in the theater (Gurr, *Playgoing* 86–104).

2. Here the film takes artistic license with historical evidence. Although female stage performers were disparaged by early modern writers concerned with morality and theology, scholars have not discovered legal statutes prohibiting women from performing.

3. It is conceivable that boys whose voices began to squeak held on to their roles longer than is suggested by Madden's film. Theater companies requested money from the crown for the care of boys whose voices had fully cracked, representing these boys as a financial burden (Chambers). But records from the period do not confirm that boys abandoned their performance careers when their high voices began to squeak at puberty, and there is even less evidence concerning how the theater dealt with male voices while they were in the process of changing.

4. I am grateful to Smith for sharing with me parts of his book when it was in progress.

5. Unless otherwise indicated, all citations of Marston's plays are taken from the collection *The Malcontent and Other Plays.*

6. For a discussion of the role of humoral ideologies in perpetuating male anxieties, see Breitenberg, esp. chap. 1.

7. Like Orgel (see n. 1), Jean Howard privileges the sights of the theater over its sounds. Her astute analysis of theatrical media focuses, for instance, on the "spectacle" of female cross-dressing.

8. See "The Castrator's Song: Female Impersonation on the Early Modern Stage." Callaghan notes the practice of castration in barber surgeon houses that were placed nearby the theaters and calls attention to the difference between the castrati of the continent, whose vocal states are virtually fixed by surgery, and the prepubescent boys of the English stage, whose voices, subject to maturation, have the propensity to crack at any time.

9. On liminal states of being and the production of gender difference in Renaissance tragedy, see Zimmerman.

10. Although many things are described as "breathing" in the period—in particular, music is often described this way, even when produced by an inanimate instrument—it is my sense that breath works metaphorically in these cases. Mellida's apostrophe, "O music, thou distill'st / More sweetness in us than this jarring world; / Both time and measure from thy strains do breathe" (*Antonio and Mellida* 2.1.190-92), imports from physiological/philosophical discourses about human breath a metaphor to describe the power of music to move the soul.

11. Historically speaking, discipline is not an inherent emphasis of vocal training. Many of today's British and American voice trainers offer the opposite advice: that pupils learn to "free" their voices. See, e.g., the writings of voice coaches Cicely Berry, Kristin Linklater, and Patsy Rodenburg.

12. Richard L. DeMollen and Michael Shapiro both count eight recorded performances.

13. DeMollen; Gurr. Credit for the revival of the Children of Paul's is usually given to Thomas Giles, who was in charge of the choir at St. Paul's. DeMollen points out, however, that several plays were performed under the name of Children of Paul's before Giles's contract began, suggesting perhaps that Mulcaster brought the children to court for these plays—one of which might have been *Antonio and Mellida*. Mulcaster has not been given credit because his name is not associated with the company during this period, but there is evidence that boys from Mulcaster's grammar school participated in plays (Nathan Field, e.g., was impressed by Blackfriars while he was a student at Mulcaster's grammar school).

14. Mulcaster has been called the most well-known pedagogue of the period. Considered the archetype of the demanding schoolteacher, his name is alluded to explicitly in one play

(Beaumont and Fletcher's *Knight of the Burning Pestle*), and DeMollen even argues that Mulcaster would have been the recognizable model for Holsefern in *Love's Labor's Lost.*

15. Mulcaster is best known by literary scholars for his "radical" ideas about education—that is, his belief that boys of all class positions should be educated in a uniform curriculum at a truly public school and that women should be educated to proficient levels of reading and writing (Barker).

16. Entrances involving running and walking; also note staging of wrestling scenes (e.g., *As You Like It*) and dancing scenes.

17. For an overview of ancient medical theories of vocal exercise, see Finney.

18. Citations, which are taken henceforth from the British Library's 1581 edition, will be noted in the text. For a modern edition that includes a useful introduction, see Mulcaster, *Positions,* ed. Barker.

19. Henrie Cuffe's *The Differences of the Ages of Mans Life* explains that male infants are born hot and wet but gradually decrease in moisture and heat until they become dry and cold in old age (115-20). There are variations on this paradigm in the period, but Cuffe's views represent the most common formulation of the relation between age and temperament.

20. Though Mulcaster believes that weeping and laughing are equally effective treatments for dislodging excess humors, he favors the latter over the former because it is more easily incorporated into a physical fitness curriculum. Mulcaster explains that a master who needs to whip his student to get him to cry risks being resented by the student. Thus weeping, while it should not be disregarded completely, is not the preferred method.

21. See Ingram's essay, "What Kind of Future for the Theatrical Past: Or, What Will Count as Theater History in the Next Millennium?"

22. The theater historian debate about style is discussed by Michael Shapiro, who, detailing the differences between various styles, points out that no single style could have been used in all plays by all characters. He halts the style debate by pointing out that children's companies likely used "different styles for different plays and parts of plays, just as directors and actors do today" (113).

23. It is on this point that I take issue with Bruce Smith's brilliant study, *The Acoustic World of Early Modern England* (1999). Bringing phenomenology to bear on historical analysis, Smith uses as evidence contemporary scientific studies of sound in order to understand what early modern theatergoers "would have heard" when they went to playhouses. I find Smith's methodology—the use of contemporary scientific discourses to shed light on early modern acoustics—to be intriguing, but I am wary of some of the positivist goals served by this methodology, with the book's overall aim of "historical reconstruction" (29).

24. All citations of Shakespeare's plays are taken from *The Riverside Shakespeare,* 2d ed.

25. Pairing the texts is especially attractive because both writers were in some way affiliated with St. Paul's. Although St. Paul's grammar school, where Mulcaster taught, and the theater company Children of Paul's, for whom Marston wrote, were entirely separate operations, there may have been some interaction between the two institutions. Nathan Field, an actor in the Children of Paul's, claimed to be a student of Mulcaster's (Shapiro 20), and scholars argue that child actors in Paul's company might have learned grammar and rhetoric at the nearby school (Gurr, *Shakespearean Stage* 70; Weiss).

26. The possession of some of England's finest young male voices helped children's

companies like Paul's gain favor with the court and attract public audiences. For a discussion of how children's drama took advantage of these fine voices, see Austern. She points out that the voices of certain characters are only or primarily used in songs, indicating that there were less intensive acting roles reserved for boys who had voice training but not much dramatic training.

27. *Antonio and Mellida* might seem like an odd choice for a feminist study of Marston. Previous studies of gender issues in Marston's work have focused on *The Dutch Courtesan*, which, with a more domestic focus, features as its protagonist an aggressive courtesan who almost manages to break up sacred male friendship. As the authors of *Engendering a Nation* point out, however, feminist readings of early modern drama need not only be concerned with the construction of female characters. Plays that center on male, public matters—on war and the politics of nations, for instance—can be useful insofar as they help us understand "the legacy affecting the lives of all women who inhabit the cultures these plays helped to shape" (Howard and Rackin 20). I find that *Antonio and Mellida,* though it presents only a handful of female characters, is rich terrain for feminist analysis.

28. Critics have noted, in particular, Marston's use of visual shows that "bewilder" and "dazzle" his audience, including complex blocking (e.g., the stage directions in act 3) and shocking set design (e.g., the body of Felice hung up in Mellida's window at the start of *Antonio's Revenge*).

29. For example, in one scene Marston has Balurdo enter partially costumed, his "beard half off, half on" (*Antonio's Revenge* 2.1.20). Scott Colley explores Marston's self-conscious theatricality, arguing that Marston distances the viewer from the fiction, provoking the audience to judge the action of the stage—Brecht's alienation effect. It makes sense, as T. F. Wharton argues, that Marston's plays found their greatest admirers in audiences of Becket and absurdist theater, where there is premium on self-referentiality, on ensuring that audience members never forget their subject positions and that they maintain critical awareness in the theater.

30. These quotations of Marston are given in Keith Sturgess's introduction to Marston, *The Malcontent and Other Plays* (ix). The first of the comments was in reference to *The Malcontent;* the second appears in Marston's letter to the reader that prefaces *The Fawn*.

31. Sturgess provides this translation in his notes for *Antonio and Mellida*. The sudden articulation of a different language contributes to the depiction of Piero's heightened emotional state, regardless of whether the auditor comprehends the meaning of these lines.

32. To make matters worse, Castilio and Balurdo are doomed to remain in this state of excessive desire, as they are unequipped to prosper in the wooing game that constitutes the subplot of *Antonio and Mellida.* They are thus unable to remedy their excess passion with what Breitenberg describes as the conventional early modern antidote to excess passion: marriage (41).

33. They gracefully put up with the jokes Rosaline delivers at their own expense, such as when she scoffs that a bad smell in the room must be the result of one of them wearing socks, a sign of a nursing child (2.1.55-56). When Rosaline spits and tells Castilio to clean up her "rheum"(2.1.81), the courtier more than obliges her; he adds, "[Y]ou grace my shoe with an unmeasured honour. I will preserve the sole of it as a most sacred relic, for this service" (2.1.82-84). Castilio and Balurdo's eagerness to give up any modicum of dignity in pursuit

of Rosaline leads Felice to compare them to dogs whom Rosaline allows "to lick her feet, / Or fetch her fan" (2.1.91-92). In short, their desire for Rosaline turns them into beasts over whom a woman has full control.

34. In a stunning enactment of the commonplace notion that men can turn into women if they behave like women, Marston transforms Balurdo into a mirror version of Rosaline. The stage directions in the middle of act 3 scene 2 instruct Balurdo to enter backward, with his page, Dildo, "following him, with a looking-glass in one hand and a candle in the other." Flavia, Rosaline's servant, follows, coming in backward holding the same props up to Rosaline. Standing in mirrored postures, the two pairs proceed to carry on separate, but intermingled, dialogues in which both servants similarly beautify and flatter their masters. Should the analogy between Rosaline, the vain woman, and Balurdo, the effeminate man, somehow be lost on audiences, Felice draws attention to the comparison: "Rare sport, rare sport! A female fool and a female flatterer" (3.2.58). Either part of Felice's description, "female fool" or "female flatterer," could apply to the "fool" and "flatterer" of each pair: if Rosaline and Balurdo are female fools, then both Dildo and Flavia flatter a female. But where Rosaline merely exhibits the "foolishness" early modern audiences might expect from a woman—women are constantly accused of vanity in early modern drama—Balurdo's womanishness is constituted by his performance of womanly behavior, in this case, vanity.

35. This effeminate trait is not easily separable from the others in early modern discourses about vocal performance. Henry Fitzgeffrey's satirical epigram about a male singer figures the cracking voice as a consequence of the man's sexual "exploits":

> See how the Gentlewomen
> Throng to his Chamber doore, but dar not come in,
> Why? least he ravish them! Tush! Laugh ye not,
> H'as done (I wosse) as great exploites as that.
> (Or else he cracks) the sweenesse of his voyce
> Ore-heard of Ladyes, hath procur'd him choyse
> Of Matches: Noble, Rich, but hee'l not meddle,
> And why (I pray?) for cracking of his Treble.
> No! hee'l with better industry make tryall,
> If hee can Match his Treble to the Violl.
>
> (Fitzgeffrey F6r-v)

The male singer's voice is so seductive that he can have his "choyse / Of Matches" with any of the women who hear him. Ironically, though, responding to women's sexual advances and becoming a sexual subject will cause his voice to crack, preventing him from remaining an object of women's desires. A cracking voice signals the man's transformation from a position of power over women to one of enslavement to them and the excessive sexual passion they induce.

36. One often finds in early modern drama descriptions of ears as passive receptors ready to be ravished by sound. The larger project of which this essay is a part examines these and conflicting accounts of ears' agency (particularly the capability to resist sound).

37. One is tempted to read this as a description of the actual sound produced by the actor playing Castilio, helping us to construct how the actor's voice likely sounded when the play

was originally performed. This, however, is a difficult conclusion to draw. The male youth playing Castilio may, in fact, have a fine, high-pitched voice, which Felice, always the critic, simply derogates. Regardless of how Castilio's voice would have sounded in any particular performance, it is worth noting that Felice and others characters *represent* that voice as aesthetically jarring, indicating, at least in the dramatic fiction, the vocalizer's inability to master his voice.

38. The stage directions, notably complex and detailed throughout the play, do not give Castilio an exit, as they do for Balurdo.

39. See, e.g., 5.2.45–71.

40. To the Romans the term "persona" referred to a mask worn by actors. In addition to producing a visual effect, the mask (used by the Greek theaters as well) helped amplify the actor's voice via a resonating chamber in its forehead. Thus, the origins of theatrical role-playing are etymologically and performatively based in the production of voice.

41. My thanks to Wendy Wall and the readers of *Renaissance Drama* for helping me work through this final formulation.

## Works Cited

Arezzo, Guido d' ("Andreas Ornithoparcus"). *Andreas Ornithoparcus His Micrologus; or, Introduction: Containing the Art of Singing. Digested into Foure Bookes. Not Onely Profitable, but Also Necessary for All That Are Studious of Musicke. Also the Dimension and Perfect Vse of the Monochord, According to Guido Aretinus.* Trans. John Dowland. London, 1609.

Aristotle. *On the Soul.* Trans. Hippocrates G. Apostle. Grinnell, IA: Peripatetic Press, 1981.

Austern, Linda. *Music in Children's Drama of the Later Renaissance.* Philadelphia: Gordon and Breach, 1992.

Bacon, Francis. *Sylva Sylvarum; or, A Naturall Historie.* London, 1626.

Barker, William. "Richard Mulcaster." *Dictionary of Literary Biography* 167 (1996).

Berry, Cicely. *The Actor and His Text.* New York: Scribners, 1988.

Boose, Linda. "Scolding Brides and Bridling Scolds: Taming the Woman's Unruly Member." *Shakespeare Quarterly* 42.2 (1991): 179–213.

Breitenberg, Mark. *Anxious Masculinity in Early Modern England.* Cambridge Studies in Renaissance Literature and Culture 10. Cambridge: Cambridge UP, 1996.

Brumwick, Ann. *Booke of Receipts.* Wellcome Western Manuscripts 160, c. 1625–1700.

Butler, Charles. *The English Grammar; or, The Institution of Letters, Syllables, and Words in the English Tongue.* London, 1633.

———. *The Principles of Musik, in Singing and Setting: With the Two-fold Use Therof (Ecclesiasticall and Civil).* London, 1636.

Callaghan, Dympna. "The Castrator's Song: Female Impersonation on the Early Modern Stage." *Journal of Medieval and Early Modern Studies* 26.2 (1996): 321–53.

Chambers, E. K. *The Elizabethan Stage.* 4 vols. Oxford: Clarendon, 1923. Vol. 2.

Colley, Scott. *John Marston's Theatrical Drama.* Jacobean Drama Studies 33. Salzburg: Institut für Englische Sprache und Literatur, Universität Salzburg, 1974.

Crooke, Helkiah. *Microcosmographia: A Description of the Body of Man.* London, 1615.

Cuffe, Henrie. *The Differences of the Ages of Mans Life.* London, 1607.

Dekker, Thomas. *The Shoemaker's Holiday.* Ed. Anthony Parr. New York: W. W. Norton, 1997.

DeMollen, Richard L. "Richard Mulcaster and the Elizabethan Theatre." *Theatre Survey* 13.1 (1972): 28–41.

Finney, Gretchen. "Medical Theories of Vocal Exercise and Health." *Bulletin of the History of Medicine* 40.5 (1966): 395–406.

Fitzgeffrey, Henry. *Satyrs: And Satyricall Epigrams. With Certaine Observations at Black-Fryers.* London, 1617.

Gair, W. Reavley, ed. Introduction to *Antonio and Mellida* by John Marston. Manchester and New York: Manchester UP, 1991.

Gurr, Andrew. *Playgoing in Shakespeare's London.* 2d ed. Cambridge: Cambridge UP, 1996.

———. *The Shakespearean Stage, 1576–1642.* Cambridge: Cambridge UP, 1970.

Howard, Jean E. *The Stage and Social Struggle in Early Modern England.* London and New York: Routledge, 1994.

Howard, Jean E., and Phyllis Rackin. *Engendering a Nation: A Feminist Account of Shakespeare's English Histories.* London and New York: Routledge, 1997.

Ingram, William. "What Kind of Future for the Theatrical Past: Or, What Will Count as Theater History in the Next Millennium?" *Shakespeare Quarterly* 48.2 (1997): 215–24.

Jonson, Ben. *Poetaster.* The Revels Plays. Ed. Tom Cain. Manchester and New York: Manchester UP, 1995.

Leggatt, Alexander. *English Drama: Shakespeare to the Restoration, 1590–1660.* Literature in English Series. London: Longman, 1988.

Lemnius, Levinus. *The Touchstone of Complexions.* Trans. Thomas Newton. London, 1576.

Linklater, Kristin. *Freeing Shakespeare's Voice: The Actor's Guide to Talking the Text.* New York: Theatre Communications Group, 1992.

Marston, John. *The Malcontent and Other Plays.* Ed. Keith Sturgess. The World's Classics. Oxford and New York: Oxford UP, 1997.

Mazzio, Carla. "Sins of the Tongue." *The Body in Parts: Fantasies of Corporeality in Early Modern Europe.* London and New York: Routledge, 1997. 53–79.

*A Midsummer Night's Dream.* Dir. Michael Hoffman. Fox Searchlight Pictures, 1999.

Mulcaster, Richard. *Positions Concerning the Training Up of Children.* Ed. William Barker. Toronto: U of Toronto P, 1994.

———. *Positions Wherin Those Primitive Circumstances Be Examined, Which Are Necessarie for the Training up of Children, Either for Skill in Their Booke, or Health in Their Bodie.* London, 1581.

Orgel, Stephen. *Impersonations: The Performance of Gender in Shakespeare's England.* Cambridge and New York: Cambridge UP, 1996.

Parker, Patricia. "On the Tongue: Cross Gendering, Effeminacy, and the Art of Words." *Style* 23 (1989): 445–65.

Playford, John. *A Brief Introduction to the Skill of Musick: For Song and Viol.* London, 1658.

Robinson, Robert. *The Art of Pronunciation.* London, 1617.

Rodenburg, Patsy. *The Right to Speak: Working with the Voice.* London: Methuen, 1992.

Shakespeare, William. *The Riverside Shakespeare.* Ed. G. Blakemore Evans. 2d ed. Boston and New York: Houghton Mifflin, 1997.

*Shakespeare in Love.* Dir. John Madden. Miramax, 1999.

Shapiro, Michael. *Children of the Revels: The Boy Companies of Shakespeare's Time and Their Plays.* New York: Columbia UP, 1977.

Smith, Bruce R. *The Acoustic World of Early Modern England: Attending to the O-Factor.* Chicago: U of Chicago P, 1999.

Stallybrass, Peter. "Patriarchal Territories: The Body Enclosed." *Rewriting the Renaissance: The Discourses of Sexual Difference in Early Modern Europe.* Ed. Margaret Ferguson, Maureen Quilligan, and Nancy Vickers. Chicago: U of Chicago P, 1986. 123-42.

Vesling, Johann. *Anatomy of the Body of Man.* Trans. Nicholas Culpeper. London, 1653.

Weiss, Adrian. "A Pill to Purge Parody: Marston's Manipulation of the Paul's Environment in the *Antonio* Plays." *The Theatrical Space.* Ed. James Redmond. Themes in Drama 9. Cambridge: Cambridge UP, 1987. 81-98.

Wharton, T. F. *The Critical Rise and Fall of John Marston.* Columbia, SC: Camden House, 1994.

Zimmerman, Susan. "Marginal Man: The Representation of Horror in Renaissance Tragedy." *Discontinuities: New Essays on Renaissance Literature and Criticism.* Ed. Viviana Comensoli and Paul Stevens. Toronto: U of Toronto P, 1998. 159-78.

# Instituting Modern Time: Citizen Comedy and Heywood's Wise Woman of Hogsdon

## GRAHAM HAMMILL

**W**HAT FORMS OF freedom might theatricality express? This question has motivated a great number, if not all, of the attempts over the past twenty years to understand the London Renaissance stage as permitting ideological and social critique. How might the theater grant the critical freedom to explore various ideological and social formations? What supports the question is the theater's place. If the London Renaissance theater had access to a "standpoint involving more freedom, or 'license,' and imagination than the particular social attitude or moral concept in question," as Robert Weimann has argued (177), then what permitted it this relative freedom of expression was its location. As Steven Mullaney has argued, locating the public theater in the liberties afforded the stage "a culturally and ideologically removed vantage point from which it could reflect upon its own age with more freedom and license than had hitherto become possible" (30). But the forms of freedom that the theater expressed tended to be those that validated market economy. "Separated, like the market, from its original ritual and hierarchical aegis, the Elizabethan and Jacobean theater furnished a laboratory of representational possibilities for a society perplexed by the cultural consequences of its own liquidity," the result of which, as Jean-Christophe Agnew has brilliantly demonstrated, was the modeling of the citizen with political and economic freedom of the professional actor (54). The relative freedom of expression afforded to the stage as it developed within the economically and politically unregulated liberties resulted in the expression of a form of freedom that went hand in hand with the liberty's version of market economy.

In a different context, this question of what forms of freedom theatricality might express has prompted Judith Butler to propose that gender performativity displaces the notion of gender identity as an expression of a stable, interior essence: sex. In *Gender Trouble,* Butler suggests that if "gender is an identity tenuously constituted in time, instituted in an exterior space through a stylized repetition of acts," then "practices of parody can serve to reengage and reconsolidate the very distinction between a privileged and naturalized gender configuration and one that appears as derived, phantasmic, and mimetic—a failed copy, as it were" (141, 146). In *Bodies That Matter* Butler attempts to reject the simplistic volunteerism that such a statement might encourage, underscoring instead both the temporality of gender and how attention to that temporality might potentially permit the taking up and taking on of repudiated identities. Butler writes, "[T]he imaginary practice of identification must itself be understood as a double movement: in citing the symbolic, an identification (re)invokes and (re)invests the symbolic law, seeks recourse to it as a constituting authority that precedes its imaginary instancing. The priority and the authority of the symbolic is, however, constituted *through* that recursive turn, such that citation . . . effectively brings into being the very prior authority to which it then defers." This turn, Butler proposes, "takes place through a set of repudiations" which invoke "the heterosexual norm through the exclusion of contestatory possibilities" (108-9). How, Butler continually asks, might the performance of these contestatory possibilities allow for the stylization of a version of freedom that resists conscription by that heterosexual norm? Her answer, somewhat disappointingly I think, tends to fall back into the very theatrical and parodic volunteerism which she expressly wishes to avoid: "[W]here the uniformity of the subject is expected, where the behavioral conformity of the subject is commanded, there might be produced the refusal of the law in the form of the parodic inhabiting of conformity that subtly calls into question the legitimacy of the command, a repetition of the law into hyperbole, a rearticulation of the law against the authority of the one who delivers it" (122). Doesn't this "inhabiting," parodic or not, also risk resubstantializing sex?

A number of Renaissance critics, influenced by Butler, have argued that because the theater reads the world through its own form, it also de facto (albeit relatively) contests dominant ideology. For example, Jean Howard proposes that as the theater was preoccupied with "the sense that in some fundamental way men and women were actors in a self-scripted theater and must forge identities once taken for granted," it "enacted ideological contestation as much as it mirrored or reproduced anything that one could call the dominant ideology of a class, class faction, or sex" (10, 7). But it seems to me that the main value of Butler's analysis for criticism of the London Renaissance stage is not the insight that identity is constructed or performatively instantiated but instead her remarkable insistence on the importance of temporality in the double instantiation of the sexed body and the juridical authority that purports to govern it, the recursive turn by which the instancing of sexed identity consolidates and supports an abstract juridical authority.[1] To this extent, I want to propose, the response especially of criticism of the Renaissance stage to Butler's analysis should not be simply to apply it but to historicize it within the fairly broadly conceived historical terms in which her argument takes place—that is, to argue that this recursive turn which Butler discusses is the modern moment par excellence, the fictional moment when, in contrast with a more theological insistence on conversion, one finds that the act of self-assertion institutes some abstract social authority to which one is subjected.

What makes this turn modern is the way it apprehends history through supersession and retrocession. The main problem here is that of Christianity and Christianity's relation to time. If the acute, immediate expectation of the Second Coming, as an effect of the eschatological pathos at Christianity's core, necessitated a turn from both history and the world as "the lust of the flesh, and the lust of the eyes, and the pride of life," as John puts it (1 John 2:16), then the very persistence of time and of the world in time necessitated an explanation by which Christianity could maintain its eschatological pathos. To sustain this turn from the world, John and Paul located the decisive events for salvation in the birth, death, and resurrection of Jesus, emphasizing faith in these past events, not action in history, as the basis for salvation. The result, as Anthony Kemp has argued, was an "ideology of time" that attempted to cancel the very passage of time by converting historical specificity into "the immediate [and imaginary] presence of the Saviour" (6): every significant event in history was significant insofar as it was also pregnant with this presence (Boyarin 34–35). It was Augustine, as Hans Blumenberg has demonstrated, who gave the problem of time's persistence its decisive, dogmatic solution. In effect, Augustine ascribed an originary freedom to mankind in order to impute to mankind, because of the Fall, responsibility for this persistence. In Augustine, Blumenberg writes, "a new concept of freedom is ascribed expressly in order to let the whole of an enormous responsibility and guilt be imputed to it" (133). Modernity readdresses this problem of time— precisely as Butler describes it—by asserting "a new concept of human freedom," one that lays "responsibility for the condition of the world *as a challenge relating to the future,* not as an original offense in the past" (137; emphasis mine). It is critical to insist, though, that this new concept of freedom is not a break with the medieval, as it imagines; rather, it redeploys the very means by which Christianity attempted to solve the problematic persistence of the world in time in the first place. Instead of making the past meaningful for the present by converting events, texts, and peoples such that each sustains an illusory, Christian narrative of continuity with the Incarnation, the modern in effect attempts a second-level conversion by which the present can be understood as a break with a theologically inflected past. But because the modern repeats the very means by which Christianity dealt with history in the first place, that is, by conversion, this break is legitimate only in its "aggression (which it fails to understand as such) against theology, from which in fact it has in a hidden manner derived everything that belongs to it" (97).

Citizen comedy, very much an early modern genre in precisely these terms, expresses a form of freedom primarily available to witty young men who break with the previous generation's paternal control. In so doing, the genre translates the allegorical and transcendental urges of a morality tradition into an allegory of historical change. To give one example, not only does Thomas Middleton's *Trick to Catch the Old One* show, in standard New Comedy fashion, the freedom of a younger generation in its undoing of the older, but the play also uses this intergenerational plot to express comic theatricality's trumping of a seemingly more allegorical morality tradition. In effect, the play's main character, Witgood, obtains a certain freedom by turning the duplicity of the Vice figure against figures of Vice. Witgood, in cahoots with a nameless courtesan, persuades his uncle, the usurer Pecunious Lucre, that this courtesan is a rich widow who will marry Witgood only if he owns his lands and has some economic security. The purpose of this ruse is to trick Lucre into absolving Witgood's mortgage and making Witgood his legal heir. Upon obtaining his mortgage—"Thou soul of my estate," as he puts it, kissing the document (4.2.86) and, in effect if not intent, successfully accomplishing what Faustus does not in his scene with the supposed Helen of Troy[2]—Witgood is detained by three creditors, who demand that he settle his accounts. "I am in hell, here," Witgood cries out, calling the creditors "devils" who prevent his escape (4.3.53-54). But Witgood is able quite easily to escape the "hell" of indebtedness by persuading the courtesan's fiancé—Walkadine Hoarde, another usurer and enemy of his uncle, who also thinks that the courtesan is a rich widow— that he had a prenuptial contract with her when they were previously engaged and that, unless Hoarde pays Witgood's debts, he will claim his rights to her hand in marriage. The economic freedom and upward mobility of the younger generation is secured by the trumping of a morality tradition itself expressed in Middleton's play both in the way in which his characters' names display his characters' purported virtues or vices and in the play's cagey drive to characterize economic ties with the older generation as demonic. However, this is not a move from allegory as much as it is a reworking of the function of allegory, from an attempt to secure a decisive continuity to an attempt to posit historical change. In order to emphasize this allegory of historical change, the play associates Lucre and Hoarde with the morality tradition immediately after they are undone, at which point the play surprisingly shifts from almost breakneck narrative action to a highly emblematic, allegorical tableau in which usurers are figured as devils and their houses as the pits of hell. This tableau has a comic and not at all a serious effect precisely because the "devils" it represents have already been overcome by the theatrical cunning of the younger generation.

From this perspective, it is possible to reformulate Butler's questions as follows: might not there be other, sexed temporalities which this recursive turn rejects, which distress or even harass this recursive turn, the forms of identity and authority it institutes, and the versions of sex it substantiates? These are not at all easy questions, but to begin I want to propose that the version of freedom that citizen comedy institutes invests a heterosexual norm that is also economic to the core. This, I suspect, will not be difficult to show. But, I also want to argue, citizen comedy's positing of an allegory of historical change depends on minor temporalities which emerge in their historical specificity. At least, such is the case with Heywood's *Wise Woman of Hogsdon*, a cross-dressing comedy which sustains a complex relation to citizen comedy. *The Wise Woman* stages citizen comedy's institution of a heterosexual norm in order to propose that this genre is organized by a cathartic enjoyment in seeing the witty young gallant renounce the possibility of sodomy, submit to the strictures of city life, and promise to get married. Claiming this cathartic enjoyment is the condition for participation in citizen comedy's mode of cultural consciousness. But, instead of arguing for potential historical identifications with the versions of enjoyment that this catharsis rejects, identifications with new articulations of the so-called lust of the flesh, I shall argue that *The Wise Woman* presents this rejected enjoyment as a minor temporality which has the capacity to desubstantiate the version of sex produced by citizen comedy's recursive turn.

## Citizen Comedy: Genre, Judgment, and Civic Being

Citizen comedy responds to the liberties as social geographies of *incoherent* jurisdiction,[3] incoherencies that were largely the product of Tudor economic policy.[4] By granting particular projectors patents for both products and techniques of production, the crown initiated a concurrent but entirely misapprehended countereconomy outside the jurisdiction of livery companies, municipal authority, and—since the crown relied on these two for a great deal of administration—ultimately outside the jurisdiction of the crown as well. In the mid-sixteenth century, the crown issued these patents in order to stimulate new domestic industries over and against the incursion of foreign imports. By the end of the sixteenth century, projects supported both the financial interest of the crown and the increasingly urgent needs of local authorities to employ the poor. The luxury items produced by projectors tended to be bought up in large quantities by unlicensed middlemen and resold in the country at "the boundaries of parishes, hundreds, or counties, where jurisdiction was disputed" (Thirsk 133–34), or in the London liberties, where the crown's confiscation of church property prevented either the city's or the livery companies' sustained jurisdiction over legal and economic matters. As might be expected, the lack of jurisdiction, when combined with the needs of governing authorities and the profit motives of private speculators, rendered the liberties something of an incoherent problem for the city, crown, and livery companies, whose separate institutional interests were overdetermined and multiple, to say the least. "What London saw when it gazed out into the Liberties were things without a proper place in the community, things that had in a certain sense already exceeded the limits of that community," as Mullaney explains (22). Moreover, the kinds of business relations and work that projects created fell outside the antiquated categories of the Statute of Artificers, Elizabeth's most comprehensive assertion of national economic policy. As Joan Thirsk has argued, because this project-based economy developed and flourished primarily in zones of disputed jurisdiction, its significance went more or less unnoticed by the official economic thought of the sixteenth and seventeenth centuries, and it wasn't until the eighteenth century that this countereconomy became the basis for the economic theory of Adam Smith (Thirsk 133–57; Agnew 49–50).

Citizen comedy reformulates this incoherency as a mode of judgment that responds to the lack of clear jurisdiction in the liberties. The cunning of citizen comedy is that this particular mode of judgment sustains cultural consciousness through disidentification. Take, for example, Ben Jonson's *Every Man out of His Humour.* Midway through, in one of the many staged commentaries that punctuate the plot, the always wrong Mitis asserts that this play would be better were it a romance, "as of a duke to be in love with a countess, and that countess to be in love with the duke's son, and the son to be in love with the lady's maid-in-waiting: some such cross-wooing, with a clown to their serving man," and not as it is, so "nearly and familiarly allied to the time" (3.6.170–74). Cordatus responds by saying that until those who criticize Jonson's comedies come up with another definition of the genre, they should be happy with the ways that these plays follow Cicero's definition of comedy as "a thing throughout pleasant, and ridiculous, and accommodated to the correction of manners" (3.6.179–80). Especially concerning "the correction of manners," this means being happy with a generic mode of judgment whose salient mechanism is rejection. In displaying judgment, one must demonstrate with some facility, call it *sprezzatura,* that the very representations which others might take as representations of oneself are not oneself. Commenting on the London audience's reception of the merchant Deliro and his wife, Fallace, Mitis worries that "the last scene will endure some grievous torture" (2.6.126–27), to which Cordatus responds (with a feigned, pedagogical naïveté): just as no member of the court would ever take offense at a satiric representation of courtiers, "no more, assure you, will any grave, wise citizen or modest matron take the object of this folly in Deliro and his wife: but rather apply it as the foil to their own virtues" (2.6.145–47). Cordatus sets it up such that, to prove oneself a "grave, wise citizen or modest matron" when confronted with this kind of comedy, one must show that one actively does not identify with these comic characters over and against the assumption that one would. This is a generic strategy in which one acts out as a mode of judgment the terse Renaissance formula for subjectivity: I am not I.[5]

Jaques explains the mechanisms for this "correction of manners" in Shakespeare's *As You Like It* when he asks the Duke Senior for a motley coat and the liberty to satirize whomever he wishes:

> And they that are most galled with my folly,
> They most must laugh. And why, sir, must they so?
> The why is plain as way to parish church:
> He that a fool doth very wisely hit
> Doth very foolishly, although he smart,
> [Not to] seem senseless of the bob; if not,
> The wise man's folly is anatomiz'd
> Even by the squand'ring glances of the fool.
> . . . . . . . . . . . . . . . . . . . . . . . . . . . . . . .
> What woman in the city do I name,
> When that I say the city-woman bears
> The cost of princes on her shoulders?
> Who can come in and say that I mean her,
> When such a one as she, such is her neighbor?
> Or what is he of basest function,
> That says his bravery is not on my cost,
> Thinking that I mean him, but therein suits
> His folly to the mettle of my speech?
> There then! how then? what then? Let me see wherein
> My tongue hath wrong'd him; if it do him right,
> Then he hath wrong'd himself.
>
> (2.7.50–57, 74–85)

What's foolish, Jaques argues, is to get angry over comic characters created by satirists of the city because getting angry displays an affective identification with the thing satirized. Or, as Jonson puts it in one of the poems in his *Epigrams,* "none e're took pleasure in sin's sense, / But, when they heard it taxed, took more offense" (94, ll. 9–10). The appropriate response to this generic representation, then, is to enact as a strategy of reading a mode of judgment that disjoins one from the thing satirized.

Citizen comedy almost always stages this mode of judgment in its final scenes as self-scrutiny, thereby consolidating as psychic space a juridical apparatus that regulates and corrects the very characters and situations produced by the liberties' lack of jurisdiction. This final staging allows the audiences of citizen comedy a cathartic identification with that mode of judgment at the plot's culmination, in effect attempting an ideological seduction through enjoyment in self-scrutiny, self-regulation, and pious disassociation from oneself and one's past actions as the instituted form of good civic being. In Marston's *Dutch Courtesan*, after Malheureux explains to Freevill that the prostitute Francischina will sleep with him only after he murders Freevill, the two agree to stage a fake duel. Malheureux will pretend to kill Freevill, even though these actions assert desire over reason, lasciviousness over virtue, folly over truth, and in effect split Malheureux from the upright citizen and friend that he previously had been. "Truth seemes folly in madnesse spectacles," he complains. "I am not now my selfe, no man" (4.2.29). Precisely in order to mend this disowning of responsibility, Freevill acts as if Malheureux really does kill him, so that, confronted with his supposed deeds, Malheureux bemoans the sinner that he has become and then gives the pious point of the satire in sententious, moral fashion:

> He thats faire of bloude, well meand, of good breeding,
> Best fam'd, of sweet acquaintance and true friends,
> And would with desperate Impudence loose all these,
> And hazard landing at this fatall shore,
> Let him nere kill, nor steale, but love a Whore.
>
> (5.3.24–28)

Only after the expression of this moral does Freevill discover himself and allow Malheureux to return to his virtuous self:

> I am my selfe, how long wast ere I could
> Perswade my passion to grow calme to you?
> Rich sense makes good bad language, and a friend
> Should waigh no action, but the actions end.
> I am now worthie yours, when before
> The beast of man, loose bloude distemperd us,
> "He that lust rules cannot be virtuous."
>
> (5.3.60–66)

As Malheureux disjoins himself from the satirized figure of the young, pleasure-seeking gallant and claims a conversion to virtuous friendship, *The Dutch Courtesan* stages citizen comedy's generic strategy of judgment as cathartic rite of passage. In so doing, the play gives the form of cultural consciousness that citizen comedy posits a point of enjoyment that links the aesthetic experience of satire with the play's social and moral lessons, effectively producing a form of cultural consciousness that "solves" the social and political problems of the unregulated liberties in psychic space.

But the condition for this solution is the assertion of "loose bloude" as an unruly sex which "distemper[s] us" unless we submit to moral self-regulation. Thus, even as citizen comedy solves the problems of the liberties, it also reinscribes in its final reckoning a more theological tradition's urges toward conversion and purification. At the end of *A Trick to Catch the Old One*, Witgood kneels, "[confesses] his follies" which he "disclaim[s]" as the "cause of youth's undoing" (5.2.167–69), and asks for the audience to approve his conversion, "for here I rise / A reclaim'd man, loathing the general vice" (5.2.181–82). It takes a great deal of trust in the power of theatricality to break with history to see this as an instance of what Mullaney calls a "virtual distance" from "reigning ideologies" (57). After all, in bringing the judgment of this transgressed moral stance to bear on himself, Witgood effectively submits to a reign of theatricality in which normative freedom is equated with a very limited subversion of a fairly naive articulation of moral rules and in which the figure of Vice that has given form to theatricality emerges as the problematicized, erotic content of the theatrical self.

## Sodometrics, Theatricality, and the Institution of the Closet in Psychic Space

In *The Wise Woman of Hogsdon*, both Chartley's actions and the effects of his actions mark him as a generic figure quite at home in citizen comedy. Like Witgood in *A Trick to Catch the Old One*, Follywit in *A Mad World My Masters*, or in a more complex way like Truewit in *Epicoene*, Chartley initiates a plot of deception and intrigue only to be deceived and tricked himself. And, quite in keeping with the generic expectations that citizen comedy sets up, this doubling back of wit and deception serves to incorporate the young gallant within the very network that he was attempting to manipulate. At the end of the play, the Wise Woman has all of the people whom Chartley has deceived hide in the small withdrawing rooms that surround the main room in her house. Eventually, one by one, the characters come out of the withdrawing rooms and charge Chartley with wrongdoing. Each time this happens, Chartley tries to shift blame onto someone whom he thinks is not present, but, immediately following his attempts to exculpate himself, the character whom he has blamed emerges to charge Chartley again—until he ends up barring himself from any place in the social order that his deception might have afforded him: "neither married man," he says, because the woman that he thinks he has married will have nothing to do with him, nor "widdow," because the woman is still alive, "nor batcheller," because he's still married to her—"whats to bee done?" (5.4.2235-36) What motivates Chartley's reincorporation into the community he had attempted to manipulate and control is the possibility of sodomy, since he unwittingly married the Wise Woman's boy apprentice. To this revelation, Chartley responds: "[T]his woman hath lent mee a glasse in which I see all my imperfections, at which my conscience doth more blush inwardly then my face outwardly" (5.4.2293-95). After this confession—this inward blush at having acted in such a way that he has married a boy—much to the surprise of all on stage, the "boy-apprentice" reveals that in fact she is Chartley's first fiancée, Luce2. Chartley completes his incorporation into the social field by disassociating himself from his past life: "Where I haue wrong'd you *Luce* forgiue. Impute my errours to my youth not mee" (5.4.2319-20).

With the phrase "not mee," Chartley renounces his faults like a snake sheds its skin: the play shows Chartley's reversal—from witty, deceptive, and manipulative youth to manipulated and deceived hooligan—to be a generically configured rite of passage that leads him toward social inclusion, cast in the role of the good husband. To call Chartley's incorporation a rite of passage, though, is a bit misleading. While it aptly names the pious movement across a produced and regulated social boundary—for Chartley, from adolescence and its slippery relation to homoeroticism to manliness and its purportedly more rigid regulation through marriage— the phrase "rite of passage" focuses on the one who moves across the boundary and, in so doing, suggests that the main significance of this ritual is individual.[6] This is the reason that Pierre Bourdieu renames Arnold van Gannep's notion "rite of institution," calling attention to the verb "to institute" and its synonyms, "to organize," "to establish," "to appoint."

By solemnly marking the passage over a line which establishes a fundamental division in the social order, rites draw the attention of the observer to the passage (whence the expression "rites of passage"), whereas the important thing is the line. What, in effect, does this line separate? Obviously, it separates a before and after: the uncircumcised child and the circumcised child; or even the whole set of uncircumcised children and the set of circumcised adults. In fact, the most important division, and one which passes unnoticed, is the division it creates between all those who are subject to circumcision, boys and men, children or adults, and those who are not subject to it, i.e., girls and women. There is thus a hidden set of individuals in relation to which the instituted group is defined. The most important effect of the rite is the one which attracts the least attention: by treating men and women differently, the rite *consecrates* the difference, institutes it, while at the same time instituting man as man, i.e., circumcised, and woman as woman, i.e., not subject to this ritual operation. (Bourdieu, *Logic* 118)

Bourdieu appropriately emphasizes the way that ritual almost offhandedly consecrates social differences, but it is also important to acknowledge the effects that rites of institution have on the formation of modes of knowing. Insofar as a rite of passage establishes a boundary between those to whom the ritual pertains and those to whom it explicitly does not, a rite of passage also institutes a boundary that separates those for whom a certain social and cultural mode of knowing is possible from those for whom this mode is most relevant insofar as they can't attain it for themselves. In other words, on the one hand, rites of passage institute psychic space and concomitant systems of temporality, historicity, and signifying apparatuses for nuanced and sophisticated self-recognition, display, and apprehension of the world through a complex interplay of knowing, not knowing, and unknowing. On the other hand, rites of passage also institute social differences by placing limitations on the accessibility of these complex and often nuanced modes of knowing in the very act of institution. A rite of institution enforces the overlay of consecrated social differences and instituted psychic spaces such that the latter are endlessly complex for some and seemingly impoverished for others.

Citizen comedy tends to emphasize and validate these social and psychic boundaries when it encourages audience identification with its dominant mode of judgment at the moment of a main character's generic transformation. But when *The Wise Woman of Hogsdon* stages citizen comedy's generic rite of passage in the context of a cross-dressed comedy, the play slows down, as it were, the positing and soliciting of citizen comedy's generic cultural consciousness and, in the process, attempts to specify what this dominant mode of knowing tries to avoid. Rather than simply forcing the institution of citizen comedy's generic cultural consciousness, through its use of the cross-dressing plot *The Wise Woman* contextualizes this institution within the broader project of consecrating social differences by means of explicitly sexed self-comprehension and display. In so doing, *The Wise Woman* emphasizes that what is at stake in citizen comedy's mode of cultural consciousness is how one becomes subject to problematized, though sanctioned, sexualities.

*The Wise Woman of Hogsdon* demonstrates that citizen comedy's rite of institution works insofar as the once manipulative young man introjects the spatial apparatuses that sustain the play's dominant mode of knowing. When the Wise Woman places each of the secret auditors in one of the small withdrawing rooms that surround the main room in her house, she creates an apparatus for the apprehension of truth based on what the play previously asserted as a strategy of the closet. After hiring Luce2 to serve as her apprentice, the Wise Woman explains the reason that she has built a small closet near the main door of her house:

[I]f any knock, you must to the doore and question them, to find what they come about, if to this porpose, or to that. Now they are ignorantly telling thee their errand, which I sitting in my Closet, overheare, presently come forth, and tell them the cause of their comming, with every word that hath past betwixt you in private: which they admiring, and thinking it to be miraculous, by their report I become thus famous. (3.1.893–900)

Because she overhears it from the position of the closet, the Wise Woman can explain "the cause of their comming" with seemingly miraculous accuracy and can, therefore, appear to have a privileged relation to truth. The play gives a comic version of this apparatus when Sencer comes to the Wise Woman for help. Luce2 meets him at the door:

2. LUCE: Whose there? What would you have?
SENCER: I would speake with the wise gentlewoman of the house.
2. LUCE: O belike you haue lost somewhat.
SENCER: You are in the wrong sweete youth.
2. LUCE: I am somewhat thicke of hearing, pray speak out.
SENCER: I say I haue not lost any thing, but wit and time. And neither of those shee can helpe me too.
2. LUCE: Then you belike are crost in Loue, and come to know what successe you shall haue.
SENCER: Thou hast hit it sweete ladde; thou hast hit it.
2. LUCE: What is it you say sir?
SENCER: Thou hast hit it!
2. LUCE: I pray come in, ile bring you to my Mistresse.                (4.3.1687–1701)

In effect, the assumption of the Wise Woman in the closet invests this exchange with a sense of produced truthfulness that Luce2's fake deafness renders comic. In much the same way that the Wise Woman can position herself as the one who knows the truth by taking the privileged position in the closet's structuring of audition and knowledge, when the Wise Woman places these characters whom Chartley has wronged in the withdrawing rooms, she situates these characters in the privileged position as overhearers of the truth.

The difference between the Wise Woman's strategic use of the closet and her manipulation of Chartley is that the apparatus that allows the Wise Woman to sustain this illusory position of truth-teller tends to be hidden to those whom she dupes, whereas in the final scene of the play the apparatus is in plain view—not just to us but eventually to Chartley as well. However, instead of pointing out these apparatuses and the constructedness of positions of knowing and unknowing by which he was manipulated, in his guilt Chartley simply accepts and introjects the privileged position of the secret auditor in the closet:

I had best bit out my tongue, and speake no more; what shall I doe, or what shall I say, there is not outfacing them all: Gentlemen, Fathers, wiues, or what else, I haue wrongd you all. I confesse it that I haue, what would you more? Will any of you rayle of mee? Ile beare it. Will any of you beate mee? So they strike not too hard, Ile suffer it. Will any of you challenge mee? Ile answer it. What would you have me say, or doo? (5.4.2214-21)

Chartley offers to marry either Luce or Gratiana, or humorously to keep both, but each refuses him. And, in order to shame him further, Gratiana's father offers his daughter to Sencer, "the more inconstant youth to spight" (5.4.2256). Chartley's final response is to introject this shame in the form of conscience ("this woman hath lent me a glasse, in which I see all my imperfections, at which my conscience doeth more blush inwardly than my face outwardly"), and then to cast off his errors as those of his now completed youth.[7]

While Chartley claims to renounce his youth, this introjection more precisely forces him to renounce his previous, naive use of performance as a way to manipulate the flows of knowledge in his social milieu. From the beginning, both in his manipulation of women and his attempts to manipulate his friends, Chartley has used role-playing and performance to conceal his (generally quite obvious) motives. For example, the play begins with Chartley having lost his money to Haringfield and Sencer; in order to get it back, he tries to pick a fight with them. But neither falls for the trick.

CHARTLEY: I say this Hatt's not made of wooll. Which of you all dares say the contrary?
SENCER: It may bee 'tis a Beaver.
HARINGFIELD: Very likely so: 'tis not Wooll, but a plaine Beaver.
CHARTLEY: 'Tis Wooll, but which of you dares say so? [Aside.] I would faine picke a quarrell with them, to get some of my money againe; but the salves now they have got it, and too wise to part with it. I say it is not blacke.
HARINGFIELD: So say wee too.                                           (1.1.53–62)

This version of performance is simply an extension of the strategies of market exchange. Market exchange assumes the good faith of its particular participants, so that customers and sellers all operate fairly; but, also, market exchange assumes a profit motive, so that customers want to pay the least amount possible for the most and highest quality of goods, and sellers want to sell the least and lowest quality for the highest price. To negotiate these two assumptions, market exchange depends on symbolically naive but practically sophisticated readers of performance. A practicing customer knows that the seller wants to sell the least and lowest quality for the highest price, and a practicing seller knows that the customer wants to pay the least amount possible for the most and highest quality of goods. But each acts as if this were not the case. At the play's beginning, Chartley's version of performance collapses the difference between symbolic and practical. Chartley assumes a practically *and* symbolically naive spectator who can't read his motives, even when these motives are obvious.

It is specifically the Wise Woman's manipulation of the logic of the closet that vitiates this version of performance because it forces Chartley to experience and subsequently to introject a practically sophisticated auditor— one who can hear his motives even when he tries to hide them. When this auditor reads with ill will, that is, when this auditor attributes a malevolence to Chartley's motives that he doesn't intend, psychoanalysis names this sophisticated listener and interpreter the superego, and psychoanalysis further argues that its function is to keep adults in line. In *The Wise Woman of Hogsdon,* the means of producing this version of a male, adult capitalist rely on spatial apparatuses, no doubt; but they need not be recognized as spatially grounded once this sense of character is produced as such. As the spatial translates into conscience, it sustains a sense of self formed by these sociospatial means as reified, psychological entity.

What mediates the social and the psychic *and* allows for the intertwining of the two is the institution of an audience for whom this rite is relevant and meaningful. When Chartley completes his incorporation into the social field, the play shows that this rite of passage depends on the complicity of an audience that acts as if it believes Chartley's claims to maturity: "*Impute* my errours to my youth." This passage institutes a virtual audience complicit with Chartley's final attempts at exculpation; that is, this passage asserts a role from which one can critique Chartley's errors as errors of his now suspended youth by judging with approval what now he is cast to be. Insofar as the play elicits an audience that approvingly judges both Chartley's shame at potentially marrying a boy *and* his impulse to characterize his shift from manipulator to being manipulated as a change in roles from lascivious, ill-mannered youth to mature, good husband, it shows the institution of an audience that is what Eve Sedgwick calls homosocial, of a reader organized by what Luce Irigaray describes as "the exclusive valorization of men's needs/desires, of exchanges among men" (Sedgwick 1–27; Irigaray 171).

These assertions may sound a little odd, so, before going on to demonstrate them, let me say a word about the general assumptions that support them. When Irigaray asserts that "women's bodies—through their use, consumption, and circulation—provide for the condition making social life and culture possible," she obviously isn't making a point about biology; rather, her point is that, even as women's bodies serve this social and cultural function, "they remain an unknown 'infrastructure' of the elaboration of that social life and culture" (171). What makes a society homosocial is not just the way it treats women but also the way it judges itself to be treating women in order to continue their exploitation as a group. Since culture is a field of strategic recognitions and misrecognitions, it is not enough for literary criticism, cultural criticism, or whatever to read for the homosocial as a textual thematics or even as a structure that explains the acknowledged and unacknowledged erotic motives that infuse social networks represented in a cultural artifact. It is also critical to pay close attention to the ways in which texts and other cultural artifacts invent, elicit, stage, frustrate, and mock homosocial audiences—the ways in which they invent homosocial readers who will read these relations synchronically and the ways in which they frustrate this reading strategy.

This rite of institution that I have been discussing in *The Wise Woman of Hogsdon* separates economic from sexual desires for an audience that wants to see this young gallant become a sexually responsible, money-making husband. When the play starts, economic and sexual desires are indistinguishable. The play begins with Chartley and three other "young Gentlemen"—Boyster, Sencer, and Haringfield—who have just come from gambling (1.1.13). The four continue to shoot dice until Chartley wins back some of the money that he had previously lost, but soon they break up in order to search out "the prettiest wenches" (1.1.143–44). Alone on stage, Chartley plots to steal Boyster's potential girlfriend, Luce, first presenting money as the means to accomplish this task:

As I live, I love her extreamely, and to enjoy her would give anything. But the foole stands in her owne light, and will doe nothing without Marriage: but what should I doe marrying? I can better indure Gives, than Bands of Matrimonie. But in this Meditation, I am glad I have won this money againe. Nay, and shee may be glad of it too: for the Girle is but poore . . . (1.1.180–86)

Up to this point, it appears that money and economic advantage will contextualize Chartley's sexual advances, but by the end of his soliloquy the language of economics becomes so infused with the language of eroticism that the two cannot easily be separated.

. . . and in my pockett I have layd up a Stocke for her, 'tis put to use alreadie. And if I meete not with a Dyce-house, or an Ordinary by the way, no question but I may increase it to a summe. Well, Ile to the Exchange to buy her some prettie Noveltie. That done, Ile visite my little Rascall, and solicite instantly. (1.1.187–92)

The shifting back and forth between a language of economic profit and erotics doesn't just point to some witty ambiguity; rather, it renders extremely unambiguous the structure of desire propelled by an enjoyment in accumulation. The demand here is quite simple: *get some!* For instance, "Stocke," at first a reference to the supply of capital that Chartley won in gambling, turns into an implicit reference to his penis once it increases into an overtly sexual "summe." To put it crudely: if he doesn't blow his wad on gambling, then he can spend it with Luce. The sexual reference becomes explicit in the scene that follows. After Chartley feigns a confession of love for Luce, she begins to negotiate marriage: "Sir, if you love me, as you say you doe / Shew me the fruits thereof" (1.2.282–83). Chartley replies, "The stocke I can, thou maiest see the fruits hereafter" (1.2.284). Luce, who gets the joke, responds by saying, "Can I beleeve you love mee, when you seeke / The shipwrack of mine Honour?" (1.2.285–86).

In this scene's presentation of motives, too, erotics and economics are inextricable. When feigning his confession of love, Chartley shows himself as an affluent young gentleman, giving Luce gifts; while Luce is concerned with protecting her chastity, her eavesdropping father is concerned with the upward mobility that such a marriage would afford him. We can see this binding of economics and erotics even in the way that the play thinks about its staging: act 1 scene 2 begins with Luce, against her preferences, sitting in her father's shop window both to protect the goods and implicitly to solicit customers; dramaturgically, she is on the market.

Only at the play's end do economic and sexual desires separate, with Chartley's rite of passage and the concurrent institution of a complicit, homosocial audience. Up to this point, Chartley's interest has been accumulating women—Luce2, Luce, and Gratiana—but now in the very last lines of the play this is exactly the form of accumulation that Chartley renounces:

> *Luce, Luce,* and *Grace,* (O covetous man) I see
> I sought to ingrosse what now sufficeth three,
> Yet each one wife enough, one Nuptiall Feast
> Shall serue three Bridalls where bee thou chiefest guest.
> (5.3.2328-31)

Whereas before Chartley tried to "ingrosse" what would fulfill three husbands, now three couples—Luce2 and Chartley, Luce and Boyster, and Gratiana and Sencer—all celebrate their marriages at one bridal feast. What is important, though, is that the language of economics doesn't end with Chartley's lesson. Rather, the economic language continues even as it articulates the moral that men shouldn't try to accumulate women. This ending functions to separate economic from erotic desires through the lesson of sexual propriety. In specifying sexual propriety as the one place in which economic desires should be forbidden, this rite of passage attempts to evacuate sex from capitalist motivations.

But note, Chartley makes this separation while someone watches: the "thou" who is his "chiefest guest." Certainly, with this "thou" Chartley could be referring to Luce2, but its position in the very last line of the play suggests that this "thou" transgresses the play's diegetic space and, in the terse manner of an epilogue, names the generic audience that the play has, at various points, elicited—the audience that has anticipated Chartley's rite of passage all along. This generic, homosocial audience from citizen comedy is the one most at home here.

The naming of this generic audience has significant consequences for the play's asserted equation between youthful femininity and theatricality. In *The Stage and Social Struggle,* Howard argues that when Luce2 and the Wise Woman get the best of Chartley, they also by implication offer a site for contesting the ideology for which Chartley metonymically stands. Because the public theater charged admission, Howard proposes, it also offered an economic leveling of class that traversed other forms of social organization and concomitant rights to social and aesthetic judgment. Thus, taking seriously the model of freedom based on economy that the Scrivener gives in the induction to *Bartholomew Fair,* where it is agreed "that every person here have his or their free-will to censure, to like or dislike at their own charge" (Induction 75–76), Howard argues that the result is a "potential gap, for certain groups, between the ideological implications of a given play and the ideological consequences of playgoing" (80). This gap, Howard argues, would possibly cause women spectators—"potentially at odds with the patriarchal injunctions governing the behavior of good women"—to view things differently: "[I]f male spectators focused on the play's palliating ending, is it not possible that at least some women might have focused on what went before: namely, the wise woman's successful domination of her aristocratic enemy and Luce2's successful achievement of her desire?" (91). And this possibility leads Howard to propose that female spectators, situated at the point of social contradiction, could identify with theatricality as the cultural and aesthetic form by which the Wise Woman and Luce2 achieved their domination and desires, even as these characters are folded back into a patriarchal world.

The most obvious problem with Howard's analysis is that Luce2's manipulation of the cross-dressing genre is entirely complicit with the solicitation of a homosocial mode of judgment. In *The Wise Woman of Hogsdon,* theatricality doesn't so much offer women a strategy for dealing with patriarchy as it is precisely the form that Luce2 uses to debunk the Wise Woman and establish, if not antagonism, at least a nonrelation between women entirely agreeable to patriarchal social arrangements. Midway through the play, Luce2 asks the Wise Woman why she has so many books, since she can neither read nor write. The Wise Woman answers that she pretends to read in order to fool those who watch, "for to be ignorant, and seeme ignorant, what greater folly?" (3.1.885–86). This woman's wisdom concerns a kind of savvy about how the symbolic order works as a system of disbelief, illusion, and belief.[8] And it is Luce2 who devalues it. In an aside, Luce2 explains, "Beleeve me, this is a cunning Woman; neither hath shee her name for nothing, who out of her ignorance, can foole so many that thinke themselves wise" (3.1.887–89).

Throughout the play, Luce2 uses theatrical form to deauthorize the Wise Woman's claims and, in the process, to authorize herself in relation to an audience that trusts the truth-figuring devices of the theater. The first time that we see the Wise Woman on stage, for example, we don't just see the Wise Woman performing magic; we see Luce2, as an example of what Weimann calls the *Figurenposition,* watching the Wise Woman magically diagnose some urine a country man has brought her.[9]

COUNTRY MAN: Here foresooth Mistresse.
WISE WOMAN: And who distill'd this water?
COUNTRY MAN: My wives Limbeck, if it please you.
WISE WOMAN: And where doth the paine hold her most?
COUNTRY MAN: Marry at her heart forsooth.
WISE WOMAN: Ey, at her heart, shee hath a griping at her heart.
COUNTRY MAN: You have hit it right.
WISE WOMAN: Nay, I can see so much in the Urine.
2. LUCE: [Aside] Just as much as is told her.
WISE WOMAN: She hath no paine in her head, hath shee?
COUNTRY MAN: No indeed, I never heard her complaine of her head.
WISE WOMAN: I told you so, her paine lyes all at her heart.          (2.1.409–22)

Surely Howard is to some extent right to read this moment as a demystification of magic (86), but also, in demystifying magic by triangulating its reception, the play replaces belief in magic with the "magic" of the theater. To believe in magic with the country man is to act as if Luce2 weren't there, and to acknowledge the presence of Luce2 is de facto to contextualize magic's (and the Wise Woman's) authority. Especially with Luce2's aside, "Just as much as is told her," the play forces upon its audience the knowledge that magic's success relies on the complicity of an audience's more or less willful unknowingness. In so doing, this staging reveals the complicity that magic assumes with an unknowing audience in order to reestablish that very complicity between an audience that suspends disbelief and a character who reveals "truth" in a theatrical aside. Theatrical form allows Luce2 to debunk and usurp the Wise Woman's authority for the play's posited homosocial audience.

Up to the very end of the play, the Wise Woman takes Luce2 to be a boy; only after her apprentice "skatters her hayre" (5.4.2308) does the Wise

Woman recognize the trick. By showing a kind of performance that fools an audience who thinks that she can control performance, this moment undermines the Wise Woman's trust in privileged listening. "My boy turn'd girl," the Wise Woman exclaims. "I hope shee'l keepe my counsell; from henceforth, ile never entertaine any servant but ile haue her searcht" (5.3.2311–13). Luce2's lesson to the Wise Woman is that theatricality over-takes and undoes those who think they can use it as a mechanism of control. But this moment also equates a contradiction concerning theatricality with femininity. By having Luce2 claim her femininity with the theatrical gesture of scattering her hair, this moment makes a rather theatrical appeal to authenticity. The play gives Luce2 no rite of passage to resolve this contradiction. Instead, in the diegesis of the play, the gesture of scattering her hair and claiming femininity is most immediately what causes Chartley to renounce his youth, to enact the generic rite of institution that I have been discussing. Of course, we need not accept this diegetic unfolding as the basis for asserting a causal relation. In practice, a rite of institution tends to respond to the impossible task of authentically acting out authen-ticity by encouraging its participants—past, present, and future—to pit the "authentic" acting of the initiates against the "inauthentic" actions of those whom ritual de facto excludes. To this extent, Luce2's contradiction is simply the flip side of Chartley's rite of passage and is the basis for an elaboration complementary to Chartley's introjection of the closet.

In short, theatricality isn't so much "a mode of empowerment for women" (84), as Howard asserts; rather, Luce2's theatricality conspires with Chartley's rite of passage and introjection of the closet to form an epistemology of heterosexuality. Luce2 responds to the Wise Woman's sexual economics with a disapproval that edges toward horror. After the Wise Woman explains the services that she provides to unmarried pregnant women, Luce2 exclaims in an aside:

Most strange, that a womans brain should apprehend such lawlesse, indirect and horrid meanes for covetous gaine! How many unknowne Trades women and men are free of, which they never had charter for? (3.1.877–81)

Not only does Luce2's aside make the Wise Woman into a figure for the sup-posed sexual secrets of London's liberties, but also the mediating theatrical-ity of her knowledge of and reaction to the Wise Woman serves to establish Luce2's epistemological distance from her as a figure of sexual and eco-nomic secrets.[10] That is, Luce2 uses theatricality to distinguish and distance herself from a trade that, upon having it explained to her, she calls "un-knowne." This use of theatricality allows Luce2 to solicit, in an aside, the ap-propriate disapproval from the homosocial viewer, the viewer who shares both Chartley's and Luce2's disapproval because a woman does these things, who will share Chartley's shame when he nearly marries a boy, who will concur with the near horror and viciousness with which Luce2 and Chartley recognize the sex-positive capitalist woman.[11] At the end of the play when Luce2 refuses her apprenticeship, when she refuses to repeat the Wise Woman's fraudulence and marries Chartley, she doesn't exactly attain some authentic femininity outside of performance and theatricality. When she renounces the relations among women, sex, and capital to which the Wise Woman points in order to become Chartley's wife, Luce2 attains a problematized femininity precisely *for generic homosocial consciousness.*

## Decathecting the Future

It remains to ask how we might locate the limits of this generic homosocial consciousness. To get at this question, let me propose that the crucial effect of the rite of institution which I have been discussing is the collapse of consecrated social differences with so-called historical reality in the formation of what Cornelius Castoriadis calls identitary time, that is, the translation of time's local irreversibility into social temporalities. Casto-riadis argues that with schedules of work, rites, festivals, and so forth, institutions lean on and conscript the implacable fact of time in order to posit and consolidate social being. In this analysis, social being isn't simply some body's identification with some socially constructed *imago;* rather, social being is grounded in an identification produced by more or less analogously expressed temporal forms (202–11).[12] In the case of *The Wise Woman,* the play strongly implies a historical allegory in which the passage of time is "correctly" experienced as the purification of manhood through the "appropriate," that is, heterosexual, configuration of sexual difference. On the one hand, Chartley's rite of passage allows him social incorporation at the cost of the introjecting into psychic space the Wise Woman's truth-producing spatial apparatuses, and, at the same time, this rite encourages the expression of femininity as theatricality. On the other hand, this rite attempts to excorporate the Wise Woman by presenting her as a figure for what both urban manhood and marriage leave in the past.

To this extent, I wish to argue, the Wise Woman figures a critical limit to the generic homosocial consciousness that the play solicits. But how so? Not as an identity to be claimed, but as an anti-identitarian cathexis, a kind of symptomatic knotting of temporality and the flesh that homosocial consciousness produces in order to reject. In somewhat the same way that, in *The Dutch Courtesan,* Malheureux becomes a supposedly better version of himself in high homosocial friendship with Freevill after renouncing his lust for the prostitute Francischina, so too does Chartley's rite of institution present him as superseding the temptations of the flesh for which the Wise Woman stands. The difference between the two plays is this: *The Wise Woman of Hogsdon* contextualizes Chartley's renunciation such that the problem of the flesh remains not simply as a temptation for some young man but as the grounds for communal possibility. This rite's process of historiation unhinges the sexed, nonreproductive woman from civic space as the ethical problem against which it defines itself, but this problem can't be forgotten because the Wise Woman also figures the very countereconomy upon whose manipulation Chartley's supposedly mature and responsible manhood is built. This "womans brain," as Luce2 puts it, knows the "lawless, indirect, and horrid meanes" for specifically *unchartered* "covetous gaine." It is this doubling that is most significant: on the one hand, the Wise Woman stands in for a kind of fantasmic wild capitalism that always exceeds attempts at market regulation; on the other hand, she stands in for the flesh. It is in this doubling that the Wise Woman figures a possible future—a futureless future, if you will—against the very social eschatology which this rite projects.[13]

I mean for this assertion to be taken in a very precise way. Generic cultural consciousness is organized such that some specifiable, anti-identitary cathexis is explicitly *not* reflected in consciousness even as it *is* presented in symptomatic social practices—rites of institution, for example—as an aporia in identitary time. To elaborate this aporia, Castoriadis also proposes a time for social doing (social *poiesis*) which identitary time constitutively denies (211–15). Especially in its relation to the overlay of social and psychic space, this time for social doing must be understood as a *poiesis* that concerns formal expression more than content, where form is understood to be an instituted and regularized relation, here between spectator and play.[14] Specifically, genre attempts to enforce an alignment between a certain mode of judgment and cathartic enjoyment. Given this understanding, Castoriadis's assertions of the time for social doing imply that this enjoyment can become unhinged from its regularized form of expression and become the basis for another, minor form of thinking that generic cultural consciousness attempts to deny and whose critical development, for this reason, tends to come from a future which, in the terms set by cultural consciousness, has no future. I want to propose that as a site of libidinal investment for Chartley and for the homosocial consciousness his character solicits, the Wise Woman figures such an anti-identitary cathexis. But also, as an aporia within the play's rituals of identitary time, the Wise Woman figures a form of future possibility situated in its historical specificity. As such, the Wise Woman counts less as an identity and more as a discursive event.

This is probably most evident in the play's accusations of witchcraft. After drinking at Mother Redcap's tavern, Chartley intrudes upon the Wise Woman in order to "make some sport" with her (2.1.506). Chartley harasses her, calling her "hagge," "shee-mastiffe," and "witch."[15] Witchcraft serves here as a fantasy screen that both indicates and hides an inconsistency that, were it to be revealed as such, would trouble the perceived coherence of the social order. Since Keith Thomas's and Alan Macfarlane's groundbreaking works in the early 1970s, it has been commonplace to accept a strategically unacknowledged complicity between an accuser of witchcraft and his or her victim—a complicity that law and jurisprudence concerning witchcraft almost insists on since the conviction of a witch demands only one witness; since the 1563 Act against Conjurations, Enchantments, and Witchcraftes makes it a felony to invoke evil spirits even if the invocation caused no harm to others; and since, as Michael Dalton explains in his *Countrey Justice* (1618), in cases against witches justices of the peace "may not always expect any direct evidence" as the grounds for conviction.[16] From within this contradictory and quite unjust juridical situation emerged a tactics for the bad-faith assertion of traditional village values in the face of historical changes which these values could not otherwise explain or even negotiate. Macfarlane proposes that accusations of witchcraft are motivated by the social guilt of the accuser over his or her failure to conform to traditional communal obligations, as a way to demonize the poor rather than care for them (196–97). Resituating this notion of guilt and obligation more explicitly within economic motives, Thomas argues that as traditional networks of care for widows and old women collapsed, these older women were left almost entirely dependent on the kindness of their often not so charitable neighbors.

Since "fear of retaliation by witchcraft was a powerful deterrent against breaking the old moral code, for to display a lack of generosity to one's neighbours was the quickest way of getting hurt," belief in witchcraft "helped to uphold the traditional obligation of charity and neighbourliness at a time when other social and economic forces were conspiring to weaken them" (564). Taken together, Thomas and Macfarlane unhinge the fantasmic witch from practices of the craft so that witchcraft becomes significant not as a practice per se but as a mediator between civic being and historical change.

Accusations of witchcraft mobilize a social fantasy of evil whose effect is to allow a community to sustain its sense of continuity in the face of economic and historical change. Elizabeth's Act against Conjurations, Enchantments, and Witchcraftes—which reinstated Henry VIII's Act of 1542, repealed by Edward's government under Somerset—characterizes witchcraft as a threat to the ideology of good neighbors. "Sythens the repeale" of Henry VIII's act, the statute proclaims, "many fantasticall and devilishe persons have devised and practiced Invocations and Conjurations of evill and wicked Spirites, and have used and practiced Wytchecraftes Enchantementes Charms and Sorceries, to the Destruction of the Persons and Goodes of their Neighbours and other Subjectes of this realme, and for other lewde Intentes and Purposes contrarye to the Lawes of Almighty God, to the Perill of theyr owne Soules, and to the great Infamye and Disquietnes of this Realme" (*Statutes of the Realm,* 5 Eliz.c.16). The brief history which the act gives promises that the reinstatement of Henry's 1542 act in 1563 will return the realm to the world of good neighbors from which it supposedly has fallen. The version of the past it posits is a specious one, since the traditional village established neighborliness through ritual festivals— neither through some release of pent-up aggression and frustration nor through manipulated feelings of communal goodwill, but instead through the systems of gifts and loans that necessarily accompanied these often extremely expensive events. Since these festivals were a costly investment in maintaining the social relations of a community, Annabel Gregory argues that "a decision to abandon festivals"—a decision that many English villages made in the sixteenth and seventeenth centuries—"would . . . depend not so much on levels of current wealth or power in a community, as on an expectation of economic and political stability in the future" (60). As Gregory argues, when these expectations falter, when the future begins to look bleaker and more unstable, charges of witchcraft accelerate.

The bad-faith instatement of this world of good neighbors is precisely the effect of witchcraft in Dekker, Rowley, and Ford's *Witch of Edmonton* (a "known true story," as the title page announces). As Elizabeth Sawyer complains:

> Any why on me? Why should the envious world
> Throw all their scandalous malice upon me?
> 'Cause I am poor, deform'd and ignorant?
> And like a Bow buckl'd and bent together,
> By some more strong in mischiefs than my self?
> Must I for that be made a common sink,
> For all the filth and rubbish of Men's tongues
> To fall and run into? Some call me Witch;
> And being ignorant of my self, they go
> About to teach me how to be one.
>
> (2.1.1-10)

It is because of her neighbor's lack of neighborliness that Sawyer begins to practice witchcraft in the first place. After being verbally abused by several of her neighbors and fellow villagers, Sawyer decides to become the thing they charge her with being. Since she is "shunn'd / And hated like a sickness," she reasons, she might as well become a witch: "'Tis all one, / To be a Witch, as to be counted one" (2.1.96-97, 114-15).[17] However much the play acknowledges Sawyer's mistreatment at the hands of her neighbors, and however much the play also implies a relation between her mistreatment and the desires for upward mobility on the part of her neighbors, Sawyer's turn to witchcraft "magically" reinstates ideal village life with Sawyer as its scapegoat. For example, after Sawyer becomes a witch, her familiar claims that he cannot kill the character who refused to let the old woman gather wood from his property. This man, the familiar explains, is "loving to the world / And charitable to the poor" (2.1.155-56)—exactly what he proved himself not to be some one hundred lines earlier. Sawyer's turn to witchcraft allows him to be judged good by the values of traditional village life, values which he himself explicitly refused to uphold.

A loose form of jurisprudence develops around the figure of the witch both in the courts of law and in culture at large, and its function is to assert a secure sense of the present's continuity with the past (a version of the past which never existed) through aggressive, violent acts of judgment in the face of an increasingly unstable and threatening future. Since the witch is presented as both the effect and the cause of communal malevolence, though, the witch can trigger the aggression of judgment in such a way that judgment need not recognize its own violence. Instead, this judgment can contextualize its actions within the bad-faith version of "good neighborliness" which it attempts to secure.

Accusations of witchcraft surface only momentarily in *The Wise Woman of Hogsdon,* and the function of these accusations is not exactly to uphold an ideology of traditional village values. This is because Chartley's charges are fairly ironic. When Chartley calls the Wise Woman a witch, he implies that she runs a house of prostitution, and, in so doing, he presents the Wise Woman as a figure constitutively split between illicit sexuality and illegal profit: "You Inchantresse, Sorceresse, Shee-devill; you Madame *Hectate,* Lady *Proserpine,* you are too old, you Hagge, now, for conjuring up Spirits your selfe; but you keep prettie yong Witches under your roofe, that can doe that" (2.1.515–18). Chartley uses the language of witchcraft to implicate the Wise Woman in illegal sexual traffic: the pretty young witches can conjure up (raise) spirits (erections) that the ugly old woman cannot—so Chartley implies. The implication of prostitution becomes more explicit further on when, after Haringfield tries to stop him, Chartley responds, "Away you old Dromadary, Ile come one of these nights, and make a racket amongst your Shee-catterwaullers" (2.1.525–26). Chartley threatens to force upon these women in the Wise Woman's house the sexual activities that he previously implied they want—a threat that calls attention more to the aggressive enjoyment that motivates his accusations than to the purported lasciviousness of these women. This aggressive enjoyment signals that much is at stake in this translation, for it indicates not some essential masculine fear of feminine sexuality but, most precisely, a refusal on the level of content to recognize the vicissitudes of historiation indicated by the accusation's form. That is, Chartley's strong implications of prostitution in his basically unserious charges of witchcraft effectively ironize the content of the accusation such that the fairly rigid forms of social time which accusations of witchcraft regularly reinforce get loosened up.

This loosening up opens the possibility for a new allegory of group formation, one that Chartley's and Luce2's solicitation of a homosocial audience cannot foreclose. Later in the play, after Chartley's accusations, we discover that the charge of prostitution is partially accurate. As the Wise Woman explains when she confides in Luce2, she has hung women's portraits over the doors of the withdrawing rooms so that "when any Citizens, or yong Gentlemen come hither, under a colour to know their Fortunes, they looke upon these pictures, and which of them they best like, she is ready with a wet finger" (3.1.851–54), a service that must remain secret, given that, since brothels were officially illegal after 1546, unlicensed sex trade tended to be policed by property owners and businessmen who profited from it (Burford 122–25, 147–61). Furthermore, the Wise Woman explains to Luce2 that "for a matter of money" (3.1.865) she provides a kind of secret birthing service for women who are pregnant with illegitimate children. What Chartley implicitly says in his "sporting" accusations, the Wise Woman admits as sexual services that she provides to the paying community. *The Wise Woman* insistently refuses to develop what from the perspective of the play's rite of institution is an almost atopic group into a viable form of identification. Rather, the play gestures toward this possibility as its rite of institution's underside, at the fantasmic boundaries of citizen comedy's mode of judgment and its assertions of civic space and time.

It would seem to me to be a mistake either to share in Chartley's excoriation of the Wise Woman or to celebrate Renaissance prostitution as a utopian ideal because both, inevitably I think, substantiate the homosocial consciousness which *The Wise Woman* so insistently stages. Nor, however, do I want simply to celebrate the ironization of modes of judgment on which these insistently unarticulated ideals are predicated. Rather, I would urge understanding the relation between ironization and allegorization as formally and, therefore, as historically as possible: on the one hand, as the specific aftereffect of the historical allegory which the institution of modern time produces; on the other hand, as a formal fracturing of possibility from its sexed substantiation that can keep open the chance for different relations among reading, history, and sexual difference.

# Notes

1. Butler develops this analysis most recently in *The Psychic Life of Power* (106–31).

2. See my analysis of this scene in *Doctor Faustus* (Hammill 328–29).

3. Since Brian Gibbons first mapped the generic contours of citizen comedy in 1968, a number of critics have developed connections between the genre and capitalist, market economy, arguing for often sophisticated and subtle relations between citizen comedy's generic conventions and the political and economic urgencies that led to the development of London as an urban center (Gibbons; Leggatt; Wells; Venuti; Leinwand; Manley 431–77). Moreover, as Rose demonstrated in 1988, these political and economic urgencies cannot be isolated from questions of gender (43–92). Bruster critiques the category of city comedy,

arguing that the plays categorized as city comedies are better conceived as part of a general trend in Renaissance drama, "a concerted attempt to map out a new paradigm for the material relations of the social world of late Tudor and early Stuart England" (40).

4. The incoherent jurisdiction of the liberties needs to be considered alongside the competing jurisdictions of London. Tudor economic policy attempted to regulate the spaces and populations of London through relatively flexible assertions of the crown's jurisdiction, often in competition with the jurisdiction of the livery companies and municipal magistrates. Rather than immobilizing London government, however, these competing assertions of jurisdiction allowed the city to develop into a fairly efficient juridical machine. In part, this was because, while the Tudor courts of the sixteenth century tended to practice local tactics of centralization that usurped the jurisdiction of municipal government and livery companies, this usurpation occurred primarily in legal definition and not in daily administrative life. When it came to London, Tudor economic policy had neither the means nor desire to assert administrative control over the livery companies or the city, but it did have a tactical urge to intervene in relations between livery companies and municipal authority in such a way that both were more securely under the legal, if not practical, jurisdiction of the crown (Rappaport 45-46, 184-214; Kramer 61-73; Pearl 34-35). The livery companies remained the basis for the maintenance of "good order" in London's daily life, even as the relations between livery companies and the crown changed fairly dramatically in the sixteenth century. The livery companies and guilds were responsible not only for the regulation of work—ordering the maximum wages a laborer could be paid, the prerequisites for setting up shop, the size of the shop, the levels and standards of production, and so forth (Rappaport 187). They also served as the ground for urban civic being. London was governed by freemen, and to obtain one's freedom one had to go through one of the city's guilds and livery companies (Loades 143-44). All in all, the crown's economic policies worked to turn the guilds into local agents that carried out and enforced "national industrial policy" (Cunningham 2:36; Kramer 88-123).

5. Joel Fineman's discussion of what he calls the subjectivity effect gets at the complexities of this formula; see, e.g., Fineman 143-64. I am trying to argue here that this subjectivity effect must be understood not simply in the unfolding diegesis of the play but also in the play's social and epistemological situation.

6. Hence, Ilana Krausaman Ben-Amos, who focuses on rites of passage from adolescence to maturity in early modern England, portrays this passage as a developmental process in which individuals gain the practical know-how necessary for social survival (208-35).

7. See Whigley's discussion of Alberti, in which the closet emerges as the discursive and material demarcation of a "space of [masculine] sexuality . . . resistant to sexuality" (342-43). See also Rambuss 103-35 and Stewart 161-87.

8. If we compare this scene with the one that precedes it, we can see quite readily that, for this play, a savvy concerning the symbolic order is particular to women. Sir Boniface, a pedantic scholar, is applying to Sir Harry for the job as his daughter Gratiana's tutor:

SIR BONIFACE: *Eques Honoratus: Ave Salutatus: non video quid est in tengo, sed salve bona virgo.*
SIR HARRY: Sir, you may call me nick-names: if you love me, speake in your Mother-tongue; or at the least, if Learning be so much ally'd unto you, that Latine unawares flowes from your

lips: to make your mind familiar with my knowledge, pray utter it in English: what's your name?

SIR BONIFACE: *Sit faustum tibi omen.* I'll tell you my *Nomen.*

SIR HARRY: Will you tell it to no men. Ile entertaine non e're I know their names: Nay, if you be so dainty of your name, you are not for my service.

SIR BONIFACE: *Intende vir nobilis.*

SIR HARRY: Not for twenty Nobles: Trust me, I will not buy your name so deare.

SIR BONIFACE: *O Ignorantia!* what it is to deal with stupidity! Sir *Henry,* heare me one word, I see, *preceptor legit, vos vero negligitis.*

TABER: I thinke he saith we are a companie of fooles, and Nigits, but I hope you shall not find us such, master Schoolmaster.                                          (2.2.765-87)

9. Weimann writes that the "*Figurenposition* should not be understood only in the sense of the actor's physical position on the stage, but also in the more general sense that an actor may generate a unique stage presence that establishes a special relation between himself and his fellow actors, the play, or the audience, even when direct address has been abandoned" (230).

10. For a discussion of licentiousness in the liberties, see Mullaney 43-44.

11. The term "sex-positive" comes from Gayle Rubin's essay "Thinking Sex: Notes for a Radical Theory of the Politics of Sexuality." The term stands in opposition to "sex-negativity," which denotes a way of thinking that considers sex to be a "dangerous, destructive, negative force" (278). One way that sex-negativity works is to divide sexual acts into expressions of "good, normal, natural, blessed sexuality" and "bad, abnormal, unnatural, damned sexuality" (281). This division recognizes all sex as more or less bad, but it also allows for the elaboration of a fairly complex ethics of "blessed sexuality." A sex-positive attitude is one that would pay close attention to the mechanisms of sex-negativity and the misrecognitions that support it, and it would also be interested in the various kinds of ethical complexities organized and expressed in different sexualities.

12. It is for this reason that I think Bourdieu's analysis of rites of institution is so important. In the somewhat magical insistence that these rites happen at certain regularized times, rites of institution serve to mark a certain social calendar in the life of the community. And insofar as these rites also posit modes of knowing, they also map a variety of possible reactions and relations to that social calendar. See Bourdieu, *Logic* 199-270.

13. For a brilliant discussion of historiography, historicity, and futureless futures, see Koselleck 3-38, 92-104. I would like to thank Dan Blanton for recommending Koselleck's work to me.

14. As V. N. Volosinov I think rightly proposes, on the level of content, "there is no basic division between the psyche and ideology." Volosinov explains, "[A]ll ideological content, without exception, no matter what the semiotic material embodying it may be, is susceptible of being understood and, consequently, of being taken into the psyche" (33). Ideological analysis—indeed, I would venture, all political criticism—must occur on the level of form. Castoriadis tends to have a fairly idealist notion of aesthetics and psychology, so he does not take his argument in this direction.

15. Although it is beyond the parameters of this essay, this argument could be expanded

through Kathleen Biddick's brilliant reading of the *Malleus Maleficarum*. Biddick argues that the *Malleus Maleficarum* should be read "as part of an epistemological break in Christianity's imaginary of its exteriority," a moment specifically when "the anti-Semitic tropes of the exterior, namely, usury and its sterility, could be shifted and at the same time doubled by the engendering of witches as a corporeal exteriority" (119). It is perhaps an overstatement to claim an epistemological break, but Biddick's point still stands: there is in the sixteenth century's interest in witchcraft an archaeological layering of the "lust of the flesh" against which Christianity and subsequently modernity defines itself. It is for this reason that, as Christopher Pye argues, the witch always exceeds any attempt at local historicism (172).

16. Michael Dalton, *The Countrey Justice* 243 (cited in Ewen 60). See also Patterson's quite suggestive discussion of witchcraft and jurisprudence (224-33).

17. See Catherine Belsey's discussion of this play in terms of the silencing of women "at the extreme edges of the social body" (185-88).

# Works Cited

Agnew, Jean-Christophe. *Worlds Apart: The Market and the Theater in Anglo-American Thought, 1550-1750.* Cambridge: Cambridge UP, 1986.

*The Authorized Version of the King James Bible.* New York: Penguin, 1974.

Belsey, Catherine. *The Subject of Tragedy: Identity and Difference in Renaissance Drama.* London: Methuen, 1985.

Ben-Amos, Ilana Krausaman. *Adolescence and Youth in Early Modern England.* New Haven: Yale UP, 1994.

Biddick, Kathleen. *The Shock of Medievalism.* Durham, NC: Duke UP, 1998.

Blumenberg, Hans. *The Legitimacy of the Modern Age.* Trans. Robert M. Wallace. Cambridge, MA: MIT P, 1983.

Bourdieu, Pierre. *Language and Symbolic Power.* Ed. John P. Thompson. Trans. Gino Raymond and Matthew Adamson. Cambridge, MA: Harvard UP, 1991.

——. *The Logic of Practice.* Trans. Richard Nice. Stanford: Stanford UP, 1990.

Boyarin, Daniel. *A Radical Jew: Paul and the Politics of Identity.* Berkeley: U of California P, 1994.

Bruster, Douglas. *Drama and the Market in the Age of Shakespeare.* Cambridge: Cambridge UP, 1992.

Burford, E. J. *Bawds and Lodgings: A History of the London Bankside Brothels, c. 100-1675.* London: Peter Owen, 1976.

Butler, Judith. *Bodies That Matter: On the Discursive Limits of "Sex."* New York: Routledge, 1993.

——. *Gender Trouble: Feminism and the Subversion of Identity.* New York: Routledge, 1990.

——. *The Psychic Life of Power: Theories in Subjection.* Stanford: Stanford UP, 1997.

Castoriadis, Cornelius. *The Imaginary Institution of Society.* Trans. Kathleen Blamey. Cambridge, MA: MIT P, 1987.

Cunningham, W. *The Growth of English Industry and Commerce.* 2 vols. Cambridge: Cambridge UP, [n.d.]; rpt., New York: Augustus M. Kelley, 1968.

Dekker, Thomas, William Rowley, and John Ford. *The Witch of Edmonton: A Critical Edition.* Ed. Etta Soiref Onat. New York: Garland, 1980.

DiGangi, Mario. *The Homoerotics of Early Modern Drama.* Cambridge: Cambridge UP, 1997.

Ewen, C. L'Estrange. *Witch Hunting and Witch Trials.* London: Kegan Paul, 1929.

Fineman, Joel. *The Subjectivity Effect in Western Literary Tradition: Essays toward the Release of Shakespeare's Will.* Cambridge, MA: MIT P, 1991.

Gibbons, Brian. *Jacobean City Comedy.* 2d ed. London: Methuen, 1980.

Gregory, Annabel. "Witchcraft, Politics, and 'Good Neighbourhood' in Early Seventeenth Century Rye." *Past and Present* 133 (1991): 31–66.

Hammill, Graham. "Faustus's Fortunes: Commodification, Exchange, and the Form of Literary Subjectivity." *ELH* 63 (1996): 309–36.

Heywood, Thomas. *A Critical Edition of Thomas Heywood's "The Wise Woman of Hogsdon."* Ed. Michael H. Leonard. New York: Garland, 1980.

Howard, Jean E. *The Stage and Social Struggle in Early Modern England.* New York: Routledge, 1994.

Irigaray, Luce. "Women on the Market." *This Sex Which Is Not One.* Trans. Catherine Porter. Ithaca, NY: Cornell UP, 1985. 170–91.

Jonson, Ben. *The Complete Plays of Ben Jonson.* 4 vols. Ed. G. A. Wilkes. Oxford: Clarendon, 1981.

———. *The Complete Poems of Ben Jonson.* Ed. George Parfitt. New Haven: Yale UP, 1982.

Kemp, Anthony. *Estrangement from the Past: A Study in the Origins of Modern Historical Consciousness.* New York: Oxford UP, 1991.

Koselleck, Reinhard. *Futures Past: On the Semantics of Historical Time.* Trans. Keith Tribe. Cambridge, MA: MIT P, 1985.

Kramer, Stella. *The English Craft Guilds and the Government.* New York: Columbia UP, 1905.

Leggatt, Alexander. *Citizen Comedy in the Age of Shakespeare.* Toronto: U of Toronto P, 1973.

Leinwand, Theodore B. *The City Staged: Jacobean Comedy, 1603–1613.* Madison: U of Wisconsin P, 1986.

Loades, David. *Tudor Government.* Oxford: Blackwell, 1997.

Macfarlane, Alan. *Witchcraft in Tudor and Stuart England: A Regional and Comparative Study.* New York: Harper and Row, 1970.

Manley, Lawrence. *Literature and Culture in Early Modern London.* Cambridge: Cambridge UP, 1995.

Marston, John. *The Dutch Courtesan.* Ed. Peter Davison. Berkeley: U of California P, 1968.

Middleton, Thomas. *The Works of Thomas Middleton.* Ed. A. H. Bullen. 8 vols. Boston: Houghton Mifflin, 1885–86.

Mullaney, Steven. *The Place of the Stage: License, Play, and Power in Renaissance England.* Chicago: U of Chicago P, 1988; rpt., Ann Arbor: U of Michigan P, 1995.

Patterson, Annabel. *Reading Holinshed's Chronicles.* Chicago: U of Chicago P, 1994.

Pearl, Valerie. *London and the Outbreak of the Puritan Revolution: City Government and National Politics,* Oxford: Oxford UP, 1961.

Pye, Christopher. " 'Froth in the Mirror': Demonism, Sexuality, and the Early Modern Subject."

*Repossessions: Psychoanalysis and the Phantasms of the Early Modern Subject.* Ed. Timothy Murray and Alan K. Smith. Minneapolis: U of Minnesota P, 1998. 171–99.

Rambuss, Richard. *Closet Devotions.* Durham, NC: Duke UP, 1998.

Rappaport, Steve. *Worlds within Worlds: Structures of Life in Sixteenth-Century London.* Cambridge: Cambridge UP, 1989.

Rose, Mary Beth. *The Expense of Spirit: Love and Sexuality in English Renaissance Drama.* Ithaca, NY: Cornell UP, 1988.

Rubin, Gayle. "Thinking Sex: Notes for a Radical Theory of the Politics of Sexuality." *Pleasure and Danger: Exploring Feminine Sexuality.* Ed. Carol S. Vance. Boston: Routledge, 1984. 267–319.

Sedgwick, Eve. *Between Men: English Literature and Male Homosocial Desire.* New York: Columbia UP, 1985.

Shakespeare, William. *The Riverside Shakespeare.* Ed. G. Blakemore Evans. Boston: Houghton Mifflin, 1974.

*Statutes of the Realm.* 11 vols. London: Dawson of Pall Mall, 1963.

Stewart, Alan. *Close Readers: Humanism and Sodomy in Early Modern England.* Princeton: Princeton UP, 1997.

Thirsk, Joan. *Economic Policy and Projects: The Development of a Consumer Society in Early Modern England.* Oxford: Clarendon, 1978.

Thomas, Keith. *Religion and the Decline of Magic.* New York: Charles Scribner's Sons, 1971.

Venuti, Lawrence. "Transformations of City Comedy: A Symptomatic Reading." *Assays* 3 (1985): 99–134.

Volosinov, V. N. *Marxism and the Philosophy of Language.* Trans. Ladislav Matejka and I. R. Titunik. Cambridge, MA: Harvard UP, 1973; rpt., 1986.

Weimann, Robert. *Shakespeare and the Popular Tradition in the Theater: Studies in the Social Dimension of Dramatic Form and Function.* Ed. Robert Schwartz. Baltimore: Johns Hopkins UP, 1978.

Wells, Susan. "Jacobean City Comedy and the Ideology of the City." *ELH* 48 (1981): 37–60.

Whigley, Mark. "Untitled: The Housing of Gender." *Sexuality and Space.* Ed. Beatriz Colomina. New York: Princeton Architectural Press, 1992. 327–89.

# "A Strange Fury Entered My House": Italian Actresses and Female Performance in Volpone

## PETER PAROLIN

THROUGHOUT THE HISTORY of London's all-male professional theater companies, audiences that wanted to see women acting on the stage could attend the performances of visiting continental acting companies, most notably companies from Italy and France. Yet to read some of the accounts of foreign women performing in England is to infer that English audiences thoroughly disapproved of such women on the stage. In a 1574 "exhortation" to the Lord Mayor of London, Thomas Norton delivered a general criticism of "that unnecessarie and scarslie honeste resorts to plaies," but he saved his specific condemnation for the "assemblies to the unchaste, shamelesse and unnaturall tomblinge of the Italion Weomen" (14). Fifty-five years later, a similar disapproval of women players appears in Thomas Brande's account of a French troupe at the Blackfriars:

Last daye certaine vagrant French players, who had beene expelled from their owne contrey, and those women, did attempt, thereby giving just offence to all vertuous and well-disposed persons in this town, to act a certain lascivious and unchaste comedye, in the French tonge at the Blackfryers. Glad I am to saye they were hissed, hooted, and pippin-pelted from the stage, so as I do not thinke they will soone be ready to trie the same againe.[1]

Contesting Brande's account of the hostile response, Stephen Orgel suggests that women players may have been welcome in England after all. Orgel notes that, Brande notwithstanding, "[t]he players performed publicly twice more during the next few weeks, at the Red Bull and the Fortune"; he also cites William Prynne's outrage at the popularity of the *"French-women Actors,* in a play not long since personated in the *Blackefriers Play-house,* to which there was great resort" (*Impersonations* 7). Even in the case of the Italian women tumblers of 1574, Thomas Norton acknowledges the assemblies of people who apparently flocked to see them; who, in other words, appreciated their presence.

Drawing criticism and audiences alike, women performers in early modern England occupied an unstable position, the cultural meanings of which have yet to be fully worked out in our scholarship.[2] What seems clear with regard to foreign women players is that their presence served as a kind of mirror that encouraged English audiences to think about their own theatrical practices. But by no means did every commentator reach the same conclusions about the theater: even Norton and Brande, who both disapproved of foreign actresses, did so for different reasons. For Norton, performance by Italian women was of a piece with the general depravity of the English theater; perhaps he even feared that the inevitable consequence of a thriving theater industry would be women on the stage. For Brande, on the other hand, the distasteful spectacle of French women on the stage implied the contrasting virility of the English theater, which had boys and young men to play the women's parts.

This article will explore some of the complex early meanings of the actress figure in English culture and argue that the actress triggers a dual anxiety: first, that performance may give women access to forms of agency typically conceived of as masculine; and, second, that theatricality itself may be an effeminizing activity even when undertaken by men.[3] This dual anxiety may initially seem paradoxical, postulating performance as both a masculinizing and an effeminizing activity. However, what is occurring is not paradoxical; rather, the actress figure forces the culture to rethink the conventional gendering of performance and theatricality. In the professional theater, the actress disrupts a previously all-male domain; in society, the actress is the theatrical woman who lays claim to the power of autonomous self-fashioning that male figures sought to reserve for themselves.[4] Women's access to various forms of performance suggests that male performers may no longer be able to hold the stage alone. In theory, men may find their performances outdone and their identities shaped by women whose theatrical skills exceed their own. In this way, the actress figure reveals performance as no longer a field for the simple display of autonomous male self-fashioning but as a field of competition in which women may challenge masculine prerogatives and men may consequently feel effeminized.

Instead of studying the actress figure by focusing on foreign players in England, I offer a reading of Ben Jonson's *Volpone* as a play that reverses the usual image of continental actresses on tour and places an Englishwoman, Lady Wouldbe, in a foreign environment, Italy, where her acting efforts can have free rein.[5] Ann Rosalind Jones has rightly said that in Renaissance England, Italy signified "another country, a country of others, constructed through a lens of voyeuristic curiosity through which writers and their audiences explored what was forbidden in their own culture" ("Italians and Others" 101). What *Volpone* does differently, though, is to put the English in among those others and to make the transgressive Englishwoman a kind of other herself.[6] As a result, the play permits not only an exploration of the culturally illicit but also of the ways in which the illicit is already a part of the dominant culture and is working to reconfigure it from within.

Italy is central to the representation of female performance in *Volpone*.[7] Its women players make Italy a place where performance itself is understood as gendered female; certainly in English writing, Italian theatricality is represented as an activity undertaken by women to disrupt male power. This model of feminized theatricality can be exploited, as it is in *Volpone,* in order to define and control for English audiences the potentially unruly implications of female performance. Karen Newman has said that "[m]anaging femininity so as to insure the reproduction of the commonwealth, great and small, was a significant ideological feature of early modern England" (16); her comment certainly applies to the theater, where femininity was insistently "managed" so as to insure the reproduction and the status of the all-male professional stage.[8] The actress figure vexes the project of managing theatrical femininity because her presence fundamentally challenges the professional theater's desired masculinity. This changing landscape is particularly visible in *Volpone*, where Jonson initially evokes an Italy dominated by actresses to define by contrast a proper, masculine English theater. If the actress figure can be discredited as a foreign aberration, the English theater can appropriate her power without the perceived taint of her femininity. Over the course of the play, however, the Italian actress comes to stand not as the English theater's opposite but as its double, forcing it to confront its fears about its own effeminization.[9]

*Volpone* foregrounds issues of theatricality and agency by staging Venice as an urban performance space in which people are free to abandon fixed identity categories and remake themselves in whatever guise they would like. This Italianate freedom causes special problems when applied to the two women characters in the play, the English Lady Wouldbe and the Italian Celia. Although they are married women, both Lady Wouldbe and Celia either have or are at times imagined to have the freedom to determine their own circulation in Venice, independent of their husbands' oversight. Identified as "free wives," the women trigger a cultural logic that associates them with a famous category of Venetian women, that of the actress. The actress's ability to circulate freely allows her to transgress the gender hierarchies that are supposed to structure marriage and social life in England. Ironically, English commentators in the late sixteenth and early seventeenth centuries frequently identify England itself as a place of gender inversion and transgression; given this context, it is significant that Jonson should so strongly identify female agency and power as Italian traits.[10] Clearly, he does so in order to displace worries that beset English masculinity; specifically, he displaces the worry that the theatrical woman may have access to effective forms of agency.

Among English writers, this act of displacement extends beyond professional theater people like Ben Jonson. English travelers like Fynes Moryson and Thomas Coryat, who wrote and published their accounts of Italy in the late sixteenth and early seventeenth centuries, chronicle the determined efforts of Italian husbands to protect their own masculinity by shutting down the possibility of their wives' agency. One of the tropes these writers repeatedly use to figure Italian marriage is that of the husband as jailer, literally locking up his wife at home and removing her from a theatrical economy of the gaze in which she would be able to watch and be watched by other men. For example, Coryat says of Venetian husbands that they "do even coope up their wives alwaies within the walles of their houses. . . . So that you shall very seldome see a Venetian Gentleman's wife but either at the solemnization of a great marriage, or at the Christning of a Jew" (265). Moryson remarks that "[t]he wemen of honour in Italy, I meane wives and virgins, are . . . locked up at home, and covered with vayles when they go abroad, and kept from any conversation with men" (409). In both of these examples, Italian husbands are seen as concerned to remove their wives from a theatrical economy of the gaze and to deny them the power of independent performance that they might enjoy if they had legitimate access to public spaces.

In Moryson's and Coryat's readings of Italian marriage, there is no room for women's legitimate performance because performance is culturally bound up with processes of self-authorization seen as properly masculine. This Italian attitude toward gender and performance is not so different from attitudes that customarily prevented women in England from appearing on the professional stage. In fact, the explicit theatricalization of the concept of all-male performance appears in *Volpone* in the male characters who are conceived of as actors and who want to monopolize access to performance. This dynamic is especially apparent in Volpone and Mosca, who play roles in order to take advantage of others.[11] The perceived masculinity of their performance mostly derives from the double meaning in the verb "to act," which means both to create theatrical illusion and also to take action, to be an agent. These two definitions often bleed into one another in ways that confer at least a measure of agency, conceived as masculine, on the actor.[12]

Volpone is a master actor in the sense of being able to purvey fantasy, and this dimension of his acting is inseparable from his status as an agent. Through his outrageous theatrical fictions, he materially alters his circumstances, enriching his coffers by swindling money from a series of gulls. More than for the money, though, Volpone embraces performance because of the power it gives him to define himself, as cunning, as audacious, as subject finally to no one but himself: "I glory / More in the cunning purchase of my wealth / Than in the glad possession" (1.1.30-32). While the male performer is thus imagined as the powerful agent of his own destiny, the woman exists to be performed upon; hence, Volpone scripts imaginary scenarios in which Celia would be entirely his construct, "Attired like some sprightly dame of France, / Brave Tuscan lady, or proud Spanish beauty; / Sometimes unto the Persian Sophy's wife, / Or the Grand Signior's mistress; and, for change, / To one of our most artful courtesans" (3.7.227-31).

It is probably inevitable that once Volpone places Celia in a theatrical context, he will imagine her as a courtesan. Like the actress, the courtesan is often imagined as a performer whose theatrical skills give her access to forms of agency not normally sanctioned for women.[13] In contrast to the strict regulations imposed on wives, Fynes Moryson notes the freedom of movement of the courtesans:

While Curtizans walke and ride in Coaches at liberty, and freely saluted and honored by all men passing by them, theire wives and virgins are locked up at home, watched by their wemen attending them abroad, have their faces covered with a vaile not to be seene, and it is death by private reveng for any man to salute them or make the least shewe of love to them. (410)

Moryson's assessment of the differences between wives and courtesans recalls William Thomas's citation of the Italian proverb, "*In Roma vale piu la putana che la moglie Romana:* that is to say, 'In Rome the harlot hath a better life than she that is a Roman's wife' " (50). Indeed, the accounts of English travelers repeatedly mention the enormous cultural prestige of Italian courtesans, whose very name connotes high status in its derivation, as Ann Rosalind Jones points out, from "*cortigiana,* the feminine form of *courtier* (*cortigiano*) in Italian" ("City Women" 304).[14] As much as their sexual availability, it may be the courtesans' high status, suggesting the possibility of independent power, that motivates husbands to distinguish them so strongly from wives.

English reporters suggest that in addition to defining performative courtesans over and against passive wives, Italian men actively use the courtesans to secure the chastity of wives. According to Coryat, for example, Italian men regard the brothels as useful domestically: "For they [the husbands] thinke that the chastity of their wives would be the sooner assaulted, and so consequently they should be capricornified, (which of all the indignities in the world the Venetian cannot patiently endure) were it not for these places of evacuation" (402-3). Although the Venetian husbands (filtered through Coryat) frame the issue of brothels in terms of the chastity of wives, the primary issue seems to be men's access to forms of sexual agency denied to women.[15] It is interesting that Coryat describes this assertion of sexual agency as "evacuation," or the loss of sexual fluids. The act of asserting control here raises the specter of the loss of control because, after contact with the courtesans, Italian men in effect lose their power of agency, being no longer able to pose a sexual threat to other men's wives. In the context of the courtesans, the assertion of male performance thus raises the specter of female performance, of women who act upon men, or, in Gail Kern Paster's words, of "women as the agents of men's humiliation and defeat" (213).[16]

Both Moryson and Coryat delight in slyly insinuating that despite the Italian husbands' rigorous attempts to circumscribe their wives' sexuality, the wives often manage to elude their control. One of the ways in which Moryson and Coryat do this is through the sheer number of their descriptions of Venetian women, whom they have earlier said are supposed to be locked up at home, out of public view. Coryat describes at length the fashion for the "Chapiney" which women wear under their shoes to make themselves appear taller (262), and he lingers over other fashions that might incite male desires: "Almost all the wives, widowes and mayds do walke abroad with their breastes all naked, and many of them have their backes also naked even almost to the middle, which some do cover with a slight linnen, as cobwebbe lawne, or such other thinne stuffe" (261). Despite the Italian husbands' efforts to lock up the wives, Coryat here implies that Venetian women do have at least limited access to public spaces. Moryson believes they also have access to agency, which he imagines as the wife's performative ability to deceive her husband and enact her own desires: "Yet for all this care, the Italyans many tymes weare the fatall hornes they so much detest because wemen thus kept from men, thincke it simpliscity to loose anye oportunity offered, though it be with the meanest servant" (410). Thus the English writer discredits the Italian husband and raises the possibility that through performance women can pursue their own agendas independently of the men who are socially authorized to control them. In an Italian world dominated by performative women like actresses and courtesans, performance itself, so bound up in men's minds with the masculine ability to act in the world, may have to be reconceived so that it no longer merely confirms privileged cultural positions but helps to subvert privilege and map out new identity positions.

In *Volpone,* the marriage of Celia and Corvino is shaped by the English image of the paranoid Italian husband who inevitably fails to foreclose the possibility of his wife's agency. Although Celia seems to be the submissive wife of patriarchal fantasy, Corvino is always aware of the possibility that she might contrive to circulate beyond his control, and this enrages him. Corvino opposes her presence at the window during Volpone's impersonation of a mountebank because to him it represents her choice to flout his power. Yet Corvino's constant opposition to what he sees as Celia's agency must represent his own knowledge that his fantasy of a completely obedient and self-abnegating wife can never be more than a fantasy.[17] He remains haunted by the fact that Celia retains her own senses, thoughts, and capacity for independent action.

Corvino's intimation that his control of Celia will never, *can* never, be complete is produced by the pervasive theatricality that saturates Venetian life. He articulates his fear of Celia's potential power by identifying it as the power of the actress to flatter and deceive her audiences. For example, in the scene where Celia appears at the window to watch Volpone play the mountebank, Corvino sees her as being on theatrical display in a way that immediately raises issues of control for him: at the window looking out, she is literally at the margins of Corvino's house and thus symbolically at the margins of his control, capable at any moment of escaping.[18] Furthermore, her appearance at the window, combined with Volpone's performance in the piazza below, exacerbates the theatricality of the scene and triggers the fear that Celia may be enacting her own theatrical scenario rather than her husband's.[19]

Given the theatrical association between windows and actresses, it makes a kind of cultural sense that when Corvino spots Celia at the window, he immediately conceives that she is willingly participating in a commedia dell'arte plotline that would cast her as the lusty young wife and himself as the comic cuckold.[20] He says to Volpone:

> What, is my wife your Franciscina, sir?
> No windows on the whole Piazza here,
> To make your properties, but mine? But mine?
> Heart! Ere tomorrow I shall be new christened,
> And called the Pantalone di Besogniosi
> About the town.
>
>                                    (2.3.4-9)

Some critics have argued that Corvino overreacts in his response to Celia here. From a modern psychological perspective there seems no question that he does overreact; however, if my argument about Italian theatricality and cultural spaces is correct, then it makes strong cultural sense for Corvino to see the scene as threatening.[21] Corvino's repetition of the possessives "my" and "mine" suggest that he is determined to reassert the stability of his identity, which he believes to be under assault when he is subjected to someone else's theatrical scenario. Significantly, Corvino shores up his identity by reasserting his status as property owner: both his house and his wife are emphatically *his*. If, as Margreta de Grazia has argued, one's identity in the early modern period derives from one's relationship to property, then Corvino is simply following a powerful cultural logic in attempting to reconstitute himself.[22] However, Corvino still has a problem because the term "property" is itself slippery: it designates the possessions that confirm his identity as property-owning subject, but it also designates the stage properties that resist permanent ownership, that are inherently transferable, and that therefore undermine any notion of the stable subject constituted by the objects he owns.

His fear of a theatrical Celia also raises for Corvino the image of a desiring and sexual Celia. At first Corvino accuses Volpone of trying to seduce Celia; however, he soon comes to consider the possibility of Celia's own theatrical agency: as an actress at the window, she may, he recognizes, be seeking to act out her own desires: "I think you'd rather mount?" he says to her, "Would you not mount? / Why, if you'll mount, you may; yes, truly, you may" (2.5.18–19). Here, "to mount" represents the complex convergence of Celia's possible desires: her desire to mount the stage theatrically; her desire to mount a lover sexually; and her desire to rise in the world, to exchange her submissive status for greater power. These various senses of "mount" coalesce in Corvino's outburst: he refers to the possibility of social mounting that theatrical mounting may hold out, yet he also ironically evokes the shame and social diminution that may attend women's theatrical mounting. It is telling that the socially and theatrically ambitious woman is described in terms that emphasize her sexual aggressiveness and that suggest the figure of the courtesan. For Corvino, Celia's theatrical performance is tantamount to her trafficking herself sexually: "Get you a cittern, Lady Vanity," he cries, "And be a dealer with the virtuous man" (2.5.21–22).

*Volpone*'s equation of the theatrical woman and the sexually promiscuous woman draws heavily on English representations of Italian theatricality, particularly on the English determination to yoke Italian theatricality to femininity and sexual transgression. A major difference between the English and Italian theaters in the late sixteenth and early seventeenth centuries was that in Italy there were professional actresses on the stage. Kathleen Lea notes the great popularity these actresses enjoyed with elite and popular audiences alike.[23] Fynes Moryson remarks on the status of one particular actress: "one Lucinia a woman player, was so liked of the Florentines, as when shee dyed they made her a monument with an Epitaphe" (465). Moryson's reference to the monument suggests that, culturally, the Italians see this actress as an alternative kind of aristocrat. Economically, the Italian actresses were so popular that companies saw them as indispensable to economic success. Ottonelli, the seventeenth-century historian of Italian theater, writes that "at times a company of these good fellows appears in a town: along with them are women experienced in the same profession, for they are convinced that without women they would make little impression and win no applause."[24] Kathleen McGill notes of the commedia actresses that "when women began to perform on stage, they immediately assumed the direction of the troupes as well, and companies became known in reference to their female 'stars' " (68). Thus for periods of time Isabella Andreini led the Gelosi company, Diana da Ponti led the Desiosi, and Vittoria Piissimi led the Confidenti.[25]

Because of the success of the Italian actresses, the commedia dell'arte plays made women, as much as men, the center of representational concerns; this may in fact be the reason their presence was so upsetting to English commentators. Lea argues that "it was the tendency of professional comedians, perhaps for economic reasons, to equalize the importance of the lovers' parts. By the introduction of actresses the dramatic value of the lady was completely changed. From being the passive, she became the active center of the play and brought the lover with her" (113). Lea specifically notes the wide range of dramatic opportunities the Italian actresses had: "The adventures of tragicomedy are designed to give them every opportunity for scenes of love-making, lamentation, frenzy, and even of duelling" (113). Actresses may not have been the center of every play, but, in the Italian theater, the advent of actresses did bring about a new cultural, economic, and representational centrality for women.

While Italian audiences clearly appreciated the presence of the actresses, contemporary records suggest that at least some English viewers felt differently. Dependent for its economic success on exploiting the dramatic possibilities in the presence of women on stage, the Italian theater accorded those women a centrality that English observers believed should be reserved for men. In *Pierce Penniless* (1592), Thomas Nashe denigrates the continental theater in comparison to the English stage specifically on the grounds that it employs women:

Our Players are not as the players beyond the sea, a sort of squirting baudie Comedians, that have Whores and common Curtizans to play womens partes, and forbeare no immodest speech, or unchast action that may procure laughter, but our Sceane is much more stately furnisht than it ever was at the time of Roscius, our representations honorable and full of gallant resolution, not consisting like theirs of a Pantaloun, a Whore, and a Zanie, but of Emperours, Kings and Princes, whose true tragedies they do vaunt. (66)

Nashe speaks of the French, Spanish, and Italian theaters here, but his reference to specific commedia figures suggests that Italy is his particular target. For Nashe, actresses inevitably degrade the material of the stage, pulling it away from manly concerns like the "true tragedies" of kings and emperors and replacing them with light and licentious comedies that are defined as feminine, immodest, and unchaste. This degradation is accomplished, Nashe believes, because of the presence of "Whores and common Curtizans" on stage; they may provoke audience laughter, but it is unchaste laughter. For Nashe, the taint of sexual promiscuity discredits the actress.

Less critical than Nashe, Fynes Moryson also feminizes the Italian theater when he reports on a play he saw in Florence during carnival time:

> The partes of wemen were played by wemen, and the cheefe actours had not their partes fully penned, but spake much extempory or upon agreement betweene themselves, espetially the wemen, whose speeches were full of wantonnes . . . and their playes were of amorous matters, never of historyes, much lesse of tragedies, which the Italian nature too much affects to imitate and surpasse. (465)

Although the commedia dell'arte is based on improvisation in *all* its parts, Moryson fixes here only on female improvisation, implying that women on the stage will inexorably lead a theater company away from the moral didacticism embedded in the fixed masculine texts of history and tragedy and toward a morally suspect wantonness.[26]

For all the attempts to feminize Italian theatricality in English writers like Nashe, Moryson, and Ben Jonson, there were significant components of female theatricality within English culture as well. First, women took their places in a theatrical milieu by being audience members at plays. Even this seemingly minimal level of women's theatrical participation provoked anxious strategies of containment, with English polemicists warning women away from the theater ostensibly out of concern for their virtue. Summarizing the logic of this position, Jean Howard writes, "[T]he female playgoer is symbolically whored by the gaze of many men. . . . She becomes what we might call the object of promiscuous gazing" (71). Yet Howard then aptly suggests that much of the problem must have been the symbolic capital women were imagined to gain, rather than lose, in the theater:

> What if one reads the situation less within the horizons of masculinist ideology and asks whether women might have been empowered, and not simply victimized, by their novel position within the theater? In the theatrical economy of gazes, could men have held all the power? . . . Is it possible that in the theater women were licensed to look—and in a larger sense to judge what they saw and to exercise autonomy—in ways that problematized women's status as object within patriarchy? (72)

The anxious cultural response to women at the theater suggests the trans-
formative power attending audience membership; far from being the most
passive aspect of the theatrical experience, audience membership encourages and enables agency. Indeed, in *Volpone* the easy passage between spectatorship and agency is precisely what is at stake in Corvino's
reprimand of Celia. To him, she may start as a spectator, watching the
mountebank perform, but she ends up as an actress:

> A crew of old, unmarried, noted lechers
> Stood leering up like satyrs: and you smile
> Most graciously, and fan your favors forth,
> To give your hot spectators satisfaction.
>
> (2.5.6–9)

Here Celia is both the woman being gazed at and the gazing woman;
as Howard's formulation suggests, it is as the gazing woman that she is
most dangerous culturally. Figured as the gazing woman, Celia looks at
her spectators, takes their measure, and turns in a performance meant to
satisfy them theatrically by arousing them sexually. As the gazing woman,
Celia learns what she needs to know in order to turn herself into the
woman being gazed at, to construct herself as the desired object of the
spectacle. The dynamics of spectatorship and performance thus help
Corvino understand that even as an object, Celia must also inevitably act
as a subject.

Again, though, it is not only fictional Italian women played by boys on the
London stage who count as actresses in an English context. English women,
too, acted at the highest levels of society, as Ben Jonson well knew. His own
work on the court masques contributed to the theatrical performances of
aristocratic women like Lucy, Countess of Bedford, Lady Mary Wroth, and
Queen Anne herself. The queen was in fact more than an actress in Jonson's
masques; she was also centrally involved as a chief sponsor of their production. Jonson in his notes acknowledges that the queen commissioned *The
Masque of Blackness;*[27] as Marion Wynne-Davies has shown, the dynamics
of Renaissance power and patronage mean that the queen's authorship
must be reckoned with in considerations of this theatrical piece.[28] Other
aristocratic women who played in Jonson's masques also exercised power
as Jonson's patrons so that, within Jonson's own working environment,
women's theatricality and their power were linked.

Jonson's uneasiness with the power of these theatrical women has been noted by commentators such as Stephen Orgel, who points out that "he was lavish in his adulation of his noble patronesses, but printed a poem in praise of the countess of Bedford immediately after an epigram asserting that the words 'woman' and 'whore' were synonyms." Orgel adds that "the play he wrote directly after *The Masque of Queens* was the openly misogynistic *Epicoene*" ("Jonson" 131). By making such choices, Jonson attempts to assert his own specifically masculine authorial control over his influential patronesses.

After *The Masque of Blackness,* Jonson reduces the range of representational options for women, thus integrating his assertion of control into the very structure of the masques. Suzanne Gossett suggests that negative responses to the queen and her ladies appearing in blackface may have caused Jonson to rethink the role of women in his masques and restructure the masque form: "If the queen could not appear briefly as a figure requiring improvement or transcendence, then transformations would have to involve two groups of characters, masquers and antimasquers" (99). With this restructuring of the masque, Jonson reduced the theatrical possibilities open to his female performers. As Gossett says of Queen Anne, "Thereafter she took parts which effectively eliminated any discrepancy between her historical and dramatic roles: Bel-Anna, Tethys, the Queen of the Orient" (99). Orgel, discussing *The Masque of Queens,* sees Jonson not so much eliminating as actively appropriating the power of female figures. In *Queens,* this power is Medusa's, despite Jonson's apparent interest in the male figure Perseus. In light of an allegorical tradition that reads Medusa as courage, knowledge, and eloquence, Orgel argues that "Jonson's attraction to Perseus looks more and more marginal, his attraction to Medusa more and more central. Perseus is there because he confers—on the poet—the power of woman, the power of the gorgon" ("Jonson" 130). Within an English context, then, Jonson is not only aware of a tradition of female performance but he also draws on that tradition in his masques, where he seems actively to try and control its significance.[29]

Given the relevance of female theatricality in England, the highly charged English accounts of female theatricality in Italy seem less like objective reports and more like motivated representations. Nashe certainly misrepresents the case when he refers to Italian actresses as "Whores and common Curtizans," but his misrepresentation is most interesting when seen as an attempt to do cultural work in an English context.[30] Nashe's reference to

Italian actresses as courtesans responds to fears about women's theatricality in England and works to create a cultural climate hostile to all forms of
female theatricality. In the late sixteenth and early seventeenth centuries,
Italian actresses offered a model of women who earned economic rewards
and cultural prestige from their theatrical and literary skills.[31] Comments
like Nashe's work to decrease the possibility that English women might
similarly advance themselves through the legitimate exercise of their own
agency. It is telling that criticism of the women's blackface in *Masque
of Blackness* also equates the actress figure and the courtesan. Dudley
Carleton reported that the women's "Apparell was rich, but too light and
Curtizan-like for such great ones."[32] Here, as in Nashe, the actress-courtesan
link is evoked in efforts to limit women's theatrical options.

*Volpone* maps the discursive connection between the actress and the
courtesan onto the physical body, which is a source of both theatrical and
sexual power. Indeed, when Corvino attempts to control Celia, he focuses
on her body. He implies sexual availability when he accuses her of having
been "too open" to a lascivious audience, and he seeks to control her
sexual options by taking away her control over her own body. Linked most
obviously to sexuality, this bodily control is also what the actress depends
on for her theatrical power. In her greatest success, *La pazzia d'Isabella,*
Isabella Andreini displayed physical dexterity in addition to her linguistic
virtuosity. Pavoni suggests in his *Diario* something of the physical exertions
she would have put herself through in her mad scene: "[Isabella] became
wholly possessed by her grief, and thus dominated by her passion, and
allowing herself to be consumed by rage and fury, was beside herself, and
like a madwoman wandered through the city stopping now one person,
now another, and speaking now in Spanish, now in Greek, now in Italian."[33]

Understanding the link between the body and theatrical power, Corvino
is suspicious of Celia's body, mistrusting even her bodily senses.[34] He rails
at her because "you will not contain your subtle nostrils / In a sweet
room, but they must snuff the air / Of rank and sweaty passengers"
(2.5.5). Even the sweetness of the prescribed "sweet room" can lead to
improvisational dangers, through its linguistic association with a forbidden
kiss: Corvino notes that Celia dropped her handkerchief, which Volpone
then "most *sweetly* kissed in the receipt" (2.5.41; emphasis mine).[35] For
Corvino, Celia's bodily senses unacceptably enable her to engage with
the promiscuous outside world regardless of the boundaries he seeks to
enforce. The symbolic power of the body enables Corvino to collapse

distinctions between Celia's theatrical power and her sexual power; in restraining her physically, he is targeting both sources of her power at once.

In addition to Celia's sense of smell, her sight becomes one of Corvino's targets: "Be not seen, pain of thy life," he says, "Not look toward the window" (2.5.67–68). Indeed, Corvino believes it is Celia's ability to *see* Volpone's enticing paraphernalia that stimulates her theatrical desire: "Were y' enamored on his copper rings? / His saffron jewel with the toad-stone in't? / Or his embroidered suit with the cope stitch, / Made of a hearse cloth? Or his old tilt-feather? / Or his starched beard?" (2.5.11–15). Celia's sight gives her access to the material trappings of theatrical performance; not only does sight stimulate desire, then, but it also enables agency, providing the theatrical tools that will allow her to pursue desire. Fearing such a situation, Corvino promises to "have this bawdy light dammed up" (2.5.50); for a moment it is eerily unclear as to whether he is referring to the light coming through the window or whether he is referring to Celia's own sight or even her life. What *is* clear is that Corvino intends to cut Celia off from a theatrical economy, to keep her from seeing or being seen outside.

Attempting to turn Celia's body itself into a boundary that she cannot transgress or exceed, Corvino exemplifies an early modern mode of patriarchal control that Peter Stallybrass has described: "In early modern England, 'woman' was articulated as a property not only in legal discourse but also in economic and political discourse. Economically, she is the fenced-in enclosure of the landlord, her father, or husband" (127).[36] As a property, Celia is not supposed to be also an actress. What Corvino opposes, then, is a process whereby the "property" remakes herself as an actress, thus giving the lie to his fantasies of patriarchal control.

Corvino further attempts to establish Celia as property by seeking to sell her for his economic gain. He discards his qualms about her sexual fidelity as soon as he realizes he can make a huge profit prostituting her to Volpone: "Go, and make thee ready straight, / In all thy best attire, thy choicest jewels, / Put 'em all on, and, with 'em, thy best looks" (2.7.13–15). Earlier, he had violently withdrawn Celia from what he saw as a sexually contaminating theatrical milieu, but here he himself uses theatrical language to prepare her for a theatrical performance that will also be a sexual performance. When Celia protests this plan on the grounds that it will taint his honor, Corvino simply reasserts her commodity status: "What is my gold / The worse for touching? Clothes for being looked on? / Why, this's no more"

(3.3.44–46). What initially seems to be a tactical shift on Corvino's part is thus not so at all but is consistent with his earlier goal of eliminating Celia's agency. Corvino can prostitute Celia because the issue now seems to be *his* power to stage and sell *her* rather than her imagined power to control her own theatrical circulation.[37] In *Volpone*'s treatment of theatricality, the issue to be decided is who will do the acting.

Corvino ultimately is publicly humiliated for striving so intensely to control Celia. His fear has been that Celia possesses the power to transform her own situation, and, despite his paranoia, he at times appears to be on to something. Celia certainly defies him when he tries to prostitute her to Volpone, and the question of precisely what she is signifying when she drops her handkerchief out of the window can likely only be decided in performance.[38] But, ultimately, Celia's power to transform her own situation within the play is minimal. She is rescued from Volpone's clutches by Bonario, and the two of them are in turn saved from Mosca's trumped-up accusations only by the chance implosion of Volpone's theatrical schemes. In the end it is less Celia who transforms her own situation than the playwright, Jonson himself, who saves her through the dramatic reversals he constructs in the concluding courtroom scene. In Celia's case, as in Queen Anne's, the potential power of the theatrical woman is appropriated by the playwright.

Celia's unrealized theatrical power is worked out differently in the figure of the English Lady Wouldbe. This character is something of an innovation on Jonson's part, because in many English plays set in Italy (such as *The White Devil, The Duchess of Malfi,* and *Women Beware Women*), it is the Italian woman who aggressively pursues her own desires. By contrast, the independent agency that so often characterizes Italian women appears in *Volpone* in the satirized figure of the Englishwoman, whose performative impulses may be the play's most explicit reference to a context of female theatricality in England. Lady Wouldbe dominates her husband Sir Politic, which is clear from the fact that she is the one who initiated their travel to Venice: Sir Politic admits that his reason for visiting Italy was "a peculiar humor of my wife's" rather than "that idle, antique, stale, grey-headed project / Of knowing men's minds, and manners, with Ulysses" (2.1.9–11). Lady Wouldbe is a remarkable character simply by being a traveler at all. Around the time that *Volpone* was first performed, Sir Thomas Palmer published a travel pamphlet specifying that "[t]he Sex in most Countries prohibiteth women [from travel], who are rather for the house then the field; and to remain at home, then travaile into other Nations" (17). Simply by traveling, then, Lady Wouldbe is signaling her break from contemporary ideologies that would seek to restrict women's behavior.

After taking the initiative in planning the journey to Venice, Lady Would-be continues to control her own circulation in Italy. When she first arrives at Volpone's house unescorted by her husband, even Volpone is surprised: " 'Fore heaven, I wonder at the desperate valor / Of the bold English, that they dare let loose / Their wives to all encounters" (1.5.100–2). Where the Venetians expect that the wife properly resides in her husband's control, the English, represented by Sir Politic, leave their wives to their own devices. Without Sir Politic watching her every move, Lady Wouldbe has a measure of power, which the Venetians find inappropriate in a wife, to control her own circulation, to be as she "would be" in public rather than as her husband would have her be. Indeed, she sees Venice as a "would-be" world in which she can indulge her desire for self-transformation, making herself into a great lady or even a courtesan.[39]

To a large extent, Lady Wouldbe expresses her agency through the tropes and techniques of the theater; once again, as in the Celia/Corvino plot, the active woman is imagined as the theatrical woman. Lady Wouldbe's basic theatricality emerges when, waiting to be ushered into Volpone's presence, she assembles and checks her costume, cosmetics, and props, much as an actress would before mounting the stage: "This band / Shows not my neck enough"; "Is this curl / In his right place, or this?"; "I pray you, view / This tire, forsooth; are all things apt, or no?"; "This fucus [makeup] was too coarse" (3.4.2–3;10–11;16–17; 37).[40] Aggressively concerned with her appearance, Lady Wouldbe is intensely aware of herself as a woman on display:

> Besides, you seeing what a curious nation
> Th' Italians are, what will they say of me?
> "The English lady cannot dress herself."
> Here's a fine imputation to our country!
>                                    (3.4.32–35)

Ostensibly striving to perform English womanhood for the Italians, Lady Wouldbe offers herself up as the object of the gaze, at least partly so that the Venetians will recognize her as a self-defining subject, as a woman in charge of her own representation.

Throughout her scenes with Volpone, Lady Wouldbe draws on theatrical improvisation to ensure that her powers of self-creation will be noticed. Volpone brings up topic after topic designed to silence her, but every time he raises a new issue, she immediately incorporates it into her conversation. Pointedly, Volpone tells her, "I dreamt / That a strange fury entered, now, my house, / And, with the dreadful tempest of her breath, / Did cleave my roof asunder"; even here, Lady Wouldbe does not miss a beat: "Believe me, and I / Had the most fearful dream, could I remember't." To this, Volpone can only lament: "Out on my fate! I ha' giv'n her the occasion / How to torment me" (3.4.40–46). Later, when Volpone brings up poetry, Lady Wouldbe responds with a long list of her favorite poets; again, Volpone asks, "Is everything a cause to my destruction?" (3.4.82). The point here is that every comment is grist to Lady Wouldbe's mill: in her eagerness to perform her own sophistication, she draws relentlessly on the strategies of improvisation characteristic of the Italian actresses. The "strange fury" that enters Volpone's house may after all be a projection of the foreign or even domestic actress taking up a place in Jonson's (play)house.

In assuming the role of actress, Lady Wouldbe asserts a power that threatens male privilege.[41] It is significant that one of the ways in which she is linked to actresses is through the application of cosmetics ("This fucus was too coarse"), because the question of cosmetics was also at the center of early modern English concerns about women's agency.[42] Frances Dolan has shown that those who opposed cosmetics for women believed that the woman who made herself up was effectively usurping the power of God, the ultimate male subject, by taking the pencil of creation out of his hand and trying to wield it herself:

Most anticosmetics treatises emphasize that a woman who paints herself refuses to submit to her passive role as a creature, a being with no legitimate capacity for self-transformation or self-determination, and insists on herself as a creator. (229–30)

Given Dolan's insights, it makes sense to look at *Volpone* as a kind of anticosmetics treatise; certainly it is a text that militates against women's pretensions to agency through the tools of the theater. But it also shows that for Lady Wouldbe, Venice is a great cosmetics as well as theatrical center that promises to recognize her power and skill at enacting her own identity.[43]

Volpone is frustrated, even terrified, when he repeatedly fails to get rid of Lady Wouldbe; part of the reason Volpone is so frantic to silence her must be that her performance completely pushes his own dramatic efforts to the sidelines of the stage. She privileges her own acting over his, forcing him to participate in her theatrical scenario rather than the other way around. When he insists that "your highest female grace is silence" (3.4.78), he seems desperate to reestablish the conditions necessary for the primacy of his own performance.[44] Clearly, then, Lady Wouldbe's theatricality evokes the disturbing image of the woman out of her place, the woman who asserts a presence and a relevance that force men to acknowledge her and share with her the stage that many of them are accustomed to occupying alone. In a specifically theatrical context, Lady Wouldbe is the actress who challenges the authority of the male actor-playwright, in this case most obviously Volpone, but also symbolically Jonson himself.

Throughout *Volpone,* Jonson attempts to discredit Lady Wouldbe as a ridiculous character who deserves to be laughed at. She may be concerned about the careful application of her cosmetics, for example, but she loses control of her makeup when she gets angry with her husband: "This heat will do more harm / To my complexion than his heart is worth" (4.2.3-4). Additionally, her anger at Sir Politic is pathetic, coming as it does from her mistaken assumption that his companion, Peregrine, is a cross-dressed courtesan. In this episode and elsewhere, Lady Wouldbe is herself discredited by being associated with the courtesans. As early as Sir Politic's first scene in the play, Peregrine asks him whether "Your lady / Lies here, in Venice, for intelligence / Of tires, and fashions, and behavior / Among the courtesans?" Sir Politic answers, "Yes, sir, the spider and the bee ofttimes / Suck from one flower" (2.1.26-31). The unintentional effect here is to blur the distinction between the spider and the bee and to identify Lady Wouldbe as a potential courtesan. Her sexual willingness later becomes apparent when she becomes attracted to Peregrine: "If you stay / In Venice, here, please you to use me, sir / . . . The more you see me, the more I shall conceive / You have forgot our quarrel" (4.3.15-16;18-19). Mosca, too, implies that Lady Wouldbe has offered sexual favors as a way of negotiating for Volpone's fortune: "Remember what your ladyship offered me / To put you in an heir" (5.3.40-41). If Celia was wrongly accused of wanting to "mount," Lady Wouldbe seems to take mounting much more seriously, in all its theatrical, social, and sexual senses.

Whether linking Lady Wouldbe to the courtesans enables Jonson to contain the sheer force of her presence likely has to be decided in performance; what is significant here is that he chooses to evoke the figure of the courtesan as part of the effort to discredit her. For all that Lady Wouldbe is the butt of jokes, she still unsettles the play by attempting to assert the power of the actress. Her theatricality signals power, a power that may, symbolically at least, put her in competition with her creator. For Jonson as for Volpone, Lady Wouldbe as actress is a disturbing figure who requires management.

The degree to which Lady Wouldbe is successfully "managed" remains unclear at the end of the play. Certainly in her marriage with Sir Politic there does not seem to have been any reversal of power: she still seems to be the dominant force. For example, after Sir Pol has been thoroughly humiliated by Peregrine, he seems still to be looking to his wife for guidance: "Where's my lady? / Knows she of this?" (5.4.80-81). Interestingly, Lady Wouldbe does not answer Sir Politic's questions, but instead, through her waiting woman, asserts her own agenda: "My lady's come most melancholic home, / And says, sir, she will straight to sea, for physic" (5.4.85-86). In her last words, then, Lady Wouldbe informs us that she is not going home to England, thoroughly domesticated, but is heading out on her own. She is still circulating.

The ambiguity surrounding Lady Wouldbe's status at the end of the play may register a larger cultural uncertainty about the power of the actress. Within the play, Italy has provided a space for female performance, but at the close of the play, Lady Wouldbe's interrogation of English gender norms cannot simply be wished or written away. Her assertion of theatrical skills provides Volpone with the first serious challenge to his ability to dominate the stage. After his scenes with Lady Wouldbe, Volpone increasingly fails in his theatrical scenarios. He fails to bend Celia to his will, and his theatrical exertions in the courtroom, far from giving him the much-desired powers of self-fashioning, increasingly subject him to the retributive powers of the state.

Another way of talking about what happens to Volpone is to say that through his theatricality, he comes to occupy a culturally feminized position. Instead of providing him with the autonomy he gloried in at the beginning of the play, his acting subjects him not only to the power of the state but also to the very physical ailments that he at first only pretended to have. The First Avocatore says:

> . . . Our judgment on thee
> Is that thy substance all be straight confiscate
> To the hospital of the *Incurabili.*
> And since the most was gotten by imposture,
> By feigning lame, gout, palsy, and such diseases,
> Thou art to lie in prison, cramped with irons,
> Till thou be'st sick and lame indeed.
>
> (5.12.118-24)

The consequences of acting have here become truly terrifying and the play's increasingly negative view of theatricality may be a mark of Lady Wouldbe's impact. *Volpone* attempts but fails to contain the feminine taint of acting by projecting it onto a demonized female actor. As a consequence, the specific fear of women acting is projected onto acting itself in a way that suggests how deeply the figure of the actress changes the meaning of theatricality. In repudiating theatricality, *Volpone* seems to be rejecting the source of its own brilliance. Generations of the play's critics have been perplexed by this conclusion, struggling to find ways to redeem theatricality even as its chief practitioners are punished.[45] I would suggest that if there is an insoluble tension at the end of *Volpone,* it responds to the presence of the actress and is rooted in the fact that her position was still unresolved, although powerfully felt, both in Jonson's dramaturgy and in his culture.

## Notes

I would like to thank Pamela Brown, Rebecca Bushnell, Leigh Edwards, Susan Frye, Jeffrey Masten, Phyllis Rackin, and my anonymous reader at *Renaissance Drama* for their generous and helpful suggestions in response to earlier versions of this essay.

1. Quoted in Bentley 1:25.

2. A growing body of scholarship is recognizing a widespread tradition of female performance in early modern England. Researching records of women's mimetic activities in Somerset, James Stokes says that "in light of the growing body of such material, women's contributions to early dramatic history in England need to be seen as much more significant than has hitherto been acknowledged or understood" (176). Ann Thompson encourages us to be more sensitive to "the relatively hidden tradition of female performance" behind the practice of men playing female roles (103). And Kim Walker and Sophie Tomlinson have explored the cultural meanings of this increasingly visible tradition of female performance, especially in a Caroline context.

3. I use the term "actress" with an awareness that it is anachronistic when applied to women players in the late sixteenth and early seventeenth centuries. However, English

audiences at that time had seen women players and, if my arguments are correct, this experience raised questions about the active woman, a doer, a sense in which, according to the *OED*, "actress" was used as early as 1589. On the provenance of the term "actress" in its theatrical sense, see Sophie Tomlinson, who suggests that it was first used in 1626 to describe Queen Henrietta Maria's role in a French pastoral played at court (189–90).

4. Stephen Greenblatt's exclusive focus on male figures in *Renaissance Self-Fashioning* perhaps reflects the dominant ideology that self-fashioning was a properly masculine endeavor, but it does not account for the many women in early modern England who more or less consciously challenged that dominant ideology by skillfully working within cultural constraints to construct advantageous identity positions for themselves. "Self-fashioning" is of course a tricky term: I use it to refer to the perception that theatricality permits the autonomous shaping of the self rather than to any social reality in which the self can take shape outside of discourse.

5. Critics have extensively studied the pervasive theatricality of *Volpone*, but they have been much less thorough in exploring the ways in which the play associates performance with women and theatricality with the feminine. David McPherson is one scholar who has paid welcome attention to female theatricality in the play by considering Lady Wouldbe as an actress figure, as I shall do below. I seek to extend McPherson's analysis, both by showing that Celia, too, is implicated in discourses of Italian theatricality and by considering this feminized Italian theatricality in relation to English practices.

6. Dympna Callaghan's reading of *The Tragedie of Mariam* is relevant here. Callaghan asserts that English women who ingore their own culture's behavioral norms are invariably represented in terms of otherness. She specifies that "racialized difference and geographical otherness, in fact, become preconditions of the representation of resisting femininity" (170).

7. Just as Margo Hendricks argues that "Venice is a crucial yet often critically neglected racial persona in *Othello*" (194), I hope to show that Venice plays a significant role in shaping the construction of the actress figure in *Volpone*. For a discussion of the play's Italian performance context, see Parker, esp. the discussion of *Volpone*'s debt to the commedia dell'arte (99–102).

8. Andrew Gurr's *The Shakespearean Stage* provides evidence of the many attractive social and financial features of a career in the theater, despite the recurrent attacks upon the profession. See esp. chaps. 1–3.

9. In *Volpone*, the English theater itself is rehearsing one of the deepest concerns of the antitheatricalists, which Stephen Orgel identifies as "the fear of a universal effeminization" (*Impersonations* 29).

10. Stephen Orgel suggests that in the later sixteenth and early seventeenth centuries, "middle-class London was a place of unusual liberty for women" (*Impersonations* 37). David Underdown argues that, at the same time, "[a]nxiety about patriarchal order was more than a literary phenomenon. Between 1560 and 1640 local court records show an intense concern about unruly women. Women scolding and brawling with neighbors, defying or even beating their husbands, seem to be distinctly more common than in the periods before or afterwards" (39).

11. Jean-Christophe Agnew has noted that, by the late sixteenth century, theatricality had become potentially suspect culturally because it enabled people to misrepresent themselves

to others, promoting their own self-interest at others' expense. Specifically, Agnew states that "theatricality itself had begun to acquire renewed connotations of invisibility, concealment, and *mis*representation. . . . It suggested the calculated *mis*representation of private meanings in the negotiated relations among men and women" (40, 60).

12. Tomlinson argues that the twin meanings of "act" also operate within the discourse of female performance: "the functional sense of acting is overlaid with a theatrical dimension"; however, where the notion of agency achieved through performance could work in favor of the male actor, Tomlinson shows that it more often works *against* the actress. Speaking of the misogynist stereotype of the woman as wrongdoer, Tomlinson says, "[I]t is a short step from this notion to the combined threat of female agency and feminine counterfeit or duplicity" (198).

13. In the context of Greek theater, Sue-Ellen Case explores the cultural association between the actress and the courtesan. Seeing this link as more ideological than historical, she suggests that "male desire projected upon the female performer created the image of the woman as 'courtesan'" (30). The case of Thomas Coryat in Venice seems to confirm Case's thesis. Ann Rosalind Jones notes that after describing a trip to see actresses in the theater, Coryat immediately switches to a discussion of the courtesans: "In a symptomatic association of ideas, he moves from this instance of feminine self-display to a first description of the courtesans for which Venice was famous" ("Italians and Others" 104).

14. Coryat, too, links the courtesans' cultural standing to etymology: "The woman that professeth this trade is called in the Italian tongue *Cortezana,* which word is derived from the Italian word *cortesia* that signifieth courtesie. Because these kinde of women are said to receive courtesies of their favourites" (264).

15. Here we see the problems in discussing the courtesans as high-status women: at the same time that their cultural cachet impresses English writers, they are also being used to enforce inequitable sex-gender relations. Nevertheless, I am interested in their perceived high status insofar as it triggers in English writers of the time anxieties about the forms women's power might take, anxieties that also attach to the figure of the actress.

16. Referring specifically to *Much Ado about Nothing,* Paster compellingly situates psychological fears of cuckoldry within their early modern social and cultural contexts.

17. Valerie Wayne cogently explicates the ideology that produces the tension Corvino is experiencing: "The ideology of marriage permitted husbands to call their wives 'ours' and to write upon their bodies, but it could not control women's desire. Since men's appropriation of women was never entire, jealousy arose from the contradictory claims of possession and desire" (173).

18. For an excellent discussion of female-dominated cultural spaces, see Mendelson and Crawford, esp. 202–12. Mendelson and Crawford show that symbolically charged liminal spaces like windows and doorways were often seen as feminine in that they "connected women in their economic role as overseers of the household to their social role as participants in village life" (208). In *Volpone,* Corvino clearly sees his house as his own space; he resists conceding Mendelson and Crawford's point that "[i]f the household was the proper place for women, then the household could sometimes become a female space" (204). Mendelson and Crawford's insights underscore why it would seem important to Corvino to control any space that Celia might inhabit.

19. Corvino's concern about Celia at the window recalls *The Merchant of Venice,* where Shylock asks Jessica to stay away from the windows, which he sees as offering a promiscuous point of contact between his "sober house" and the carnivalesque world outside: "when you hear the drum / And the vile squealing of the wry-necked fife, / Clamber not you up to the casements then, / Nor thrust your head into the public street / To gaze on Christian fools with varnished faces" (2.5.30–35). It is worth remarking that for Shylock, too, the presence of the woman at the window is linked to a theatrical setting, a night of masking and revelry in Venice. In *Women Beware Women* another form of theatricality, this time civic pageantry, causes problems when connected to a woman at the window. In this case, Bianca watches from Leantio's window as the duke of Florence takes part in the procession of the festival of Saint Mark. Seeing Bianca, the duke is determined to possess her sexually. Here, as elsewhere, the window is believed to make possible the threat to the woman's virtue: Guardiano says, "The Duke himself first spied her at the window" (2.2.9).

20. According to Kathleen Lea, the commedia dell'arte, as opposed to the commedia erudita, foregrounded the presence of women at windows, partly as a result of having actresses to play women's parts: "For the convenience of academic representation, and in accordance with the convention that honest women were not seen in the street or at the windows, the object of the technique of the Commedia erudita was to conceal the lady. . . . When the practical difficulty of boy-actors taking women's parts was obviated, it became the concern of the popular playwright to invent excuses for letting the actress appear as much as possible" (113).

21. For examples of critics who stress Corvino's overreaction, see Marchitell 287 and Beaurline 161–62.

22. Countering the Enlightenment premise of the separation of the subject and the object, Margreta de Grazia compellingly shows in an analysis of *King Lear* that objects constitute the subject: "Through the lives of both titular and subtitular characters, the play dramatizes the relationship of being and having. As we shall see, removing what a person *has* simultaneously takes away what a person *is.* If having is tantamount to being, *not* having is tantamount to *non*-being—to being nothing. . . . Subjects and objects are so tightly bound in the play's economy that a subject cannot survive the loss of his or her possessions" (21–22, 24).

23. Lea notes that Henry III of France, watching a play in Venice in 1575, particularly admired "La femme appelee Vittoria" (262). As evidence of the broad range of elite and popular support for the actresses, Lea cites the Mantuan diarist Rogna, who compares two different plays by referring primarily to the star actress of each company: "Both had good and crowded audiences, but Flaminia drew more nobles and played the tragedy of Dido as a tragicomedy with great success" (114).

24. Quoted in Richards and Richards 28.

25. See Richards and Richards 56, 67, and 221.

26. It is worth noting that McGill *does* see women as being especially linked to improvisation in the commedia dell'arte. Citing several examples of sixteenth-century praise for women's improvisation, McGill argues that "it was the women performers who introduced, developed, and excelled at the practice of comic repertory improvisation" (65).

27. Jonson writes, "And because her Majestie (best knowing, that a principall part of life in these Spectacles lay in theyr variety) had commaunded mee to think on some *Daunce,* or

shew, that might praecede heres, and haue the place of a foyle or false-*Masque;* I was carefull to decline not only from others, but mine owne stepps in that kind." See Jonson, *Ben Jonson* 7:282.

28. Wynne-Davies notes the seventeenth-century attribution of *The Masque of Blackness* to Queen Anne; she also notes that the Venetian ambassador, speaking of *The Masque of Beauty,* identifies Anne as "authoress of the whole" (Jonson, *Ben Jonson* 10:457). Wynne-Davies acknowledges the "lexical mutation" of the term "author," but she maintains the term's relevance for an understanding of Anne's role: "The earlier definition [of author] was much looser, allowing the 'author' to be the initiator or instigator of a work, someone who gave existence to something in any number of ways. What the Venetian secretary is suggesting, then, is that the masque was a production by diverse people of whom the Queen was the most politically notable force" (79–80). Kim Hall and Clare McManus have also discussed the queen's central role in the masques.

29. Clare McManus questions how effective any authorial attempt at controlling the significance of female performance can ever be. In a reading of *The Masque of Blackness,* McManus argues that the masque form attempts to use the corporeality of the elite female performers to subject them to the gendered ideologies of courtly society. Yet, as McManus points out, the female body always frustrates the imposition of one authorial meaning. Multiple, sexual, and open, that body cannot be reduced to a single signification: "Within the very discourse that attempts to constrain the significance of the female through confinement to the physical is a recognition of the corporeal creation of meaning which offers the female masquer expressive possibilities" (107).

30. Kathleen McGill helpfully addresses the question of the historical relationship between commedia actresses and courtesans. McGill shows that the evidence sometimes adduced to identify early commedia actresses as courtesans is inconclusive at best, and she warns that even symbolically to conflate the two categories "collapses a very real distinction between the actual status of women and the range of male desire" (63).

31. Isabella Andreini is the notable example of an example of an Italian actress with literary credentials. Her pastoral *Mirtilla* was published in 1588; her *Rime* and *Lettere* were published posthumously in 1607.

32. Jonson, *Ben Jonson* 10:448.

33. Quoted in Richards and Richards 75.

34. Corvino's attempt to control Celia's independence by controlling her senses functions similarly to the "monumentalizing" of women that Valerie Traub sees at work in a number of Shakespearean plays: "In *Hamlet, Othello,* and *The Winter's Tale,* male anxiety toward female erotic power is channeled into a strategy of containment; the erotic threat of the female body is psychically contained by means of a metaphoric and dramatic transformation of women into jewels, statues, and corpses" (26).

35. The many critical discussions of the specifically sexual valences of the handkerchief in *Othello* apply here as well. Lynda Boose suggests that with the handkerchief, Shakespeare was representing "a visually recognizable reduction of Othello and Desdemona's wedding-bed sheets, the visual proof of their consummated marriage" (363). Peter Stallybrass argues that the handkerchief in Shakespeare's play is "an emblem of Desdemona's honor . . . above all, [her] chastity" (137). Valerie Wayne contends that "[t]he handkerchief serves as proof of

married chastity. . . . It is an emblem of Desdemona's body that does not circulate because her body is not supposed to circulate" (172).

36. In *Volpone*, Corvino works to make his wife into what Stallybrass calls a "patriarchal territory," a process that involves the policing of her body as if it were a piece of land. Woman as property, Stallybrass argues, is seen as a rigidly "finished" body in that "her signs are the enclosed body, the closed mouth, the locked house" (127).

37. Stallybrass argues that the controlled wife "becomes her husband's symbolic capital"; certainly Celia functions throughout the play as symbolic capital for Corvino, but here she moves out of the realm of the symbolic when he tries to stake her as literal capital to advance his own economic interests (128).

38. Pamela Brown pointed out to me that Celia's dropping of the handkerchief might very well signal her own independent desire not just to Corvino but also to the audience.

39. See McPherson, who argues that Lady Wouldbe "is in the city chiefly to imitate the fabled courtesans" (107).

40. This scene in which Lady Wouldbe checks her clothes and makeup predicts a scene in Coryat's *Crudities* in which Coryat describes the techniques used by Venetian women to make the hair on their foreheads stand up in peaks. Coryat concludes his account: "That this is true, I know by mine owne experience. For it was my chaunce one day when I was in Venice, to stand by an Englishmans wife, who was a Venetian woman borne, while she was thus trimming of her haire: a favour not afforded to every stranger" (261). Just as Coryat puts the Englishman's Italian-born wife on display for his readers in the midst of her hair curling, so Jonson puts the presumably English-born Lady Wouldbe on display for his audience in the midst of her final preparation of her appearance. The point here is not to suggest that one account influenced the other (the *Crudities* did not appear in print until 1611, about six years after the first performance of *Volpone*) but rather to suggest that the slippage from English to Italian femininity via theatricality was a common trope available to English writers.

41. Although he does not specifically mention the figure of the actress, Marchitell astutely reads this scene as centered on questions of female autonomy: "male domination depends, in large part, upon denying women access to language" (299).

42. Moryson suggests the degree to which the question of cosmetics was specifically bound up with ideas about Italian women. He reports that in Venice "[b]oth honest and dishonest wemen are *Lisciate fin'alla fossa,* that is paynted to the very graue" (412).

43. It has often been suggested that the materialistic Volpone negates divine power by replacing God with gold; Lady Wouldbe, I suggest, is here doing something similar, replacing God's creative arts with her own.

44. In his compelling account of the play, Stephen Greenblatt has noted Volpone's fear of the cessation of theatricality. Greenblatt argues that Volpone's frenetic theatricality, especially apparent in act 5, is meant to counter his fears of standing still, of vanishing, of death. When Volpone acknowledges the precariousness of theatrical fictions, Greenblatt contends that "for a brief moment we glimpse that void which is perceived again more powerfully at the false ending, that sense of emptiness against which Volpone struggles" ("False Ending" 98). I would simply add that it is here, in his scene with Lady Wouldbe, that Volpone is first forced to confront the limitations of theatricality and the void that those limitations imply. As I have

been suggesting throughout the article, female performance, among other things, forces a recognition of the fact that limitless male autonomy is a myth.

45. In the Epistle, Jonson himself voices uneasiness that "my catastrophe may in the strict rigor of comic law meet with censure" (32). Later critics and editors have discussed this tension between the comic spirit and the punishments that conclude the play, but they have not resolved it. C. N. Manlove argues that the instructive and delightful elements of *Volpone* are "increasingly opposed during the play," and he finds an ultimate ambivalence on Ben Jonson's part: "As he wrote he came to admire his own creation [Volpone] to the extent that he could not find it in him to give the creation fully adequate motives answering the governing notion of evil being self-detonating" (239, 252). In his edition of the play, R. B. Parker says, "Jonson leaves us no excuse for misunderstanding his moral condemnation; nevertheless theatrically and imaginatively the Fox survives because he represents something permanent in all of us, a corruption that is closely linked to our vitality" (44). And Anne Barton argues that "Volpone cannot be forgiven within the play. . . . But the Fox . . . can rely on the spectators to acquit him of any crime committed against the spirit of comedy" (119).

## Works Cited

Agnew, Jean-Christophe. *Worlds Apart: The Market and the Theater in Anglo-American Thought.* Cambridge: Cambridge UP, 1986.

Barton, Anne. *Ben Jonson, Dramatist.* Cambridge: Cambridge UP, 1984.

Beaurline, L. A. *Jonson and Elizabethan Comedy: Essays in Dramatic Rhetoric.* San Marino, CA: Huntington Library, 1978.

Bentley, G. E. *The Jacobean and Caroline Stage.* Oxford: Clarendon, 1941–68. Vol. 1.

Boose, Lynda. "Othello's Handkerchief: 'The Recognizance and Pledge of Love.' " *ELR* 5 (1975): 360–74.

Callaghan, Dympna. "Re-Reading Elizabeth Cary's *The Tragedie of Mariam: Faire Queene of Jewry."* *Women, "Race," & Writing in the Early Modern Period.* Ed. Margo Hendricks and Patricia Parker. London: Routledge, 1994. 163–77.

Case, Sue-Ellen. *Feminism and Theatre.* New York: Routledge, 1988.

Coryat, Thomas. *Coryat's Crudities.* 1611. London: Scolar Press, 1978.

De Grazia, Margreta. "The Ideology of Superfluous Things: *King Lear* as Period Piece." *Subject and Object in Renaissance Culture.* Ed. Margreta de Grazia, Maureen Quilligan, and Peter Stallybrass. Cambridge: Cambridge UP, 1996. 17–42.

Dolan, Frances. "Taking the Pencil out of God's Hand: Art, Nature, and the Face-Painting Debate in Early Modern England." *PMLA* 108 (1993): 224–39.

Gossett, Suzanne. "Man-maid, Begone!: Women in Masques." *ELR* 18 (1988): 96–113.

Greenblatt, Stephen. "The False Ending in *Volpone." Journal of English and Germanic Philology* 75 (1976): 90–104.

———. *Renaissance Self-Fashioning: From More to Shakespeare.* Chicago: U of Chicago P, 1980.

Gurr, Andrew. *The Shakespearean Stage, 1574–1642.* 3d ed. Cambridge: Cambridge UP, 1992.

Hall, Kim. "Sexual Politics and Cultural Identity in *The Masque of Blackness*." *The Performance of Power: Theatrical Discourse and Politics*. Ed. Sue-Ellen Case and Jenelle Reinelt. Iowa City: U of Iowa P, 1991. 3–18.

Hendricks, Margo. " 'The Moor of Venice,' or the Italian on the Renaissance English Stage." *Shakespearean Tragedy and Gender*. Ed. Shirley Nelson Garner and Madelon Sprengnether. Bloomington: Indiana UP, 1996.

Howard, Jean. "Women as Spectators, Spectacles, and Paying Customers." *Staging the Renaissance: Reinterpretations of Elizabethan and Jacobean Drama*. Ed. David Scott Kastan and Peter Stallybrass. New York: Routledge, 1991. 68–74.

Jones, Ann Rosalind. "City Women and Their Audiences: Louise Labe and Veronica Franco." *Rewriting the Renaissance: The Discourses of Sexual Difference in Early Modern Europe*. Ed. Margaret Ferguson, Maureen Quilligan, and Nancy Vickers. Chicago: U of Chicago P, 1986. 289–316.

———. "Italians and Others: Venice and the Irish in *Coryat's Crudities* and *The White Devil*." *Renaissance Drama* 18 (1987): 101–19.

Jonson, Ben. *Ben Jonson*. Ed. C. H. Herford, Percy Simpson, and Evelyn Simpson. 11 vols. Oxford: Oxford UP, 1925–52.

———. *Volpone*. Ed. Alvin Kernan. New Haven: Yale UP, 1962.

———. *Volpone*. Ed. R. B. Parker. Manchester: Manchester UP, 1983.

Lea, Kathleen. *Italian Popular Comedy: A Study in the Commedia dell'Arte, 1560–1620*. New York: Russell and Russell, 1934.

Manlove, C. N. "The Double View in *Volpone*." *SEL* 19 (1979): 239–52.

Marchitell, Howard. "Desire and Domination in *Volpone*." *SEL* 31 (1991): 287–308.

McGill, Kathleen. "Women and Performance: The Development of Improvisation by the Sixteenth-Century Commedia dell'Arte." *Theatre Journal* 43 (1991): 59–69.

McManus, Clare. " 'Defacing the Carcass': Anne of Denmark and Jonson's *The Masque of Blackness*." *Refashioning Ben Jonson: Gender, Politics, and the Jonsonian Canon*. Ed. Julie Sanders. London: Macmillan, 1998.

McPherson, David. *Shakespeare, Jonson, and the Myth of Venice*. Newark: U of Delaware P, 1990.

Mendelson, Sara, and Patricia Crawford. *Women in Early Modern England*. Oxford: Oxford UP, 1998.

Middleton, Thomas. *Five Plays*. Ed. Bryan Loughrey and Neil Taylor. London: Penguin, 1988.

Moryson, Fynes. *Shakespeare's Europe*. Ed. Charles Hughes. 2d ed. New York: Benjamin Blom, 1967.

Nashe, Thomas. *Thomas Nashe*. Ed. Stanley Wells. London: Edward Arnold, 1964.

Newman, Karen. *Fashioning Femininity and English Renaissance Drama*. Chicago: U of Chicago P, 1991.

Norton, T. *Instructions for the Lord Mayor of London* (1574). *Illustrations of Old English Literature*. Ed. J. Payne Collier. Vol. 3 (1866). Repr. New York: Benjamin Blom, 1966.

Orgel, Stephen. *Impersonations: The Performance of Gender in Shakespeare's England*. Cambridge: Cambridge UP, 1996.

———. "Jonson and the Amazons." *Soliciting Interpretation: Literary Theory and Seven-*

*teenth-Century English Poetry*. Ed. Elizabeth D. Harvey and Katherine Eisaman Maus. Chicago: U of Chicago P, 1990. 119-39.

Palmer, Thomas. *An Essay of the Meanes How to Make Our Travailes into Forraine Countries the More Profitable and Honourable*. London, 1605.

Parker, Brian. "Jonson's Venice." *Theatre of the English and Italian Renaissance*. Ed. J. R. Mulryne and Margaret Shewring. New York: St. Martin's Press, 1991. 95-112.

Paster, Gail Kern. "*Much Ado about Nothing:* A Modern Perspective." *Much Ado about Nothing*. Ed. Barbara Mowat and Paul Werstine. New York: Washington Square Press, 1995. 212-30.

Richards, Kenneth, and Laura Richards. *The Commedia dell'Arte: A Documentary History*. Oxford: Blackwell, 1990.

Stallybrass, Peter. "Patriarchal Territories: The Body Enclosed." *Rewriting the Renaissance: The Discourses of Sexual Difference in Early Modern Europe*. Ed. Margaret Ferguson, Maureen Quilligan, and Nancy Vickers. Chicago: U of Chicago P, 1986. 123-42.

Stokes, James. "Women and Mimesis in Medieval and Renaissance Somerset (and Beyond)." *Comparative Drama* 27 (1993): 176-96.

Thomas, William. *The History of Italy*. Ithaca, NY: Cornell UP, 1963.

Thompson, Ann. "Women/'Women' and the Stage." *Women and Literature in Britain, 1500-1700*. Ed. Helen Wilcox. Cambridge: Cambridge UP, 1996.

Tomlinson, Sophie. "She That Plays the King: Henrietta Maria and the Threat of the Actress in Caroline Culture." *The Politics of Tragicomedy: Shakespeare and After*. Ed. Gordon McMullan and Jonathan Hope. London: Routledge, 1992.

Traub, Valerie. *Desire and Anxiety: Circulations of Sexuality in Shakespearean Drama*. London: Routledge, 1992.

Underdown, David. *Revel, Riot, and Rebellion: Popular Politics and Culture in England, 1603-1660*. Oxford: Oxford UP, 1987.

Walker, Kim. "New Prison: Representing the Female Actor in Shirley's *The Bird in a Cage*." *ELR* 21 (1991): 385-400.

Wayne, Valerie. "Historical Differences: Misogyny and *Othello*." *The Matter of Difference: Materialist Feminist Criticism of Shakespeare*. Ed. Valerie Wayne. Ithaca, NY: Cornell UP, 1991. 153-79.

Wynne-Davies, Marion. "The Queen's Masque: Renaissance Women and the Seventeenth-Century Court Masque." *Gloriana's Face: Women, Public and Private, in the English Renaissance*. Ed. S. P. Cerasano and Marion Wynne-Davies. Detroit: Wayne State UP, 1992. 79-104.

# From Imagination to Miscegenation: Race and Romance in Shakespeare's The Merchant of Venice

## ELIZABETH A. SPILLER

IN EARLY MODERN studies, debate recently has centered on the question of whether race is a valid category for analysis.[1] Some readers have expressed concern that in identifying skin color as a crucial component for defining race we in effect project backward contemporary understandings that would have made no sense to early modern readers.[2] While recognizing the risks of being anachronistic, most critics have nonetheless agreed that the early modern period comprises the moment at which skin color becomes the determining feature of racial identity. Where Michael Neill suggests that "color emerg[es] as the most important criterion for defining otherness" (367), Margo Hendricks has shown that this definition replaces an earlier, more traditional understanding of race as a category defined in genealogical terms (42).[3] If the term "race" once meant who were you born of, in the early modern period it comes to mean what you look like. Following this line of thought, racial studies in the Renaissance have focused on the historical and cultural implications of this shift. As instructive as these discussions have been, insufficient attention has been paid to how this new definition of race is realized through the generic forms in which it is enacted. Understanding race in terms of physical color can only underscore how the question of race also becomes a question of representation, since physical appearance is now seen as a sign that marks who or what one is.

137

As the meaning of race shifts in the early modern period, so do the conventions of romance. *The Merchant of Venice* recognizes this fact when it introduces competing definitions of race to rethink a model of romance traditional both in Shakespeare's own works and in the genre as a whole. By defining what Jean Howard describes as a "community that cut across national lines" (102), traditional courtly romance transcends questions of ethnic identity. On the other hand, it is a genre organized by genealogy, since who you were born of and, by implication, who you give birth to are central topics of romance. If this major concern of romance is congruent with genealogical understandings of race, romance nonetheless also anticipates color-based definitions of race. By defining nobility of blood and spirit through a materialist model of physical appearance (the fair are "fair," the rich "worthy," the nobility "noble"), this romance convention helps to shape a generic form that participates in the way that race is defined in this period. Where commitment to a nobility of birth and appearance once made romance a conservative literary genre, these conventions now allow not just different subjects but also hybrid forms. Early modern subjects thus apprehend and rethink questions about race through the already assimilated, if newly heterogeneous, conventions of romance. Where readers such as Hendricks and Neill have identified the early modern period as a moment of transition from an understanding of race as genealogy to one of physical appearance, Shakespeare's *The Merchant of Venice* enacts the shift to reflect on the changing relationship between the genre of romance and the racial representations it allows.

Reframing recent debate about race through the perspective provided by romance reveals not so much two distinct ways of thinking about race but rather how, in this genre, understandings of race as genealogy provide the terms for new arguments about race as physical appearance. Shylock's story of how Laban's once pure white sheep become "spotted" is one which most readers have found puzzling as an explanation for usury. As I discuss, however, read alongside the racially oriented readings of this remarkable genealogical narrative in Genesis by Luther, Gervase Babington, and Ambrose Paré, Shylock's use of the Jacob and Laban story becomes important not so much as an argument about usury but as a narrative about imaginative miscegenation. The getting of "parti-color'd" sheep through what is in important ways an imaginative act provides a model for understanding how racial difference becomes important in *The Merchant of Venice* not just in political terms but in representational ones.

This perspective thus allows us to see how the play's cuckoldry jokes—involving Portia, Jessica, and Launcelot—move us from the infidelity of adultery to the adulteration of infidels. Recognizing how the play enacts its own genealogical adulterations likewise explains how we as audiences retake our own casket tests by making discriminations based on "blood" and "complexion," terms that extend from physical qualities to moral attributes. These responses—theatrical versions of the "spotting" of Laban's sheep—involve us in imagining and, thus, in some sense producing various forms of racial adulteration throughout *The Merchant of Venice*.

In act 1 scene 3, Shylock offers Antonio what begins as a justification for his taking of usurious interest by telling a version of the story of Jacob and Laban from Genesis. As it is more fully told in Genesis, when Jacob desires to return to his father's homeland, he agrees with Laban that he will at the end of the season take "all the black amongst the sheep" and those that are "ringstraked, and of diuers colours," those "spotted and coloured," among the goats (Gen. 30:32, 35).[4] Initially agreeing to Jacob's terms, Laban responds by sending his sons to pastures three days away from Jacob's (Gen. 30:35–36). This gesture seems to be motivated not just by greed but by a desire to reassert a kind of "purity" within the flocks that represent his life and family. Laban thus gives to his sons the culled livestock—which would have produced the "wages" that he would otherwise have to give to his interloping and half-foreign son-in-law—as a way of preserving the integrity of his immediate family. Jacob reacts by practicing yet another "separation" within the remaining flocks. First, he divides the ewes, strong from weak. To ensure that the new lambs will be black, he "did separate these lambes," so that the ewes breed only with the white rams rather than with the black or spotted ones (Gen. 30:40). In the case of the goats, however, Jacob mixes them. He does so not by breeding spotted to pure but by placing white wands in front of the remaining black goats during the mating season. The image of the white wands at the moment of "conception" marks the resulting offspring, so that they are no longer black but instead "spotted and speckled." In the act of "conception," the resulting kids are marked through an imagining of "whiteness."[5]

Recognizing how anomalous Shylock's story is as a "defense of usury," most readers have followed Antonio in seeing this attempt to "make interest good" as evidence of Shylock's tendency to understand everything in monetary terms (1.3.90). From this perspective, Shylock confuses gold and silver with ewes and rams, just as he will later be unable to distinguish the loss of his daughter from the theft of his money (1.3.91; 2.8.15). Readers have long commented on how Shylock's use of the Jacob and Laban story does not accord with contemporary debate about usury. Assessments of Shylock's arguments generally take as their point of departure Shylock's remarkable failure to cite the standard biblical passages concerning usury.[6] Yet, if Shylock unexpectedly does not refer to Deuteronomy or Leviticus in making his case, it is equally important to recognize that contemporary readers of Genesis do not understand the Jacob and Laban story in terms of usury.[7]

Shylock's argument is more than a little dubious as a defense of usury, but it becomes considerably less surprising in the context of the play's use of Genesis as a narrative of racial identity. Understood by early modern readers as an account in which the moral fall of man was expressed in terms of his genealogical "descent," Genesis became a text into which early modern readers interjected their concerns about racial lineage and difference. Benjamin Braude concludes in this context that biblical genealogy of the kind found throughout Genesis is the "most politically responsive of traditional genres." As a result, stories "that had no central theological significance" became the site for often contradictory readings "that reflect a range of the ethnic and geographical assumptions of each age" (107-8).[8] Shylock's life becomes a kind of early modern revision of Genesis: his wife is Leah; Tubal and Chus are his "countrymen"; his servant, Launcelot, is no better than "Hagar's offspring" (3.2.101; 3.2.284; 2.6.42). In his powerful analysis of the Jacob and Laban scene, Marc Shell shows how Shylock begins with a distinction between "brothers and others"—members of the Jewish tribes and "members of any other tribe" (*Money* 48-55).[9] Shylock then uses this story of ewes and rams, in part, to tell a kinship narrative that distinguishes members of his family, from whom he does not demand interest, and those outside his "flock," from whom he does take interest. Yet, if Shylock understands himself to be Jacob's descendant, the play's references to Genesis that follow the Jacob and Laban story suggest that what begins as an act of separation ultimately produces an intermixture of races.

Whatever its original lesson, the Jacob and Laban story is one that highlights how definitions of race are changing in the early modern period. As Genesis makes clear, the composition of Jacob's animal "flocks" is impor-tant because it also defines that of his "tribe" of people. In this particular case, Jacob does not just manipulate the rods he puts in front of the sheep, he also takes advantage of Laban's perfectly reasonable expectation that genetics and appearance will conform to one another. Jacob is able to separate the flocks in such a way that physical appearance, not breeding, determines the identity of the flock. As Jacob manages it, what the sheep look like, not how they were bred, determines whose they are. He has in some sense imposed a new definition of the "flock" upon Laban, a definition that looks surprisingly like early modern models of racial identity. That is, where Laban might be regarded as representing an older definition of race, Jacob establishes a newer one. Equally important, although Shylock understands himself to be telling a story about what separates his "tribe" from Antonio's "flock," the actual content of his story suggests that an act of imagination is enough to confound, to "compromise," those distinctions. A narrative about racial separation thus becomes, in ways that Shylock almost certainly does not intend, one about imaginative miscegenation.

While the Bible itself does not identify Jacob's "work of generation" as a type of adulteration, early modern readers clearly brought their own concerns about miscegenation to this text. Shell's conclusion that "generation, or production, is the principal topic of Shakespeare's *The Merchant of Venice*" (*Money* 48) can thus be extended by comparing Shylock's reliance upon the Jacob and Laban passage to contemporary readings of this Genesis story. In particular, analysis of contemporary commentaries on Genesis shows that while early modern readers did not identify Genesis 30 as a key theological text, they did, in the ways that Braude's work suggests, read the stories about Jacob through their own concerns about how racial difference was produced and what it meant.[10] In discussing the "spotting" of Jacob's flocks in Genesis 30, most readers thus explain how through the power of the maternal imagination "special forms of marks are imprinted on the young" (Luther 5:380). These discussions occasionally deal with various forms of animal husbandry—a number of readers, for instance, refer to the "well knowne" practice of Spanish horse breeders to show mares in heat the "fairest" horses to generate better foals (Babington 122v).[11] More typically, however, commentators use the episode with Jacob and Laban as an occasion to introduce stories not about livestock but about women who give birth to what seem to be but are not actually mixed-race children. Martin Luther in his *Commentary on Genesis* thus tells of "a queen who gave birth to a child with the form and face of an Ethiopian as a result of a strong mental image of an Ethiopian painted on a tablet near her bed" (5:380–81). Andrew Willet's *Hexapla in Genesin* includes both a version of this story and its reverse: "The Hebrewes report of an Aethiopian, that had a faire childe, and a Rabbin being asked the reason therefore showed the cause to be a white table that was in her sight at the time of conceaving" (319). Incorporating accounts of a woman who unexpectedly gave birth to "a most faire childe" and another who brought forth a "black More," Gervase Babington moves in a kind of covert pun from the original adulteration in Jacob's "spotted" cattle to the supposed adulteries of these mothers (121v).

Although not an exegetical commentary on Genesis, Ambrose Paré's influential and controversial *De monstres et prodiges* (1575) draws on the story of Jacob's flocks in a way that makes explicit the generic implications of reading the Jacob and Laban story as a narrative of imaginative miscegenation.[12] As a supplement to Paré's more central treatise on obstetrics, *De monstres et prodiges* instructed its readers on monsters as reproductive pathologies, the rare exceptions that in some sense defined what surgeons might normally expect to see in patients. Surveying possible causes for monstrous births, Paré uses the Jacob and Laban story to introduce a chapter on "monsters that are created through the imagination" (38). This widely accepted medical theory was a by-product of Aristotelian understandings of conception as not just analogous to but indeed predicated on an act of intellection: monsters of the imagination result when the force of female imagination interferes with the normal model in which the idea (male) of conception is imposed on its matter (female). As Thomas Laqueur concludes, "[S]ince normal conception is, in a sense, the male having an idea in the woman's body, then abnormal conception, the mola, is a conceit for her having an ill-gotten and inadequate idea of her own" (59).[13] Paré thus explains that any "ardent and obstinate imagination that the mother might receive at the moment she conceived" may mark the resulting offspring. Jacob's breeding of spotted livestock shows how "the imagination has so much power over seed and reproduction that the stripe and character of them remain [imprinted] on the thing bred," thereby shifting the emphasis away from reproduction as maternal intellection to a kind of imaginative wand-waving (38).

Paré substantiates his claims by using material taken not from the scientific sources he knew that dealt with this topic but rather from two works that exemplify a romance reading of racial difference: Heliodorus's *Ethiopian Romance* and Pierre Boaistuau's *Histoires prodigieuses* (1560).[14] The stories from Heliodorus and Boaistuau provide more than just the context for Paré's understanding of the Genesis story as imaginative miscegenation. Critically, they also supply what might be called the narrative of miscegenation that, while never fully realized, establishes a model for the audience's responses to the play. In the case of the *Ethiopian Romance,* the heroine, Charicleia, is virtuous, brave, and fair in ways that are understood by all as "marks" of a noble birth. In the concluding book of the romance, the fair Charicleia is indeed revealed to be noble but as the daughter of the king and queen of Ethiopia. Her white skin is, as Paré recounts, "because of the appearance of the beautiful Andromeda" that her mother "summoned up in her imagination, for she had a painting of her before her eyes during the embraces from which she became pregnant" (38).[15] Pierre Boaistuau's book of wonders provides Paré with a narrative obverse to Heliodorus's: in this widely retold story, a princess is "accused of adultery" after she gives birth to a child "as black as a Moor," "her husband and she both having white skin" (38). The princess is saved "upon Hippocrates's persuasion that it was [caused by] the portrait of a Moor, similar to the child, which was customarily attached to her bed" (39).

As Patricia Parker has emphasized, Paré elsewhere signals his interest in stories of "Barbarie" through his use of material taken from Leo Africanus's *Geographical Historie of Africa* (1550) (84–86). Here, however, I would emphasize how familiar these narratives are: even as they are wondrous, they are familiar in the forms that their wonder takes. As stories of Ethiopian queens and Greek princesses, these stories invoke the genealogy of family lineage but in a way that underlines how an old impulse to maintain the purity of the family line is reconfigured through narratives of racial difference. In this respect, the element common to these stories is the implied recognition that the danger is not the possibility of miscegenation itself. Rather, these "monsters" are the consequences of acts of imagination: it is a picture of the Greek Andromeda, the portrait of the African Moor, the "white wands" of Jacob that produce what are apparently if not actually mixed-race offspring. These stories—themselves clearly the product of various forms of imaginative excess—allow readers to indulge in speculations about new races produced not through physical admixture but through the perhaps more troubling power of the imagination. That is, Paré localizes a general structural distrust of romance as a passion-invoking genre by connecting it to romance's racially heterogeneous subjects. Romance, as a genre that is centrally concerned with defining nobility of blood and spirit, here becomes a story of cultural miscegenation that dangerously mixes elements from different peoples and different races in its narratives.

Paré further suggests that what the female imagination creates is inherently a form of romance. Heliodorus's *Ethiopian Romance* and Boaistuau's *Histoires prodigieuses* exemplify what might be called a new romance of otherness in this period. Heliodorus's work seemed to be the product of a real-life romance as wondrous as the story it told: written in Greek by an author who identified himself as "a Phoenician of Emesa, of the race of the sun," a complete manuscript was found in the sacked library of Matthias Corvinus (Stechow 144). Boaistuau's work was likewise read as a type of romance: the first and most influential of the Renaissance works on "monsters," Boaistuau's *Histoires prodigieuses* compiled a kind of cabinet of monsters, marvels, and wonders.[16] Although Paré's work has sometimes been criticized for its own susceptibility to romance, Paré in this passage implies that these exotic narratives are inherently dangerous in their force on the imagination. Paré thus allows that his own readers may themselves be subject to dangerous forms of imaginative miscegenation as a result of reading *De monstres et prodiges*. In a later comment that refracts concern about allowing those who are not physicians access to unsuitable sexual materials contained in medical texts through the more prominent apprehension that romances were dangerous to women because they incited passion in readers, Paré warns that pregnant women should not read his book. Admonishing his readers with "how dangerous it is to disturb a pregnant woman" by showing her images or pictures of anything "deformed and monstrous," Paré anticipates possible objections about his own practices: "For which I am expecting someone to object to me that I therefore shouldn't have inserted anything like this into my book on reproduction. But I will answer him in a word, that I do not write for women" (55).[17] That is, of the many monsters described throughout the text, these "monsters of the imagination" become a kind of metafiction that critically defines Paré's relationship to his own readers.

It is this aspect of Paré's account of Jacob and Laban that becomes relevant to understanding why Shakespeare should through Shylock introduce this story into *The Merchant of Venice*, in part as a model for understanding literary representations of racial difference. The imaginative miscegenation against which Paré explicitly warns his readers is realized, albeit diffusely, throughout *The Merchant of Venice*. The Jacob and Laban story signals how miscegenation is not only a key theme of the play but structurally central in generic terms. Without suggesting that Shakespeare understands his audience to be sheep, the miscegenation that is both a mixing of races and of generic kinds is realized in the audience through their own acts of perception.[18] Like Paré, Shakespeare uses the story of Jacob and Laban to rethink the relationship between race and romance that characterizes works such as *As You Like It, A Midsummer Night's Dream, Much Ado about Nothing,* and *Twelfth Night.* The rhetoric of appearance that typifies the romantic comedies is concerned primarily with genealogy: outer appearances manifest inner essence not just as a consequence of birth but through the act of birth itself. Yet, at the same time, the romantic comedies also suggest that ultimately all that matters in the social world is outer appearance. This established interaction between romance and comedy, between imagination and reality, changes when an account of race as a visible difference produced through the imagination enters this generic dynamic in *The Merchant of Venice.*

In romances such as *A Midsummer Night's Dream,* genealogy plays a key role in determining the ideal suitor. Lysander is loved over the "spotted" Demetrius not because he comes from a better family but implicitly because his more faithful love insures better—or at least more often legitimate—progeny (1.1.110). When Portia first considers her suitors, however, this logic is inflected through racial difference. Seen from the perspective of the other comedies, Portia's suitors seem to meet the most significant criteria that "princely suitors" should have: a Neapolitan prince, a county Palatine, a Duke's nephew, a baron, and two lords, these are the sons of European nobility and gentry (1.2.34-83). Yet Portia dismisses them as creatures who, although they may be noble, are scarcely men. Whatever excuses she gives, Portia's denigration of the suitors reveals a conflict between changing definitions of racial identity. While Portia's admirers ought to qualify as worthy suitors under definitions of race as genealogy, they are here rejected. The birth that once testified to nobility now expresses the racial difference, the almost inhuman foreignness, of the "stranger" (1.3.103).

Caricaturing not just the suitors but the emergence of a kind of identity based on national affiliation rather than family descent, Portia's comments about the suitors become a series of ethnic jokes—jibes at the melancholy Frenchman, the "neighbourly charity" of the Scotsman (1.2.66), the drunken German, and the "dumb show" Englishman (1.2.61). The way in which such "national" ethnicities—a concept at odds with traditional understandings of universal nobility—themselves depend on a shift in underlying theories of racial identity is signaled by Portia's dismissal of the first suitor, the Neapolitan prince. Although not foreign, the Neapolitan prince is equally illegitimate in Portia's mind:

> Ay, that's a colt indeed, for he doth nothing but talk of his horse, and he makes it a great appropriation to his own good parts that he can shoe him himself: I am much afeard my lady his mother played false with a smith. (1.2.39-43)

The familiar cuckold joke introduces Portia's subsequent jokes not as an exception but rather to suggest how the meaning of race is moving away from genealogy toward national ethnicity. Portia's jokes concerning the foreignness of the other suitors are in effect new versions of the colt joke, except in this case they point to an anxiety about classifying people according to categories that are inextricably ethnic and national.

While cuckoldry in Renaissance drama is a recurring subject for "nervous jokes" that are a consequence of patriarchal interest in genealogy (Maus 563),[19] Portia's suggestion that "my lady his mother played false with a smith" is somewhat remarkable. Ordinarily, this is the kind of joke in which Portia would be her father's daughter only as the subject of the joke, not as its teller, given that cuckoldry jokes are most often told by men, to men, and about men (Cook 188-89).[20] On the other hand, the apparent anomaly involved in Portia's telling of this joke can be comprehended by recognizing how this particular joke must be told by a woman for it to work. What Portia uses to explain this "colt" of a prince critically involves not just an imagined adultery but also, anticipating Shylock's use of the Jacob and Laban story, an imaginative adulteration. On one level, Portia's joke suggests that the most elitist of the Neapolitan prince's pretensions—the skill at horsemanship that he understands as chief among "his own good parts"—may be a mark of his illegitimacy rather than of his nobility (1.2.37). Yet, while illegitimacy might explain why the prince would love horses so excessively, it does not entirely make clear, even as an easy joke, how his birth has made him into one. Just as Spanish horses were famous for breeding the best colts through looking at the "fairest" horses, here the quick metonomy of Portia's jibe also allows us to imagine that the prince's mother engendered such an "adulterated" colt by thinking too much of horses.

Portia's joke is thus told by a woman because, as Paré's warning suggests, such hybrid monsters, which Portia ultimately dismisses as "little worse than a man" and "little better than a beast," are created through the power of the female imagination (1.2.84–85). As the first of a series of jokes that, in the ways Shell suggests, clearly dehumanizes these "unnatural" suitors (*Money* 55–56), this joke enacts itself in a way that demands that we, too, take part in the adulterate imagination that characterizes Portia's speculations. In doing so, Portia's joke participates in what Katharine Maus identifies more generally as the metatheatrical element characteristic of cuckold jokes in Elizabethan drama: cuckold jokes engage the audience in a "theatrical enactment" in which "the dynamic of sexual jealousy provides a complex analogy to theatrical performance and response in a culture that tends to conceive of theatrical experience in erotic terms" (563). Portia precedes her attacks on the other, more obviously foreign suitors in a manner that reflects a larger historical shift from definitions of race based on genealogy to race thought of as national and ethnic origin. Her dismissal of her countryman thus recontextualizes familiar cuckold jokes through the new forms of racial difference being introduced into Belmont with these various "strangers."

The famous casket test also shows what happens when the genealogy of romance as it is accepted by romantic comedy is disrupted by the intrusion of foreign elements into that once largely homogeneous, and thus endogamous, world. As other readers have noted, the test of the caskets is a traditional romance device, taken here from the *Gesta Romanorum*, that is generally used to determine nobility along precisely the lines initially suggested by Portia's overview of the suitors (1.2). When Shakespeare adapts his sources in *Merchant*, however, what begins as a test that might typically regulate sexual access becomes one that controls reproductive possibility. In the *Gesta Romanorum*, the correct casket contains "precious jewels"; in Shakespeare's version, a scroll and portrait (Holmer 54–57; Lewalski 336).[21] This alteration of course distinguishes material wealth from the "spiritual richness" that is needed to choose the golden Portia. Yet, at the same time, it is important to recognize that through this substitution Portia does not, in contrast to Jessica, thus become herself a "precious jewel," the "gem richer than all others" (Holmer 56). Shylock emphasizes the "precious, precious jewels" (3.1.74) in his complaints about Jessica's elopement because the loss of his daughter as a sexual property also involves the loss of a masculinity that is tied to his religious identity. What Shylock implicitly understands as the raping and pillaging of his house by Jessica does not just unman him in sexual terms;

it also threatens the descent that makes him part of the tribe of Israel. That is, Shylock needs to control his daughter's sexuality as a somewhat illogical way of retrospectively confirming his ancestry. If the "precious jewels" in the Jessica narrative reflect concern about establishing ancestry, Shakespeare thus removes them from his adaptation of the casket test to suggest that the Portia story is primarily about securing progeny.

With the introduction of the portraits and scrolls, the casket test shifts from "getting" to "begetting." When Bassanio finds the portrait of Portia, he does not just get the right of sexual access implied in claiming a kiss (3.2.138). By finding the reproduction of Portia, Bassanio also critically obtains the right to reproduce. Promising "never to speak to lady afterward in way of marriage," the unsuccessful claimants renounce marriage and the lawful progeny that marriage makes possible (2.2.40-42).[22] Gratiano, speaking the truth of the comic register, makes explicit that this end of marriage is legitimate reproduction. Even as Bassanio uses the language of courtesy to express how "much honoured" he and Portia are by the marriage of their servants to one another, Gratiano offers to wager them "the first boy for a thousand ducats," "stake down" (3.2.213-15). In this context, the picture of Portia contained within the casket—her "portrait," "form," "counterfeit," and "shadow" (2.7.11, 2.7.61, 3.2.115, 3.2.127)— should remind us that her father had this portrait made just as he did Portia herself. That is, it is not just that, Apelles-like, the painter is a "demi-god" who "hath come so near creation" (3.2.115-16). More important, the metaphor also works the other way. As other Shakespearean fathers make clear, the reproduction of children is literally that: Portia is herself a portrait of her dead father, his image and positive "counterfeit."[23] It is thus critically appropriate that it is not careful and "deliberate" reasoning that wins Portia (2.9.79). Rather, Bassanio engages in an act of imaginative passion that emulates her father's originary act of creation.

Through this emphasis on reproduction, the caskets become not only a test of the suitors but also a critique of romance assumptions about procreation as a mechanism that makes ineffable qualities—honor, virtue, fairness—visible. As it has been traditionally understood, Bassanio wins because he is able to see beyond external qualities to "choose not by the view" (3.2.131). His choice of the lead casket over the more visibly alluring "temptations" of the gold and silver is in keeping with the Christian practice of recognizing the ineffable. The prince of Morocco thus loses because he cannot see beyond external "shows" to recognize that "all that glisters is not gold" (2.8.65). More recently critics have suggested that the prince of Morocco loses Portia not so much because he sees only exterior appearance but because of how his own exterior appearance, his "complexion," is seen by others (2.1.1, 2.8.79). On this reading, there is also a suspicion that Bassanio is able to imagine what is inside the right casket through the inside help he receives from Portia rather than through any ability to look beyond the merely visible.[24] Despite different interests, these two apparently incompatible critical perspectives ultimately collapse into one another. The prince of Morocco sees only the outside because he is an outsider. Bassanio sees within the premises of the game because he is the insider that the test was designed to select: he is, on this understanding, no more able to "choose"—or "refuse"—than Portia herself (1.2.20).

By emphasizing oppositions such as inner/outer and visible/invisible, recent readings continue to replicate the structure of the test itself. In some sense, these critical determinations involve retaking the test in ways that make it difficult to find a perspective outside the test's structure. Ironically, the prince of Morocco provides just such a perspective by placing the text's romance conventions in jeopardy through his appearance on stage, an appearance that is carefully bracketed at his first entrance and his ultimate departure by references to his "complexion" (1.3.110, 2.1.2, 2.8.79). Although not fair, the prince is emphatically not a villain: he is noble in both birth and bearing. Portia refers to him as "noble prince," as he names her "fair Portia." Morocco emphasizes how he has been feared by the valiant as much as he has been loved by the "best regarded virgins of our clime" (2.1.10). He describes feats of personal bravery against the infidel— killing religious rulers in Persia and reclaiming battlefields from the Turks under Suleiman—that should make him a worthy knight (2.2.25–26). In imagining how because of the princes in search of Portia "the Hyrcanian deserts and the vasty wilds/ Of wide Arabia are as throughfares," Morocco understands the odyssey for Portia as a high romance of courtly nobility.

It is thus precisely this traditional romance sensibility that determines his choice of the golden casket. The prince insists:

> I do in birth deserve her, and in fortunes,
> In graces, and in qualities of breeding:
> But more than these, in love I do deserve.
> (2.7.32–34)

Seen in the larger generic context provided by romance, Morocco's under-standing of himself in this passage reiterates almost precisely the terms of

Lysander's suit to Hermia's father in *A Midsummer Night's Dream* (1.1.99–104) and likewise anticipates Othello's defense against Desdemona's father in *Othello* (1.2.31-32). Believing in the genealogy that defines romance, the prince of Morocco adheres to a traditional understanding of outer appearances (wealth, rank, feature) as true manifestations of inner reality (worth, nobility, virtue).

If Morocco expresses a desire for the idealism of romance, Bassanio's rejection of the "beauty" of the golden casket shows how the romance associated with those traditional values has been rewritten through new understandings of who and what is a stranger.

> Look on beauty,
> And you shall see 'tis purchas'd by the weight,
> Which therein works a miracle in nature,
> Making them lightest that wear most of it:
> So are those crisped snaky golden locks
> Which make such wanton gambols with the wind
> Upon supposed fairness, often known
> To be the dowry of a second head,
> The skull that bred them in the sepulchre.
> Thus ornament is but the guiled shore
> To a most dangerous sea: the beauteous scarf
> Veiling an Indian beauty.
>                                    (3.2.88-99)

Bassanio's choice obviously depends on identifying beauty as a material adulteration. Foreign to the self, beauty becomes a foreign import—a cosmetic "purchased by the weight" in the distant ports of Tripoli, Barbary, and India; a scarf "[v]eiling an Indian beauty." Beauty becomes a foreignness in the seemingly lost homogenous world that Belmont represents: European trade with the various "guiled" ports brought back both cosmetics and "Indian beauties" as exotic luxury goods.[25] In this rejection of the golden casket, Bassanio thus critically rethinks his description of Portia in the opening scene of the play—there the "four winds" blow in suitors for Portia; her "sunny locks" are not a wig but a "golden fleece"; far from being a treacherously "guiled shore," Belmont is a distant, heroic outpost, "Colchos' strond" (1.1.168-71). Rejecting these earlier assumptions that represent a more traditional definition of romance, Bassanio now sees the universal attraction that before had made the pursuit of Portia a romance "quest" as a dubious, mercenary adventuring (1.1.172). Although

Bassanio's changed attitude may indicate a new recognition of the paradox that the only means to true beauty is through a renunciation of it, this realization seems to be achieved only through the play's contact with the "outside" world, represented most literally on stage by the prince of Morocco.[26]

This romance logic motivates the prince of Morocco's suggestion that a different sort of test be used to "prove" the worthiest suitor (2.1.7). Although no drop of blood is of course ever actually spilled, *The Merchant of Venice* is a play that turns centrally on questions of blood. Demonstrating that questions about blood are "almost always narratively overdetermined," Gail Kern Paster thus emphasizes how in *Merchant* "the resolution of the central crisis comes to hinge upon the privilege secured by a difference in blood" (84). What has not been fully recognized, however, is how Morocco as a suitor defines the terms by which blood will be understood later in the play.[27] Seeming as impatient as Portia herself at the casket test as "cold decree" that tries to "devise laws for the blood," the prince of Morocco suggests, as an alternative, a test not "for" the blood but of it:

> Bring me the fairest creature northward born,
> Where Phoebus' fire scarce thaws the icicles,
> And let us make incision for your love
> To prove whose blood is reddest, his or mine.
> (2.1.4–7)

Morocco's suggestion—comparing blood to see whose is "reddest"— should not be understood simply as evidence of the kind of materialism that makes him lose the casket test.[28] By using the anatomical term "incision," Morocco proposes a kind of symbolic phlebotomy to prove himself to Portia. This offer thus would seem to accord precisely with the category of controlled bloodletting, which Paster identifies as "the cultural inversion of involuntary bleeding" that shames women in menstruation or symbolically weakens men wounded in battle (91). As such, the prince's offer should, in the ways that Paster suggests, be a means of demonstrating the kind of masculine power that a patriarchal society seeks to preserve in its bloodlines through marriages like the one in question. Certainly, Morocco's willingness to "make incision" is implicitly paired in this scene with the involuntary bleeding that he has inflicted with his scimitar on "the Sophy, and a Persian prince" (2.1.25). Morocco's willingness to bleed for Portia likewise anticipates yet also contrasts with the symbolic bloodletting that so critically emasculates Antonio.

Understanding why this proposed test of blood does not, in fact, "prove" the prince of Morocco requires recognizing how such a test throws into relief two competing definitions of blood. Emphasizing both his breeding and his bravery, Morocco seems in some sense to be reading from the account of true love elaborated by Lysander in *A Midsummer Night's Dream:* for Morocco, the first and most significant potential obstacle to true love is to be "different in blood" (*Midsummer* 1.1.135). Morocco follows Hermia in comprehending blood as a natural sign of the hierarchy of rank, "too high to be enthralled to low" (*Midsummer* 1.1.136). Like most editors of the play, Morocco thus understands "red" blood according to romance codes as a mark of bravery and nobility. The material terms under which Morocco would "prove" this otherwise ineffable difference, however, invoke a new language of physiology that is itself in part the result of changing theories of racial and ethnic difference. Surgery, anatomy, humoral theory: as the example of Ambrose Paré makes clear, the sciences of the body are in the early modern period extremely responsive to European encounters with "other" peoples.[29] In referring to his "complexion" as "the shadowed livery of the burnished sun" and proposing a comparison to the "fairest creature northward born," Morocco reminds his audience that both dark skin and warm climates were associated with what were thought to be less fully concocted and thus physiologically weaker forms of blood.[30] These prejudices are not themselves unexpected. Potentially troubling to the world represented by Belmont, however, are the implications of what Morocco wants to prove: in this new medical context, the "reddest" blood would be as much a mark of reproductive potency as a sign of valor.[31] Thus, as soon as the possibility is raised that the "qualities of breeding" that the prince of Morocco claims for himself might refer as much to progeny as to ancestry (2.7.33)—and that those qualities might be empirically verifiable—that possibility must be passed over.

In this moment, the play allows its audience to see a nobility in Morocco on his own terms while nonetheless encouraging, under a seemingly scientific "objectivism," a racialized judgment against him. Thus, even though the very possibility of a public bleeding from Shylock's much-whetted knife is enough symbolically to transform Antonio into a "tainted wether of the flock" (4.1.113), the prince of Morocco is not obversely transformed by his proposal into a powerful man. Critically, the whole scene with Morocco is designed to evoke and yet immediately dispel the possibility later imagined, in the provocations of Iago and the dreams of Brabantio, of the black man as "an old black ram tupping / Your white ewe" (*Othello* 1.1.88–89). Morocco does not get to prove his blood and ultimately departs from Belmont under a promise not to marry that makes him as "tainted" as Antonio will be.

If the prince of Morocco calls attention to the way that the meaning of blood changed with that of race, Jessica shows us how these questions are framed through the narrative conventions of romance. As the "infidel" who does marry across racial lines (3.2.217), Jessica realizes what the prince of Morocco fails to achieve. What distinguishes Jessica, remarkably enough, is the relationship between her blood and her complexion. Salerio thus taunts Shylock over the loss of Jessica by insisting: "There is more difference between thy flesh and hers, than between jet and ivory, more between your bloods, than there is between red wine and Rhenish" (3.1.33–35). While theories about blood were used to discriminate between other races in the ways suggested by the prince of Morocco, Salerio's comment reminds us that the most consequential use of blood as a form of racial differentiation in early modern Europe did not involve Samuel Purchas's exotic "others"— the "tawney Moore, black Negro, duskie Libyan, ash-colored Indian, olive-colored American" (546), whose internal differences might be extrapolated from their external otherness. Rather, blood became the identifying characteristic for a category of people who were threatening expressly because there were no visible physical, cultural, or religious differences to distinguish them from the rest of society: the New Christians. As Jerome Friedman makes clear, the "pure blood laws" of the Spanish Inquisition were instituted not against "alien" Jews like Shylock (4.1.345) but against New Christians, who as a group had assimilated into Spanish society in ways that were making them a troublingly invisible minority within a culture that increasingly wanted race to be physically visible (16–19, 21, 25).[32]

As one "sav'd" by the husband who will make her a Christian, Jessica is in some sense the newest of the New Christians, and it is thus at this moment that attention shifts from her outer "complexion" to her inner blood (3.5.17–18). Yet, even as these scenes with Jessica evoke contemporary discussion surrounding pure blood laws, they depart notably from that historic context. As a retroactive response not simply to three centuries of religious conversions but to intermarriages like that between Lorenzo and Jessica, the Spanish pure blood laws assumed that Jewish blood was always fundamentally different in ways that made it impervious to the transformations of grace or baptism.[33] Part of a remarkable Christian appropriation of the kinds of genealogical distinctions that govern Shylock's understanding of the Jacob and Laban story, the blood laws would admit no "difference" between the blood of Jessica and her father: "it is not enough for the Jew to be three parts aristocrat or Old Christian for one family-line [i.e., one Jewish ancestor] alone defiles and corrupts" (Friedman 16–17). Although through transubstantiation bread and wine might become body and blood, a thousand masses could not transform Jewish flesh and blood. Given this understanding, Jessica in her blood would always retain the essential qualities of her ancestors.[34]

While this racial theology offered no model for the transformation of Jessica, romance does. Knowable from the "complexion" of her flesh to that of her soul (3.1.27), Jessica can in some sense be read as a romance text. That is, Lorenzo believes that he can see inside Jessica for precisely the reasons and in precisely the terms that Morocco would see Portia inside the golden casket. Jessica's fairness becomes the romance confirmation of her innately Christian soul: Lorenzo can easily identify her "fair hand" (2.4.112, 114), while Salerio and Solanio speak confidently of her "ivory" flesh and her "Rhenish" blood (3.1.33–35). Most critically, Lorenzo determines her inner being through her outward actions:

> For she is wise, if I can judge of her,
> And fair she is, if that mine eyes be true,
> And true she is, as she hath prov'd herself:
> And therefore like herself, wise, fair, and true,
> Shall she be placed in my constant soul.
>                                       (2.6.53–57)

Where Morocco loses Portia by interpreting the gold casket as a sign of her soul, Lorenzo ascertains the love of the "wise, fair, and true" Jessica through her actions of leaving her father and giving him her own gold casket. This disparity involves neither an inconsistency in plot nor the simple racism of preferring a Christian gentleman from Venice over a noble black Moor from Morocco. Identifying the powerful "racializing potentiality of the matrix," Jonathan Crewe suggests that the mother's womb is a site for producing racial purity that nonetheless always carries the potential to engender racial admixture through physical adulteration (21). Jessica's foreignness as a Jew is thus less problematic than Morocco's primarily because her capacity to reproduce—the end of romance as well as of marriage, after all—involves an adulteration already inherent in a woman.

Jessica and Lorenzo consequently become representative figures of the successful cross-cultural marriage through their rereading of the romances of Dido and Aeneas, Troilus and Cressida, Jason and Medea, Pyramus and Thisby. Most contemporary readers understood these stories—narratives in which the woman is always a foreigner, the love always fatal—as necessarily doomed romances of otherness that defined Western culture. Jessica and Lorenzo, however, banter them as sentimental love stories. Placing themselves in "such a night as this," they insert themselves into this lineage of stories (5.1.1). Importantly, they understand themselves as the inheritors of these prior romances without being implicated in their tragic consequences. Achieving the union that their antecedents could not sustain, Jessica and Lorenzo provide in some sense an alternative, happy ending to those other stories. They do so, however, not by transcending racial difference and its threat of otherness but by domesticating it, as their role as symbolic gatekeepers to Belmont suggests.

While Jessica and Lorenzo dramatize how a romance of otherness can become assimilated, the seemingly marginal example of Launcelot Gobbo more pointedly reflects the way that miscegenation remains a representational problem. With Jessica and Lorenzo, the audience is not asked to imagine miscegenation as something that might intrude into their pretty story. With Launcelot, though, Shakespeare offers a ludic joke about miscegenation as adulteration. Where Chrétien de Troyes's Launcelot figures the romance love that exceeds its rightful bounds to become adultery, Shakespeare's Lance-alot is a comically fertile debasement of that romance ethos. His "adventures" are always sexual and scarcely noble. For instance, when Launcelot predicts that he will have fifteen wives, eleven widows, and nine maids, the language he uses ("trifle," "nothing," "a simple coming-in for one man"; 2.2.153–55) suggests that the terms of his possession will be strictly sexual. Perhaps thinking of marriage as a sexual misadventure, Launcelot thus worries that he will be "in peril" of his life "with the edge of a feather-bed" (2.2.156–57).

Discussions of Launcelot Gobbo's role in the play have understandably focused on how his trickery of his blind father enacts a debased version of Jacob stealing Esau's birthright (2.2).[35] In doing so, Launcelot thus offers the audience a comic model that enables the supplanting of an older order with a newer one.[36] At the end of act 3, Launcelot returns to the question of supplanting patriarchy in a way that again involves the audience. Expressing the belief that "the sins of the father are to be laid upon the children," Launcelot suggests that Jessica is almost certainly going to be damned to hell because of her father. Her only hope, he concludes, is "but a kind of bastard hope" that she may not be in fact be Shylock's daughter after all (3.5.1-10). When Lorenzo hears a report of this discussion about Jessica's conversion to Christianity, he tells Launcelot that he "shall answer that better to the commonwealth than you can the getting up of the negro's belly" (3.5.35-36). In this scene, Launcelot is implicated in an act of adultery that registers the shifting meaning of race for *The Merchant of Venice* as a romantic comedy. The various sexual promiscuities that Launcelot had earlier predicted for himself are realized here as a mixing of kinds that accompanies his own participation in a debased romance narrative. In getting the "Moor with child," Launcelot has committed some form of adultery that is detrimental to the commonwealth. As Lorenzo sees it, Launcelot's illicit sexual activity will also produce a potentially dangerous "adulteration" of racial kinds.[37] This moment dramatizes how the standard comic fear that the end of marriage will be adulteration has been transformed through the way that the new interracial, interdenominational context for *The Merchant of Venice* has changed the meaning of race. Adulteration no longer means just a single bastard offspring but the larger possibility of "bastard races" that were understood to be the dangerous consequences of miscegenation.

Shylock's "work of generation" becomes something that the audience participates in through the telling of one last cuckold joke—this time about Launcelot himself. Launcelot responds to Lorenzo's news by replying, "It is much that the Moor should be more than reason: but if she be less than an honest woman, she is indeed more than I took her for" (3.5.37-39). In turning this joke of a "bastard hope" on Launcelot himself, the unsettling implications originally associated with Portia's inappropriate joke about the Neapolitan prince have returned to their proper place. The "sins of the father are visited upon the children," as Launcelot suggests: at this moment, Launcelot goes from being a sometimes erring son to an unwitting father. In the elaborate pun on more/Moor/much/less, we are asked to imagine an "infidelity" in the Moor that extends from the exogamy of her religious affiliation to a lack of monogamy in her sexual behavior. Yet, at the same time, these consequences occur through Launcelot's participation in his own cuckolding. By putting to rest the various acts of imaginative miscegenation in which we have participated by "looking into" the racial affiliations of this play, Launcelot's joke establishes the terms for the final judgments of the play and thus provisionally contains the problems inherent in the shift from an understanding of race as genealogy to one of race as ethnic identity. Just as Launcelot represents a rewriting of a familiar romance ethos, so does *The Merchant of Venice* rewrite what in Shakespeare's other romantic comedies is a comparatively pure form into a new hybrid. The miscegenation of *Merchant* involves a mixing of generic kinds that dramatizes the reciprocal relationship between new understandings of race and new types of romance.

## Notes

1. Certainly, to the extent that "race" can be identified as a category in early modern Europe, it overlaps and competes in at times contradictory ways with distinctions involving religion, nationality, physical appearance, and family origin—hence, the recurrence of texts that distinguish between white and black Africans, Christian and Muslim Turks, Counterfeit Jews and False Christians, and Indians from the New World and those of the Far East. For important work that considers various understandings of how "race" intersects with other subject categories, see Neill; Shapiro 13–42, 167–93; Vitkus; Singh.

2. For a useful warning against reading a contemporary "taxonomy of color" into early modern texts, see Boose 35. Lupton provides a brief critical history of "the current color-based approach" (74n2). See also Walvin 32–47; Washington 70–101.

3. See also Smith 171.

4. I have used the *Bishop's Bible* rather than the *Geneva* because Shakespeare did not begin relying on the *Geneva Bible* until the period after 1596 (Berry 20). Citations from *The Merchant of Venice* follow the Arden Shakespeare (ed. Brown); all other Shakespeare plays follow Greenblatt's *Norton Shakespeare*.

5. In his more compressed version, Shylock simply refers throughout only to Jacob's "sheep"—rather than to the sheep and goats or to the cattle. Shakespeare may just be simplifying a notoriously corrupt and confusing passage. At the same time, I include this more complete version of the story as it was generally accepted by early modern translators and commentators. I do this less to suggest that either Shylock or Shakespeare got it wrong than to remember how this story—like the others involving Jacob—is concerned not just with "multiplying" the flocks through "the work of generation" but also with separating, dividing, and remixing them. Informed readers were aware of the problems with this passage: Jerome complains that "the meaning is greatly disordered" (66), while Luther attempts conscientiously to sort out the complexities even as he admits the confusion of the passage: "But there are four kinds, namely, rams, ewes, she-goats and he-goats. But by synecdoche sometimes only one kind is named, sometimes more. All are not counted. This is the source of the difficulty" (5:374).

6. As Yaffe points out, the biblical texts that figure in most contemporary discussions about usury include Exod. 23.24–26; Lev. 25.35–55; and Deut. 15.1–11, 23.19–21 (180n62).

Assessments of the strength of Shylock's use of Jacob and Laban instead of the more usual passages vary: Danson sees the Jacob and Laban story as the "strongest part" of Shylock's case (148-50), while Yaffe comments on Shylock's "rather loose and self-serving" interpretation of Genesis (62). More generally, Draper demonstrates how consistently Shylock uses in this defense "the very reasons urged most bitterly against" usury (43). For contemporary attitudes toward and more typical arguments about usury, see Nelson 73-89, 141-51.

7. The only reading of Jacob and Laban that I am aware of which refers to usury is Martin Luther's and there indirectly: speaking of what readers widely agreed was the avarice of Laban, Luther concludes that "usurers, robbers, and greedy-guts are not human. They have eyes, and they do not see. They have ears, and they do not hear . . . they are loveless, monstrous, and cruel men" (5:377).

8. Although Braude is primarily concerned with a fluidity of meaning that he sees as characteristic of preprint culture, many of his findings and warnings remain relevant for understanding early modern biblical commentary.

9. See also Nelson 73-89.

10. See Williams. These conclusions need to be balanced, however, against López's argument that an overemphasis on skin color—"a dichotomy between black and white"—tends to obscure what are for Renaissance readers the more fundamental categories of race and religion (51).

11. See also Luther 5:381; Jerome 66, 203-4; Willet 319.

12. An early version of this work was published in the second part of his obstetrical tract, *Deux livres de chirurgie* (Paris, 1573); the longer, familiar *De Monstres et prodiges* was included in his *Oeuvres de M. Ambroise Paré* (1575, 1582, 1585). For an analysis that connects these kinds of reproductive monstrosities to the "horrible conceits" of *Othello*, see Aubrey 234-37.

13. Some aspects of Laqueur's influential account of the history of sexual difference have been challenged: see, e.g., Park and Nye; Adelman 25-39. Belief in theories of maternal intellection provides an example of what Butler refers to as a "culturally constructed desire that is interpreted through a naturalistic vocabulary." While the maternal imagination seems literally to embody a kind of "principle of pure generativity," it can only be expressed through the language and representation of its imprinting (91). On the basis for accounts of the pregnant imagination in the context of Aristotelian reproductive theory, see Maclean 41; Park and Daston, *Wonders* 173-214.

14. Paré notes discussions of this theory as being "taught" by Aristotle, Empedocles, and Hippocrates but does not otherwise rely on their works here (38). On the classical sources for this fairly widespread belief, see Reeve.

15. Although the *Aethiopica* has been reread by classical scholars recently, it remains surprisingly neglected by readers interested in rethinking questions of race in the Renaissance. While critics have long recognized Heliodorus's influence on writers such as Cervantes, Sidney, Spenser, and Tasso, more work needs to be done on how this wildly popular romance set the terms for a racially inflected materialism that informs Renaissance reinventions of romance. The idea of a "visible" character in which skin color and other aspects of physical appearance indicate moral qualities is in Heliodorus from the start entangled with questions about race. What I am calling the genealogy of Shakespeare's romantic comedies is an

inheritance from Heliodorus. Written in Greek c. A.D. 220-250 by a writer of apparently Ethiopian descent who describes himself as being "of the race of the sun," the *Aethiopica* seems to enact in its central narrative a mythic version of Heliodorus's own situation as an author (Heliodorus 277). The story of how Charicleia's mother gazed on a picture of Andromeda as an explanation for her daughter's light coloring is itself clearly a narrative of the cultural assimilation of other races into the Greek Empire. In particular, Heliodorus's suggestion that a picture of Andromeda might produce a fair-skinned child calls attention to the somewhat anomalous fact that although Andromeda was herself the daughter of Cepheus and Cassiopeia, the king and queen of Ethiopia, most classical writers nonetheless implicitly assumed that this legendary beauty was fair-skinned. As such, the Andromeda story at the center of the *Aethiopica* thus becomes in Heliodorus an image of the "whitening" of Ethiopia that anticipates the narrative transformations undergone by Charicleia and the authorial one enacted by Heliodorus himself. On Heliodorus's use of biological genealogy as a model for creating generic genealogy in a new kind of novel, see Whitmarsh; for a tradition in Renaissance art of a dark-skinned Andromeda, see McGrath.

16. The intrinsic relationship between the *Histoires prodigieuses* and the genre of romance is underlined by Boaistuau's first English translator, Edward Fenton, who advertised his book as an alternative to "the fruitlesse Historie of king *Arthur*" and the "trifeling tales of *Gawain* and *Gargantua*" (*Certaine Secrete Wonders of Nature* [1569]; cited in Park and Daston, "Unnatural Conceptions" 37).

17. On the dangers that romance was thought to have for women, see Ife 1-48. For examples of the common concern that writing in the vernacular might "expose" the "private parts" of gynecological works to unsuitable readers, see Roesslin Biiiv-ivr; Guillemeau sig. ¶¶ 2-3.

18. Without focusing on the play's structural interest in miscegenation, Hall identifies how miscegenation provides "a powerful subtext" to *The Merchant of Venice* ("Guess" 89). See also Palmer; Hall, *Things of Darkness* 125.

19. For similar conclusions about the importance of often brief jokes about cuckoldry, see especially Cook 187-90; Kahn 106; Bruster 47-62.

20. Compare *Tempest* 1.2.55-57; *Much Ado* 1.1.105.

21. The test in the *Gesta Romanorum* does involve some emphasis on begetting as the end of marriage in its reference to Deut. 30:19, "chuse life, that both thou and thy seede may live" (cited in Lewalski 336).

22. Some readers have understood what appear to be differences in the fates of the princes of Arragon and Morocco as racially inflected. Comparing the promise that Morocco makes never to wed with the scroll in Arragon's lead casket, Shell thus concludes that "unlike the black Muslim, the white Christian is allowed to try to generate kin in wedlock" (*Money* 57). At the same time, this reading may not account fully for the context in which Arragon is imagined as marrying: the scroll, "Take what wife you will to bed / I will ever be your head" (2.9.69-70), explains the meaning of the fool's head in the casket. As a man who in bed will have at least "two, fool's heads," Arragon may differ from Morocco in being able to take a wife. Having certain knowledge only of his own cuckoldry, however, Arragon will as effectively lack true heirs as Morocco.

23. See, e.g., *Midsummer Night's Dream* 1.1.49-50; *Winter's Tale* 1.2.122.

24. On how the play encourages speculation on this point, see Berger 157-61.

25. For attacks on cosmetics as foreign to both women and England, see Dolan 229, 231; on the public display and sale of "imported" indigenous peoples, see Mullaney 69. Given that makeup was so often regarded as a material adulteration used by women, it is not surprising that it should be associated with the corporeal adulterations associated with reproduction: Dolan cites in this regard Thomas Tuke's argument in *A Treatise against Painting and Tincturing of Men and Women* (1616) that mercury sublimate, like original sin and venereal disease, was passed on to women's offspring (237n9).

26. Any reading that relies on a significant transformation in Bassanio needs to be set against our profound intuition, expressed by Auden, that in the romance world that is being put to the test with the caskets, there is no becoming, only being (221). We have no more reason to attribute a transformation to Bassanio than doubt that he will choose correctly.

27. In contrast to the prince of Morocco, Bassanio notably does not refer to his good "blood" until after he wins Portia (3.2.25-54).

28. On the strong materialism associated with questions about blood in this period, see Rogers 1-38. The prince of Morocco's desire to "make incision" differs in ways that are not always recognized from Shylock's famous "If you prick us, do we not bleed?" (3.1.54). Where Shylock takes blood as a sign of common humanity, the aristocratic prince understands it as a mark of distinction. The prince is not suggesting, as Webster's Zanche will, that his blood is as red as anyone else's; he wants to "prove whose blood is reddest" and expects to win.

29. On how early modern anatomists understood their work in terms of a "discovery" of "a remote and strange terrain" comparable to those charted by Columbus, see Sawday 22-32. For background on early modern sciences of the body, see Siraisi.

30. On the association of fair complexions with greater quantities of seed, see Aristotle, *History of Animals* 7.2.583a 10-14. For an example of how this humoral theory could be adapted in the context of early modern concerns about race, see Paster 67-68.

31. Although the symbolism of blood is complex, the best blood was generally characterized as the reddest, thinnest, and warmest. In males, the best of the best blood was concocted into seed; those who were weak in some way—fat, sick, old, and perhaps even foreign—produced both less semen and children who were more often deformed. See, e.g., Aristotle, *Generation of Animals* 1.724b 22-725b 25; Aristotle, *History of Animals* 7.4.584b 7-11.

32. On the status of so-called New Christians, intermarriage rates, and pure blood laws, see Shell, "Marranos"; Shapiro 13-43; Sicroff; Netanyahu 64-66, 70-72.

33. Friedman argues that it was not so much religious or even social assimilation but ultimately intermarriage that precipitated the pure blood laws (11). Shapiro suggests that the English feared that many of the most noble families were of Jewish descent (18, 39-40).

34. The way that the pure blood laws became a model applied to other races can be seen in Fray Prudencio de Sandoval's comparison in the Jews of "the evil inclination of their ancient ingratitude and lack of understanding, just as in Negros [there persists] the inseparability of their blackness. For if the latter should unite themselves a thousand times with white women, the children are born with the dark color of the father" (*Historia de la vida y hechos del emperador Carlos V* [1604]; cited in Friedman 16).

35. On the importance of the Jacob and Esau story to *Merchant,* see Lewalski; Shell, *Money* 52; Colley; Fortin.

36. Ishmael is supplanted by Isaac, Esau by Jacob, Jews by Christians: these narratives that

Colley characterizes as "ambiguous (yet divinely inspired)" acts of usurpation become types for the choices that Jessica and Launcelot make in leaving Shylock. They also model our response as an audience to the trial scene judgment against Shylock (Colley 188).

37. Although most readers assume that Launcelot Gobbo is a Venetian Christian, some scholars have understood Shylock's characterization of him as "Hagar's offspring" as an indication that he is Muslim, while others have thought his surname suggests Jewish, rather than Italian, origin (Shell, *Money* 52; Fortin 261n7). This critical question is part of what has become a kind of ongoing speculation about various points of identity affiliation in *Merchant*—for instance, what does it mean for the traditionally Ethiopian Chus, the son of Ham who was conceived white but born black, to be identified as Shylock's "countryman" (3.2.284)? Fixing on these questions is at once almost irresistible and yet also critically problematic. It is not so much that the questions are ultimately unanswerable but that the need for a determinable answer runs counter to the play's own enactment of genealogical adulterations, its ongoing demand that our aesthetic response involves imagining and thus producing various forms of admixture.

## Works Cited

Adelman, Janet. "Making Defect Perfection: Shakespeare and the One-Sex Model." *Enacting Gender on the English Renaissance Stage.* Ed. Viviana Comensoli and Anne Russell. Urbana: U of Illinois P, 1999. 23–52.

Aristotle. *The Complete Works of Aristotle.* Ed. Jonathan Barnes. 2 vols. Princeton: Bollingen, 1984.

———. *Generation of Animals.* Trans. A. Platt. *Complete Works.* Ed. Barnes. 1:1111–1218.

———. *History of Animals.* Trans. d'A. W. Thompson. *Complete Works.* Ed. Barnes. 1:774–993.

Aubrey, James R. "Race and the Spectacle of the Monstrous in *Othello.*" *Clio* 22 (1993): 221–38.

Auden, W. H. "Brothers and Others." *The Dyer's Hand and Other Essays.* New York: Random House, 1948. 218–37.

Babington, Gervase. *Certaine Plaine, Briefe, and Comfortable Notes upon Euerie Chapter of Genesis.* London, 1592.

Berger, Harry, Jr. "Marriage and Mercifixion in *The Merchant of Venice:* The Casket Scene Revisited." *Shakespeare Quarterly* 32.2 (1981): 155–62.

Berry, Lloyd E. "Introduction." *The Geneva Bible: A Facsimile of the 1560 Edition.* Madison: U of Wisconsin P, 1969. 1–24.

Boose, Lynda E. " 'The Getting of a Lawful Race': Racial Discourse in Early Modern England and the Unrepresentable Black Woman." *Women, "Race," and Writing in the Early Modern Period.* Ed. Margo Hendricks and Patricia Parker. New York: Routledge, 1994. 35–54.

Braude, Benjamin. "The Sons of Noah and the Construction of Ethnic and Geographical Identities in the Medieval and Early Modern Periods." *William and Mary Quarterly,* 3d ser., 54.1 (1997): 103–42.

Bruster, Douglas. *Drama and the Market in the Age of Shakespeare.* Cambridge: Cambridge UP, 1992.

Butler, Judith. *Gender Trouble: Feminism and the Subversion of Identity.* New York: Routledge, 1990.

Colley, John Scott. "Launcelot, Jacob, and Esau: Old and New Law in *The Merchant of Venice.*" *Yearbook of English Studies* 10 (1980): 181–89.

Cook, Carol. " 'The Sign and Semblance of Her Honor': Reading Gender Difference in *Much Ado about Nothing.*" *PMLA* 101.2 (1986): 186–202.

Crewe, Jonathan. "Out of the Matrix: Shakespeare and Race-Writing." *Yale Journal of Criticism* 8.2 (1995): 13–29.

Danson, Lawrence. *The Harmonies of "The Merchant of Venice."* New Haven: Yale UP, 1978.

Dolan, Frances E. "Taking the Pencil out of God's Hand: Art, Nature, and the Face-Painting Debate in Early Modern England." *PMLA* 108.2 (1993): 224–39.

Draper, John W. "Usury in *The Merchant of Venice.*" *Modern Philology* 33.1 (1935): 37–47.

Erickson, Peter. "Representations of Blacks and Blackness in the Renaissance." *Criticism* 35.4 (1993): 499–527.

Fortin, René E. "Launcelot and the Uses of Allegory in *The Merchant of Venice.*" *SEL* 14 (1974): 259–70.

Friedman, Jerome. "Jewish Conversion, the Spanish Pure Blood Laws, and Reformation: A Revisionist View of Racial and Religious Antisemitism." *Sixteenth Century Journal* 18 (1987): 1–29.

Guillemeau, Jacques. *Child-birth, or the Happy Delivery.* London, 1612.

Hall, Kim F. "Guess Who's Coming to Dinner? Colonization and Miscegenation in *The Merchant of Venice.*" *Renaissance Drama* n.s. 23 (1992): 87–111.

———. *Things of Darkness: Economies of Race and Gender in Early Modern England.* Ithaca, NY: Cornell UP, 1995.

Heliodorus. *An Ethiopian Romance.* Trans. Moses Hadas. Ann Arbor: U of Michigan P, 1957.

Hendricks, Margo. " 'Obscured by Dreams': Race, Empire, and Shakespeare's *A Midsummer Night's Dream.*" *Shakespeare Quarterly* 47.1 (1996): 37–60.

Hendricks, Margo, and Patricia Parker, eds. *Women, "Race," and Writing in the Early Modern Period.* New York: Routledge, 1994.

Holmer, Joan Ozark. "Loving Wisely and the Casket Test: Symbolic and Structural Unity in *The Merchant of Venice.*" *Shakespeare Studies* 11 (1978): 53–76.

*The Holy Bible, Conteining the Olde Testament and the Newe.* London, 1584.

Howard, Jean E. "An English Lass amid the Moors: Gender, Race, Sexuality, and National Identity in Heywood's *The Fair Maid of the West.*" *Women, "Race," and Writing in the Early Modern Period.* Ed. Margo Hendricks and Patricia Parker. New York: Routledge, 1994. 101–17.

Ife, Barry. *Reading and Fiction in Golden-Age Spain: A Platonist Critique and Some Picaresque Replies.* Cambridge: Cambridge UP, 1985.

Jerome, Saint. *Hebrew Questions on Genesis.* Trans. and ed. C. T. R. Hayward. Oxford: Clarendon, 1995.

Kahn, Coppélia. "The Cuckoo's Note: Male Friendship and Cuckoldry in *The Merchant of Venice.*" *Shakespeare's "Rough Magic": Renaissance Essays in Honor of C. L. Barber.* Ed. Peter Erickson and Coppélia Kahn. Newark: U of Delaware P, 1985. 104–12.

Laqueur, Thomas. *Making Sex: Body and Gender from the Greeks to Freud.* Cambridge, MA: Harvard UP, 1990.

Lewalski, Barbara K. "Biblical Allusion and Allegory in *The Merchant of Venice.*" *Shakespeare Quarterly* 13.3 (1962): 327–43.

López, Judith A. "Black and White and 'Read' All Over." *Shakespeare Studies* 26 (1998): 49–58.

Lupton, Julia Reinhard. "*Othello* Circumcised: Shakespeare and the Pauline Discourse of Nations." *Representations* 57 (Winter 1997): 73–89.

Luther, Martin. *Lectures on Genesis, Chapters 26–30.* Vol. 5 of *Works.* Ed. Jaroslav Pelikan. 55 vols. St. Louis: Concordia, 1955.

Maclean, Ian. *The Renaissance Notion of Woman: A Study in the Fortunes of Scholasticism and Medical Science in European Intellectual Life.* Cambridge: Cambridge UP, 1980.

Maus, Katharine Eisaman. "Horns of Dilemma: Jealousy, Gender, and Spectatorship in English Renaissance Drama." *ELH* 54.3 (1987): 561–83.

McGrath, Elizabeth. "Black Andromeda." *Journal of the Warburg and Courtauld Institutes* 55 (1992): 1–18.

Mullaney, Steven. *The Place of the Stage: License, Play, and Power in Renaissance England.* Chicago: U of Chicago P, 1988.

Neill, Michael. " 'Mulattos,' 'Blacks,' and 'Indian Moors': *Othello* and Early Modern Constructions of Human Difference." *Shakespeare Quarterly* 49.4 (1998): 361–74.

Nelson, Benjamin. *The Idea of Usury: From Tribal Brotherhood to Universal Otherhood.* 2d ed. Chicago: U of Chicago P, 1969.

Netanyahu, Benzion. *The Marranos of Spain: From the Late Fourteenth to the Early Sixteenth Century, According to Contemporary Hebrew Sources.* 1966. 3d rev. ed. Ithaca, NY: Cornell UP, 1999.

Palmer, Daryl W. "Merchants and Miscegenation: *The Three Ladies of London, The Jew of Malta,* and *The Merchant of Venice.*" *Race, Ethnicity, and Power in the Renaissance.* Ed. Joyce Green MacDonald. Madison, NJ: Farleigh Dickinson UP, 1997. 36–66.

Paré, Ambrose. *On Monsters and Marvels.* Ed. and trans. Janis L. Pallister. Chicago: U of Chicago P, 1982.

Park, Katharine, and Lorraine J. Daston. "Unnatural Conceptions: The Study of Monsters in Sixteenth- and Seventeenth-Century France and England." *Past and Present* 92 (1981): 20–54.

———. *Wonders and the Order of Nature, 1150–1750.* New York: Zone Books, 1998.

Park, Katharine, and Robert Nye. "Anatomy Is Destiny." *New Republic.* 18 February 1991. 3–7.

Parker, Patricia. "Fantasies of 'Race' and 'Gender': Africa, *Othello,* and Bringing to Light." *Women, "Race," and Writing in the Early Modern Period.* Ed. Margo Hendricks and Patricia Parker. New York: Routledge, 1994. 84–100.

Paster, Gail Kern. *The Body Embarrassed: Drama and the Disciplines of Shame in Early Modern England.* Ithaca, NY: Cornell UP, 1993.

Purchas, Samuel. *Purchas His Pilgrimage; or, Relations of the World and the Religions Observed in All Ages.* London, 1613.

Reeve, M. D. "Conceptions." *Publications of the Cambridge Philological Society* n.s. 35 (1989): 81–112.

Roesslin, Eucharius. *The Byrth of Mankynde.* Trans. R. Jonas. London, 1540.

Rogers, John. *The Matter of Revolution: Science, Poetry, and Politics in the Age of Milton.* Ithaca, NY: Cornell UP, 1996.

Sawday, Jonathan. *The Body Emblazoned: Dissection and the Human Body in Renaissance Culture.* New York: Routledge, 1995.

Shakespeare, William. *The Merchant of Venice.* Ed. John Russell Brown. Cambridge, MA: Harvard UP, 1959.

———. *The Norton Shakespeare.* Ed. Stephen Greenblatt et al. New York: W. W. Norton, 1997.

Shapiro, James. *Shakespeare and the Jews.* New York: Columbia UP, 1996.

Shell, Marc. "Marranos (Pigs), or From Coexistence to Toleration." *Critical Inquiry* 17.2 (1991): 306–35.

———. *Money, Language, and Thought: Literary and Philosophical Economics from the Medieval to the Modern Era.* Berkeley: U of California P, 1982.

Sicroff, Albert. *Les Controverses des statuts de "pureté de sang" en Espagne du 15e au 17e siècle.* Paris: Didier, 1960.

Singh, Jyotsna. *Colonial Narratives/Cultural Dialogues: "Discoveries" of India in the Language of Colonialism.* London: Routledge, 1996.

Siraisi, Nancy G. *Medieval and Early Renaissance Medicine.* Chicago: U of Chicago P, 1990.

Smith, Ian. "Barbarian Errors: Performing Race in Early Modern England." *Shakespeare Quarterly* 49.2 (1998): 168–86.

Stechow, Wolfgang. "Heliodorus' *Aethiopica* in Art." *Journal of the Warburg and Courtauld Institutes* 16 (1953): 144–52.

Vitkus, Daniel J. "Turning Turk in *Othello:* The Conversion and Damnation of the Moor." *Shakespeare Quarterly* 48.2 (1997): 145–76.

Walvin, James. *The Black Presence: A Documentary History of the Negro in England, 1555–1860.* New York: Schocken, 1972.

Washington, Joseph E. *Anti-Blackness in English Religion, 1500–1800.* New York: Edward Mellen, 1984.

Whitmarsh, Tim. "The Birth of a Prodigy: Heliodorus and the Genealogy of Hellenism." *Studies in Heliodorus.* Ed. Richard Hunter. Cambridge: Cambridge Philological Society, 1998. 93–124.

Willet, Andrew. *Hexapla in Genesin.* Cambridge, 1605.

Williams, Arnold. *The Common Expositor: An Account of the Commentaries on Genesis, 1527–1633.* Chapel Hill: U of North Carolina P, 1948.

Yaffe, Martin D. *Shylock and the Jewish Question.* Baltimore: Johns Hopkins UP, 1997.

# Notes on Contributors

GINA BLOOM is a doctoral candidate in English language and literature at the University of Michigan, where she is also a graduate fellow at the Institute for the Humanities. Her contribution to this volume is part of a dissertation project about the materiality of vocal communication, entitled "Choreographing Voice: Staging Gender in Early Modern England."

GRAHAM HAMMILL received his Ph.D. in English from Duke University and is an assistant professor at the University of Notre Dame, where he teaches Renaissance literature and literary theory. He is the author of *Sexuality and Form: Caravaggio, Marlowe, and Bacon* (Chicago, 2000) and is currently working on the baroque.

JONATHAN GIL HARRIS, associate professor of English at Ithaca College, is the author of *Foreign Bodies and the Body Politic: Discourses of Social Pathology in Early Modern England* (Cambridge, 1998) and co-editor, with Natasha Korda, of the forthcoming *Staged Properties: Props and Property in Early Modern English Drama*. He is currently at work on a book-length project, *Etiologies of the Economy: Commerce, Disease, and Nation in Shakespeare and Jonson*.

PETER PAROLIN is an assisant professor of English at the University of Wyoming. The present essay is part of a project on the cultural uses of Italy in early modern England.

ELIZABETH A. SPILLER is an associate professor at Texas Christian University.

She has published articles on Renaissance literature, most recently in *Renaissance Quarterly, SEL, Modern Language Quarterly,* and *Studies in Philology.* She is completing a book entitled *Experiments in Fiction: Science, Imagination, and Poetry, 1580–1660.*